How to Raise Independent and Professionally Successful Daughters

Also by the authors:

Practical Approaches to Individualizing Instruction: Contracts and Other Effective Teaching Strategies

Educator's Self-Teaching Guide to Individualizing Instructional Programs

Administrator's Guide to New Programs for Faculty Management and Evaluation

By Kenneth J. Dunn and Jack Tanzman:

Using Instructional Media Effectively

How to Raise Independent and Professionally Successful Daughters

Dr. Rita Dunn / Dr. Kenneth Dunn

PRENTICE-HALL, INC., Englewood Cliffs, N.J.

How to Raise Independent and Professionally Successful Daughters
by Dr. Rita Dunn and Dr. Kenneth Dunn
Copyright © 1977 by Dr. Rita Dunn and Dr. Kenneth Dunn
All rights reserved. No part of this book may be
reproduced in any form or by any means, except
for the inclusion of brief quotations in a review,
without permission in writing from the publisher.
Printed in the United States of America
Prentice-Hall International, Inc., London
Prentice-Hall of Australia, Pty. Ltd., Sydney
Prentice-Hall of Canada, Ltd., Toronto
Prentice-Hall of India Private Ltd., New Delhi
Prentice-Hall of Japan, Inc., Tokyo
10 9 8 7 6 5 4 3 2 1

Library of Congress Cataloging in Publication Data
Dunn, Rita Stafford
    How to raise independent and professionally
successful daughters.
    Bibliography: p.
    Includes index.
    1. Daughters. 2. Child development.
3. Success. 4. Children—Management. I. Dunn,
Kenneth J., joint author. II. Title.
HQ777.D86 649'.133 77-1898
ISBN 0-13-430710-0

To our daughter Rana and all the
other young ladies in this world
who deserve the opportunity
to realize their full potential.

About the Authors

Dr. Rita Dunn is the first (and only) woman to hold the rank of full professor in the School of Education at St. John's University, New York. She is the former regional director of the New York State Teacher Reserve Center and director of the School-University Graduate Teacher Education Program. Dr. Dunn earned her Ed.D. from New York University, where she was awarded the N.Y.U. Research Scholarship Award for her dissertation on those factors that motivated successful, professional women toward their respective careers. She is the author of more than forty articles and books, including *Practical Approaches to Individualizing Instruction: Contracts and Other Effective Teaching Strategies, Educator's Self-Teaching Guide to Individualizing Instructional Programs,* and *Administrator's Guide to New Programs for Faculty Management and Evaluation.*

Dr. Kenneth Dunn is Superintendent of Schools, Hewlett-Woodmere, New York, and adjunct professor at Hunter College. He is the former deputy superintendent of schools for the Board of Cooperative Educational Services in Nassau County, and executive director of The Education Council for School Research and Development. He was the coauthor of the three books listed above, as well as *Using Instructional Media Effectively, Visuals into Words, Quest for Questions,* and other booklets on curriculum subjects.

The Dunns have four teenagers living at home. Both authors have trained teachers and administrators in the areas of teaching and learning and have been involved in a number of research projects, including career aspirations, learning and teaching styles, individualized instruction, and curriculum topics such as reading, writing, and arithmetic.

Contents

How to Cope with the Influences of Family, Friends, and School • Understanding Your Daughter's Thinking and Language Development during Adolescence • Understanding Your Daughter's Physical Development during Adolescence • Understanding Your Daughter's Career Choices • Teaching Your Daughter to Cope With and Control Her Future through the Continuing Development of Thinking Skills

Acknowledgments

We wish to acknowledge the special contributions of selected New York University faculty to the development and completion of the original research on which a portion of this text is based. Dr. Ethel J. Alpenfels, professor emerita of Anthropology and recipient of the Great Teacher Award for 1972, Dr. Henrietta Fleck, professor emerita and former chairperson of the Department of Home Economics and Nutrition, and Dr. Ellis F. White, former chairperson of the Department of Higher Education at New York University, now dean emeritus, University of Northern Florida, were constant in their availability, guidance, encouragement, and support. They each richly deserve the honor intended by this recognition.

A special word of appreciation is given to Isobel Cameron who typed the manuscript with the kind of dedication and professionalism that we advocate for all people.

Acknowledgment is gratefully made to the following copyright holders for permission to reprint from previously published and/or original materials.

The National Association for Better Broadcasting, 2315 Westwood Boulevard, Los Angeles, California, for an excerpt from *Television for the Family*, printed annually as part of the winter quarterly, *Better Radio and Television*, subscription rate $4.00. Copyright © 1976.

D. C. Heath and Company, Lexington, Massachusetts, for an excerpt from *Children's Literature: An Issues Approach*, by Dr. Masha Rudman. Copyright © 1976.

Women on Words and Images, P.O. Box 2163, Princeton, New Jersey, for an excerpt from *Dick and Jane as Victims*, copyright © 1975, and for an excerpt from *Channeling Children*, copyright © 1975.

The Parker Publishing Company, Nyack, New York, for an excerpt from *The Educator's Self-Teaching Guide to Individualizing Instructional Programs*. Copyright © (1975).

Foreword

By Dr. Wayne W. Dyer

When I first heard about Rita and Ken Dunn's projected new book, I had hopes that, at last, someone had undertaken to provide parents with practical guidelines for channeling their daughters' growth so that the more common mental health problems and emotional tensions of adult women might be avoided. These expectations were realized, for after I read the manuscript, I knew that *How to Raise Independent and Professionally Successful Daughters* was a real breakthrough for overcoming many of the restrictive attitudes that tend to narrow our expectations—and, therefore, the horizons—of most females.

I am impressed with the Dunns' detailed advice which helps girls to build a sense of identity without guilt, independence without constant need for approval, and increasing success without the need to blame anyone for the obstructions that must be overcome along the way. In fact, this important work is "must" reading for parents of girls because its positive messages and specific suggestions will be effective for all human beings.

This original, informative book provides well-researched and documented, long-term guidelines for overcoming negative, self-defeating patterns of behavior. It mirrors and extends much of my own recent work in *Your Erroneous Zones* with specific and practical advice for fostering, nourishing, and instructing young girls from the cradle through their teens.

If you want to help your daughter reach her maximum potential and become internally controlled, independent, and professional, then what follows will become an indispensable resource.

Introduction

This book is a guide whose time has come; indeed, it is long overdue. It is a step-by-step developmental text for parents on how to raise independent and professionally successful daughters. It is a guide that begins at the beginning——at birth—and carries parents through the difficult teen years.

Our view, that the road to independence and professional success for girls begins at birth, or at least in the early years, grows out of a decade of our own research, the basis of which was Rita Stafford Dunn's comprehensive study of outstanding professional women, conducted during the mid-sixties.* One of the startling revelations of this original investigation was that many professional women recognized their interest in their respective fields *long before* they entered college. In fact, a very large proportion of those several hundred independent females were motivated toward their professions before they entered high school! For example, nearly two-thirds of the women doctors and dentists in the population surveyed, more than half the female attorneys, and nearly three-quarters of the nursing administrators had made their basic career

*Rita Lynne Stafford. "An Analysis of Consciously Recalled Motivating Factors and Subsequent Professional Involvement for American Women in New York State." Doctoral dissertation, New York University (1966). This study earned the N.Y.U. Research Scholarship Award (Alice Crowe), 1966.

decisions *before* they completed high school. Further, more than 50 percent of these early choices were made during their elementary and junior high school years.

Thus, it is essential that parents become involved directly in building positive attitudes, skills, and individual identities in their daughters early, when it counts most, as it has for boys since the beginning of time. Moreover, it is our belief that there are specific, developmental steps that parents can take to ensure independence and professional involvement for their daughters. These concrete and practical approaches are drawn from the authors' research and a decade of applications with thousands of school children of all ages.

Programs for the development of career aspirations, time management skills, learning styles identification, self-instructional techniques, basic skills, and kinesthetic and tactual—as well as visual and auditory—learning resources are a few of the major areas in which the authors successfully have bridged the research-practice chasm. This cumulative knowledge is herein focused on the release of females from their inferior placement in our society—a level determined by deep-rooted prejudice against women which starts the instant they are born, *or before.* The basic thesis of this book, therefore, is that the recalled perceptions of successful, outstanding professional women, when combined with a developmental program of planned experiences and activities, a designed environment, and positive attitudes, will aid daughters to become both independent and professionally successful women themselves.

On a broader scale, the feminist movement will receive the effective momentum it requires and deserves in order to reach its goal of equality. In this regard, women's-rights authors consistently have tended to define the problems of females as adults, when it is too late. Moreover, feminist writers, by and large, have not identified many practical solutions, nor have they established a source for obtaining answers to channeling young girls toward an improved existence. Actually, a review of the many fine articles and books by feminists supports our view that most of their work, to date, has been more theoretical than practical. Many recognize that they have identified more problems than solutions. Betty Friedan's classic *The Feminine Mystique*, for example, clearly identified the needs of women but offered little or no concrete assistance to our daughters.

This problem persists for adult women, too. Indeed, as reported in recent journals, news articles, and Sunday magazine sections, many adult women during this decade have become more confused than ever in their search for independence, success and self-fulfillment. An increasing number of grown females are frantically seeking fuller orgasms, open marriages, homosexual or bisexual relationships, plastic beauty, children out of wedlock, higher wages, and better positions. After a brief fling at glamour and adventure, some even declare themselves for motherhood in an archaic style—barefoot and pregnant in the kitchen, a kind of negative imprisonment, rather than the freedom that the choice to raise children can provide.

The reason for continuing and escalating frustrations for adult women—feminist or not—is that the realization and attempted change begins too late. Indeed, the recognition of an inferior status produces indignation and unhappiness—but little hope. Thus, for some women the "equality" and self-identity they seek, as individuals and as professionals with appropriate careers and salaries, may be fading farther into infinity, as is their universe—and just as society is beginning to permit individuals greater latitude in the selection of their life styles!

This personal deprivation of self-fulfillment for many adult women often is caused by their nonentrance into the professions, even though they have the basic ability and talent. More important, not having the right start results in the tragic loss of their unrealized contributions to humankind. If encouraged and supported from birth, girls could aid in the conquest of cancer, heart-disease, the elimination of pollution and poverty, the acceleration of space exploration, and possibly, the removal of pain and death itself from the human experience. For we literally are wasting half, or more, of our most precious resource—people—when females generally are treated (and thus react) like a subservient minority group without professional aspirations. Obviously, all individuals, including women, should be given the opportunity to grow and to contribute at their highest level of potential, but, to date, this has not been the practice in most of the world. There is hope, however, for the solution is clear: Female consciousness and fulfillment must *begin at birth by providing each newly born daughter with the environment, knowledge, attitudes and developmental experiences* that will overcome the stereotypes and societal shackles that restrain today's women from becoming self-realizing adults.

This book, then, will aid parents to nurture their daughter's life between delivery and career decisions. It will suggest what to say, what to read to her, what should be done in various real life situations, and what she should and should not see on television or at the theater. It is a blueprint Magna Carta designed to release daughters from future serfdom in a man's world; for while it is not too late for some grown women to choose or change their vocations, the change that is needed to sustain the future of the women's movement must begin at the cradle—not the podium.

We believe that this book is badly needed, because it is the first that is written specifically to help parents raise daughters. Cognitively, socially, and emotionally most girls are crippled from infancy on; this text will aid mothers, fathers, grandparents, guardians, and teachers to help young girls to become healthy, happy, independent, and professionally successful.

The women's movement should not allow itself to fail because it starts too late in each girl's lifetime. This book begins early—before it grows too late.

1.
The Problem:
Parents Prevent Their Young Daughters from Growing Up as Successful, Professionally Oriented Individuals

Our twentieth-century daughters, with few exceptions, are bound up emotionally in restrictive tape just as severely as were the feet of little Chinese girls in times gone by. Our daughters' natural creativity, ambition, desire for self-realization, and chances for success and independence are confined in social-adhesive roles that prevent growth as surely as the crippling gauze applied by well-intentioned parents to the infant females of Cathay. To the Chinese culture of that era small feet and short strides were feminine and beautiful; to the American society of today lack of aggressiveness and the absence of professional ambition are feminine and appropriate. The roar of pain from adult women in the various liberation movements often comes too late to change their chances to obtain normal achievement through equal growth and opportunity.

Without early development of the basic ten attributes required to achieve independence and success, such as ambition, persistence, poise, and individuality, girls cannot achieve personally what boys do in this social and economic system designed to enhance male superiority. Society's tragic error, therefore, is apparent—girls are enslaved emotionally during their formative years and thus are doomed to inferior roles and a kind of minority status.

Boys, on the other hand, receive career involvement attitudes from

1

the cradle through the toddler stage, when they begin to receive plastic baseballs, cars, guns, airplanes, space ships, and medical kits or have children's books like *The Little Engine That Could* read to them. Girls receive negative attitudes toward career involvement, individual identity and personal choice of life style from the moment they are given their first dolls, dressed daintily, encouraged to bake, prevented from climbing and dirtying their clothes, and are read the same *The Little Engine That Could.* This widely heralded *and accepted* story deleteriously describes the weakness of "she" trains and the power, persistence and triumph of "he" trains. Subtle as the comparisons may be, they are reiterated time after time in much of the literature to which our children are exposed.

The stereotypes of male strength, aggressiveness, destined professional ability, or superior intelligence for boys and the clichés of female weakness, passiveness, and satisfaction with motherhood as the major goal for girls begin with the first blue outfit and baseball teething ring you supply boys in the nursery and the pink layette (complete with ribbons and lace) that mothers bring to dress their daughters at the hospital. Also, in several conscious and unconscious ways, boys seem to be preferred by parents of both sexes[1]—an attitude which is destructive to the identity development of girls.

Research, however, evidences an even more insidiously debilitating pattern of continuing parental repression of female development. When girls exhibit ambition, we call it "aggressiveness"; when they demonstrate a thirst for knowledge, we suggest that they not rush and that they should enjoy their childhood; when one of them is energetic, we urge her to "act like a lady"; when they become involved actively, we disparagingly call them tomboys; and when they are creative, we deplore their uniqueness by questioning why they can't "do what they're supposed to, like other little girls." Parents often exhibit subtle displeasures which discourage their daughter's personal growth. This basic blunder is expressed in several ways, including "she's only a little girl" and extending to "she won't be popular, liked, or accepted." These phrases have undoubtedly blunted the self-confidence and aborted the dreams of more daughters than most adults realize.

Liberation or, better still, freedom to grow for all children must begin at birth because it is—

TOO LATE AT AGE FOURTEEN!

It is difficult for many parents to realize that the future of a high percentage of their daughters has been determined prior to the age of fourteen.[2] Indeed, by that time the aspirations, attitudes, and future professional directions for a substantial number of likely-to-succeed young ladies are set, as surely as if they had been programmed by some diabolical technology of the future. For example, of the population of professional women studied in Rita Stafford Dunn's award-winning doctoral research, 40 percent of the dentists, 29.7 percent of the attorneys, 37.5 percent of the physicians, 15.8 percent of the educational administrators, and 25.8 percent of the nursing administrators initially recognized their interests in their fields *prior* to the age of fourteen. If combined with those who had identified their professional selections *prior to college,* the totals include 60 percent of the dentists, 52 percent of the attorneys, 65.5 percent of the physicians, 32.6 percent of the educational administrators, and 71 percent of the nursing administrators. These figures suggest that career decisions tend to be made very early in the lives of professional women. Therefore, what they will be, how they will live, and how well they will cope with our changing society are largely determined long before they ever apply for admission into college and are essentially irreversible. Serendipity has very little to do with these life prognostications, and, as a matter of research fact, knowledgeable and determined parents undoubtedly can influence their daughter's pattern of existence and be relatively certain as to the positive outcome of their plans.[3] It is essential, therefore, that parents involve themselves positively in their daughter's future *early—before* it is too late.

THE "GIRLS DON'T DO THAT" SYNDROME
AND OTHER PARENTAL BLUNDERS

Despite strong gains by the feminist movement, "girls don't do that!" and similar expressions still may be overheard among too many families across the United States. The problem, of course, is that advances toward equality for women have been limited thus far to feminist advocates, sophisticated intellectuals, selected educators, and a small percentage of the book-reading public. Too many grandparents, parents, and relatives born prior to the early 1950s continue to project attitudes that are the result of generations of sexist brainwashing. Here are some examples that persist in too many homes and apartments:

1. The Well-Meaning Uncle
Uncle Charley is well-liked by the family. He's good-natured and humorous but rarely serious about things that are important. Good old Charley always boasts that his "beautiful" ten-year-old niece, Lisa, will never have to worry about supporting herself, because many rich men will undoubtedly pursue her until she accepts one for marriage. Once, someone asked Lisa what she wanted to be when she grew up. In Charley's presence, she responded, "A doctor who takes care of babies." Uncle Charley took her into his arms and said, "Lisa, you're too pretty and feminine to get into the rat-race and struggles at colleges of medicine. All you'll have to do is smile at your doctor-husband, and he'll buy

you anything you want." Lisa looked at Mom, who smiled but didn't contradict Uncle Charley. Dad wasn't even listening.

2. The Playful Grandpa

Six-year-old Sue frequently was eased onto Grandpa Ed's lap with a great deal of affection. He insisted that she be "dressed up" whenever he came, and he particularly loved pink ribbons, pink frills and pink lace all over his adored granddaughter. Until recently he'd enjoyed placing her on his shoulders and marching around with her as if she were a toy. In fact, he called her "doll" more often than "Sue" or "Susy." He especially looked forward to each Easter, when she wore the pink bunny costume he'd bought for her. Grandpa was thinking of getting a larger size for her next year.

3. The "Don't Rush Her" Father

Bill was proud of his three sons and his daughter. They were all doing well academically; the two older boys were in college, and the youngest lad was in a high school honors class. Betsy was in eighth grade, and one night she explained the school's new career guidance workshop to her mother. Father Bill came downstairs at about that time and overheard Besty's mom encouraging her to register for it and to explore various vocations. He exploded with exasperation, "For goodness sake, Martha! Don't rush her! Let her enjoy her childhood. The world of work is difficult enough for men without thrusting girls, especially young ones, into it. She's got plenty of time to think about things like that!"

4. The "Girls Don't Do That" Mother

Mary worked hard to provide a loving and well-kept home for her husband and four young children. The two boys, however, were permitted to be exuberant in their activities, whereas the two girls were protected from injuries through the encouragement of passive play. One night, the boys played "cowboy," with one acting as a horse. They asked the girls to do the same. Mother came upon the scene just as Ann, on top of Lil, and Bob, aboard Richard, were about to ride out after the rustlers. Mary immediately pulled Ann off Lil and scolded them both. "Will you please act like girls!" she shouted, "Only tomboys behave that way!"

The incidents above represent a small sampling of the damaging words, actions, attitudes, and repeated negative or restricting behaviors still exhibited by well-intentioned parents, relatives, and friends toward young girls. They constitute a few of the frequent, insidious blunders that restrict the growth and development of our daughters.

The well-meaning uncle discouraged Lisa's budding ambition to become a pediatrician by implanting fears of a difficult, insurmountable course ahead. Uncle Charley equated beauty with success and offered it as a means of gaining an accomplished or wealthy husband, rather than encouraging Lisa to achieve that status for herself. Mother and Father either acquiesced to Uncle Charley's philosophy or were unaware of how his statements might affect ten-year-old Lisa's aspirations.

Many people in our society treat young girls as plaything bunnies and dolls. As a result, our daughters' thoughts and attitudes are molded into narrow or limited expectations for themselves as adult women. A few become Playboy Bunnies, in keeping with their earlier roles as children; most simply accept positions or a way of living far below their potential. They permit (and sometimes encourage) manipulation by other adults—primarily men.

Father Bill's "concern" for his daughter effectively destroys interest, stimulation, energy, ambition, curiosity, growth, and other positive attributes needed by girls to achieve equality of knowledge and opportunity. His, "Don't rush her, Martha" increases her dependence and delays or may even eliminate independence. Little Betsy is exposed to the concept that college and work are all right for boys but that girls should remain childish and protected longer than boys and should not be concerned about the various exciting fields of career involvement legally open to all.

Mary's inconsistent attitudes toward what boys and girls do when playing will develop similar values and beliefs in her daughters. They will begin to believe that roughhousing and aggressive play are for boys and are inappropriate or "wrong" for girls. Her daughters' feelings, emotions, and attitudes may be distorted—perhaps forever.

INVESTMENT IN BOYS; DIVESTMENT OF GIRLS

These common mistakes, repeated by many adult relatives, are reinforced by the widely held belief that boys are an "investment" in the future; that girls merely procreate and "continue" the future. Thus, too many families consider only the boys when attempting to cope with the costs of college. The happiest words in these households are, "My son's becoming a doctor; my daughter's getting married."

Occasionally, a daughter succeeds, despite a father's (or mother's) attitude about college for girls. One woman pediatrician told us:

My father resented my mother's insistence that we attend college and become income-producing. He said there was "no money for foolishness like sending girls to school." My mother went back to nursing so that she could support us through our undergraduate education. He never stopped grumbling about how hard we were making Mother work in order to satisfy *our* ambitions. Now he tells everyone he meets about his "doctor-daughter." Mother doesn't talk . . . she just glows. . . .

Most girls are not that fortunate. Fathers, and mothers too, often prevent their intelligent daughters from attending college or graduate school because they consider it a luxury, saying that "they'll marry and never *use* their education." Therefore, investment in a daughter's future becomes related to her ability to attract and marry a desirable or potentially successful husband and, subsequently, to fulfill her many housekeeping roles.

Unfortunately, the outdated misconceptions of the parents are perpetuated and passed along to each succeeding generation which continues to raise daughters (and sons) with a handbook of society's most cherished and worn-out clichés, stereotypes and hand-me-down narrow viewpoints or shallow values.

ANALYZING THIRTY-TWO OVERUSED AND UNDERREFUTED CLICHÉS

Unfortunately, parents too often believe the frequently joked-about clichés concerning girls and women; inaccurate and incorrect statements that are repeated often enough become familiar to the ear and begin to sound like truth. Despite statistics to the contrary, women do not challenge their negative image as "poor drivers" or "emotional thinkers." By their silence and acquiescence, mothers reinforce the various myths of inferiority with daughters and permit them to believe that their mission in life is to be the "caretaker of a man's castle."

A listing of thirty-two of the more commonly repeated clichés permit us to recognize the magnitude of the problem. Only *four* are true. Can you identify which ones they are?

SEX BIAS INVENTORY CONCERNING FREQUENTLY USED CLICHÉS ABOUT WOMEN

Directions: Read each statement and then check either TRUE or FALSE on the appropriate line. Then compare your answers with the explanations that follow this exercise.

CLICHÉ	TRUE	FALSE
1. In order to succeed, a woman must be "better than a man."		
2. Women are more emotional than men.		
3. Men are more logical than women.		
4. Women are less intelligent than men.		

CLICHÉ	TRUE	FALSE
5. Men are stronger than women.	_____	_____
6. Women have more difficulty making decisions than men.	_____	_____
7. Women are influenced more by their fathers than by their mothers.	_____	_____
8. The best place for a woman is at home.	_____	_____
9. A career woman's marriage and children suffer.	_____	_____
10. It is easier to take care of a home than to hold a job.	_____	_____
11. There are more professional men than women, because men outnumber women.	_____	_____
12. Many graduate and professional schools continue to restrict the number of women who may enter—and therefore continue a quota system.	_____	_____
13. A daughter's education is less important than a son's.	_____	_____
14. Medical schools are correct to limit the number of females admitted, because men will practice medicine for many years, while women will marry and become mothers.	_____	_____
15. The more intelligent and accomplished a girl, the less sexually attractive she is.	_____	_____
16. Successful professional women (particularly those in medicine and law) are usually "old maids."	_____	_____
17. Men hate to work for women.	_____	_____
18. Women prefer to work for men.	_____	_____
19. Women receive lower salaries than men for the same job.	_____	_____
20. Men should be "boss" in the family.	_____	_____
21. Daughters should be "seen but not heard."	_____	_____
22. Men do not feel comfortable with "brainy women," and therefore a girl shouldn't appear to be overly intelligent.	_____	_____
23. A woman who really loves her husband and children does not become very involved in activities outside the home.	_____	_____
24. Divorce is more likely to occur when the wife is professionally involved.	_____	_____
25. Women who work experience more headaches and backaches than women who stay home.	_____	_____
26. Your daughter's marriage is more likely to succeed if she leaves school to support her husband, so that he can complete his education.	_____	_____
27. Your daughter is likely to go to college if you did.	_____	_____

CLICHÉ	TRUE	FALSE
28. Mother love is naturally stronger than marital love.	——	——
29. A woman's behavior is more difficult to understand than a man's.	——	——
30. A good mother loves all her children equally.	——	——
31. It is safer to ride in a car driven by a man than by a woman.	——	——
32. Women have no mechanical ability.	——	——

Now compare your answers and thoughts with the reasoning or research noted for each of the above statements. Never again fall prey to loosely stated and unsupported clichés about women. Fortify your daughters (and sons) against the perpetuation of nonsense.

     1. In order to succeed, a woman must be "better than a man."
False.
It is not true that "in order to succeed a woman must be better than a man." It is only true that women *believe* this to be so. They accept this fallacy because of the decades of discouragement from parents, guidance counselors, teachers, college admissions officers, personnel directors, and male executives. They succumb to this negative concept because they are not aware of and do not know how to use recent Title IX antidiscrimination legislation to eliminate insidious practices, such as arbitrary promotions, quota systems, and biased salary differentials. In this regard, the United States Department of Labor booklet, *A Working Woman's Guide To Her Job Rights*, will aid in equalizing opportunities for persons of similar abilities. Low grades also tend to discourage women more than men,[4] because they have been conditioned to believe that their chances for success are poor unless they are academically superior. Actually, self-motivation and persistence are more important than academic ability in achieving success.[5]

     If, as parents, we can help our daughters to overcome those negative attitudes that tend to limit their professional aspirations and simultaneously encourage them to challenge illegal and discriminatory educational and employment practices, the next generation will realize that each woman *can* succeed just as well as men with similar abilities.

     2. Women are more emotional than men.
False.
Men and women are equally emotional, depending on the individual makeup of each person. Little boys, however, are taught to *suppress* their emotions ("Be a man! Only sissies cry!"), while girls are encouraged to *express* them. This disparity in early training has been suggested as one of the reasons that more men than women are prone to ulcers and heart failure.

     3. Men are more logical than women.
False.
Men and women are equally logical, depending on the individual. It is true,

however, that society's attitudes toward the intellectuality (and, therefore, logic) of women frequently *cause* girls to *act* less rationally, in order to retain what they believe to be the appropriate characteristics of femininity. Girls often have been made aware that they "should never act smart around a boy"[6]—a misconception that may have developed out of statements such as this one made in 1944:

> . . . only exceptionally talented girls can carry a surplus of intellect without injury to their affective lives . . . [for] . . . women's intellectuality is, to a large extent, paid for by the loss of valuable feminine qualities. . . .[7]

Fourteen years after this "bromide" was published, the Tiedman, O'Hara, and Mathews findings began to counteract the theories of necessitated intellectual restrictions for "feminine" women:

> The damage to the feminine core development may result from the injury to the woman's self-concept that results from society's views of intellectual activity in women, rather than from the process of intellectualization itself.[8]

One study of the lives of successful women executives found that although their mothers represented the traditional feminine role model, they also actively supported their daughters' total freedom of exploration of what were considered male roles.[9] This might have been an emotionally laden issue for the mothers, but they unanimously (and independently) treated it in a most logical way.

    4. Women are less intelligent than men.

False.

Men and women are equally intelligent, depending, again, on the individual. Women, however, ". . . are given greater freedom to fail."[10] In addition,

> In a thousand subtle ways, a young college woman is exposed to the concept that women are less capable, less intelligent, less serious, more emotional, and less important than men. It propels her toward "soft" courses, pushes her into "women's" occupations and away from science, and finally, closes the door on many kinds of work for which she may be well suited.[11]

Despite these factors, girls continually achieve higher grades in school than boys do.

    5. Men are "stronger" than women.

False.

Men are frequently more *muscular* than women but are not as resistant to sickness. Insurance companies indicate that women live longer and contract fewer illnesses than men. Indeed, Ashley Montagu, world-renowned scientist and writer, claims that women are stronger than men in every way except muscular strength, which, in part, results from cultural expectations and habit patterns. In his classic *The Natural Superiority of Women*, Montagu suggests that women are emotionally more flexible and stable, physically more durable, socially more capable, and probably more intelligent.

      6. Women have more difficulty making decisions than men.

False.

Depending on the individual, women are as capable of reaching decisions as men. Women, however, frequently must take into account additional considerations (husband's employment, lack of domestic help, care of children, and lack of financial independence) that do not necessarily affect men.

      7. Women are more influenced by their fathers than by their mothers.

False.

Both parents tend to influence their daughters, but in terms of education, achieving girls tend to be more influenced by their mother's experiences than by their father's.

      8. The best place for a woman is at home.

False.

The best place for a woman is where she truly wants to be. Each parent "belongs" at home (and involved with the children) some of the time, but Rita Dunn's study revealed that of the outstanding professional women interviewed, 85 percent of the physicians, attorneys, dentists and administrators believed that their career involvements were "equally appropriate" or even "more appropriate" for women than for men. More than 95 percent of this sample believed that their professional lives had either "strengthened," "enriched," been "entirely compatible with," or had had "no relationship to" their married lives, and the majority had met their husbands in either college, professional school, graduate school, or after they had entered their professions. It should be noted, too, that less than 4 percent of the physicians and educational administrators, *none* of the dentists, and less than 13 percent of the attorneys and nursing administrators stated that they would *not* encourage their own daughters into the same profession. Interestingly, most of the women in nursing said that they preferred that their daughters choose *medicine.*

      Countless studies describe the emotional tensions experienced by intelligent and/or talented women who face the discrepancy between their personal needs for achievement and society's feminine role model, as witnessed through the realities of a homemaker's existence. This is not to suggest that *all* women *should* or *are able to* choose combined career and home roles, but certainly, daughters should be prepared, so that, should they *want* their lives to include either or both options, they will not be "boxed into" (or out of) a narrowly defined, traditional role.

      It is interesting to note that an extensive study of college coeds found that those young women overwhelmingly viewed work as a very important and meaningful way of satisfying a wide range of values such as self-fulfillment, security, and interpersonal satisfaction but that the same young women said that they also looked forward to family life—which they viewed as largely *tedious, monotonous* and *routine!*[12]

9. A career woman's marriage and children suffer.

False.

It is the *quality*, not the quantity of time spent by parents with children in the home that determines the well-being of both. Working mothers, however, should be certain to have someone at home when children are not in school. A daughter (or son) must know that there is a supportive person available to care for and protect her when the mother is away.

Close examination of the lives of many vocationally successful women reveal enhanced marriages and major contributions to society. Further, their children were not affected negatively.[13]

10. It is easier to take care of a home than to hold a job.

False.

Essentially, this answer must be determined by each woman. It must be noted, however, that many career women say that when they return to the home they discover that "housework is physically and mentally tiring." Fewer major and minor illnesses occur among working women, and although it may be true that sick women usually do not work (which might account in part for these statistics), it is also true that many women who experienced continuing minor ailments while at home were happy to report a total loss of symptoms once they became employed. In addition, since school girls tend to achieve better than boys academically,[14] as women they may find it easier to use their mental abilities in employment than their physical abilities in caring for a home.

11. There are more professional men than women, because men outnumber women.

False.

The U.S. Department of Labor reports that in the United States there are more women than men.[15] The lesser percentage of women in the professions usually is caused by the persisting cultural images of masculine and feminine roles and the resulting lack of motivation in women which reduces strong academic, vocational and professional commitments.

12. Many graduate and professional schools continue to restrict the number of women who may enter—and therefore continue a quota system.

True.

A distinction must be made between legal equality of admissions policies and practical equality based on educational and occupational statistics. Women's rights to the same training and professional opportunities as men are formal, legislated national objectives under Title IX. In *Barriers to Women's Participation In Postsecondary Education* . . . , however, Westervelt describes the five major sets of institutional factors that tend to exclude women from education beyond high school: (1) admissions practices, (2) financial aid practices, (3) institutional regulations, (4) deficiencies in curriculum planning and student services, and (5) faculty and staff attitudes.

The combined effect of these factors has been noted by a variety of sources concerned with equal educational opportunities for women,[16] and specific ways of coping with and bypassing insidiously inhibiting factors (such as requirements for residency, full-time enrollment, credit transfers) are described in a 1971 Office of Education document, *Report On Higher Education*, by Frank Newman and members of a special governmental commission.

13. A daughter's education is less important than a son's.

False.
An educated woman serves as an excellent role model and motivating example for her children (particularly for her daughters), and all those with whom she comes into contact. Extensive research verifies that the more educated the *mother*, the more educated the daughter, and *one of the few significant relationships that are repeatedly verified in research studies is the one between a mother's education and encouragement of her daughter's educational achievement and/or subsequent professional involvement.*[17]

A woman's cycle may easily include education, career preparation, marriage, motherhood and entrance into or return to a professionally rewarding life. Her contribution to society will be equal to her mate's, but, perhaps of greater personal importance, she is less likely to suffer both mental and physical breakdowns.[18]

14. Medical schools are correct to limit the number of females admitted, because men will practice medicine for many years, while women will marry and become mothers.

False.
Rita Dunn's research, conducted among outstanding women physicians, attorneys and dentists in New York State, verified that professional women can continue in practice while simultaneously rearing well-adjusted, academically achieving children and maintaining long-term marital relationships. In addition, women have contributed enormously to the advancement of medicine, and because of longer life spans and rotating career involvements (time out for child-rearing and eventual return to the world of work), a woman may engage in her profession for as many years as most males.

15. The more intelligent and accomplished a girl, the less sexually attractive she is.

False.
Sexual attractiveness is a quality determined by each individual, based on his or her own perceptions. An intelligent, accomplished male will appreciate those qualities in a woman and may find her additionally desirable because of them. Also, there has been some evidence which suggests that independent, secure, and successful women tend to be more aggressive and self-fulfilled in sex than are their more passive, timid, "feminine" sisters.

16. Successful professional women are usually "old maids."

False.

As revealed through Rita Dunn's study conducted at New York University, successful professional women tend to achieve successful marriages. More important, however, is the fact that successful professional women have options, and should their marriages prove to be unrewarding, they need not face the economic deprivation that noneducated, nontrained women inevitably do. It may be this very independence and self-sufficiency that saves the marriages of professional women who do not, as Betty Friedan describes in *The Feminine Mystique*, cause ". . . the growing aversion and hostility that men have for the feminine millstones hanging around their necks. . . ."

17. Men hate to work for women.

False.

Most men who actually have worked under the supervision of women do not support this cliché, whereas men who have had little experience in the employ of women frequently do. In recent studies, three-fourths of the male executives surveyed expressed favorable attitudes toward women managers for whom they had worked.[19] More interesting, perhaps, than whether men prefer working under the supervision of either women *or* men is that, in the *majority* of cases, men do not like to work for others of *either* sex and prefer to be self-employed.

18. Women prefer to work for men.

True.

In the survey referred to above, the majority of female secretaries responded that they had no preferences, although some stated that they would prefer working for males. The secretaries who indicated they preferred males, however, had little or no experience working for women, and the reasons they gave for their choices verified that their decisions had been reached on a male-female basis rather than an employee-employer basis.

19. Women receive lower salaries than men for the same job.

True.

Despite the fact that legislation has been passed to protect women against lesser salary schedules for similar responsibilities, *U.S. Working Women: A Chartbook* reveals that virtually every profession reports that women with the same or better qualifications are paid less than men for assuming similar responsibilities. This 1975 Department of Labor publication verifies that annual earnings of women varied by occupation, but that in no salaried group were they as much as two-thirds of those of men employed in similar work, and after allowing for changes in federal income and social security taxes and consumer prices, the ten-year increase in gross median earnings was 21 percent for men and only 8 percent for women.

20. Men should be "boss" in the family.

False.

The concept of a family "boss" or "ruler" has no place in society today. Husbands and wives should be partners and should reach joint decisions that will affect them both individually and as part of a cooperative team. A man who needs to feel that he is the "boss" is one who is less secure than he should be in relation to his wife, women, or society.

21. Daughters should be "seen but not heard."

False.

Although it is easier to live with children who are essentially quiet, the concept of passivity for daughters is incorrect. Children must be taught to think, discuss, state, interact, participate, and share their thoughts, feelings, and reactions. An emotionally healthy daughter will utilize the opportunities for polite verbal interaction with others to develop highly desirable skills which will serve her advantageously as she grows.

22. Men do not feel comfortable with "brainy" women.

False.

"Brainy" men do.

23. A woman who really loves her husband and children does not get involved in activities outside the home.

False.

"Really loving" a husband and children implies that you have learned to give, share, respect, and care for them. It does not imply that you should devote every moment of your life to their needs and desires. Martyrdom is not motherhood or marriage—it is masochism.

24. Divorce is more likely to occur when the wife is professionally involved.

False.

The findings in Rita Dunn's research suggest that divorce is probably less likely to occur when the wife engages in professional practice. It may be that she feels less "trapped" and more in control of her destiny, but among the women in that study, none of the dentists, less than 6 percent of the attorneys, and only 6.5 percent of the physicians had divorced. When compared with the statistics that describe the divorce rate among the remainder of the population, it is apparent that the marriages of professional women have a six to eight times' better chance for permanence. Further, professional wives can contribute immeasurably to the stability of their marriages by being better informed, more financially solvent, less dominating, and more interesting.

Even among nonprofessionals, and despite their comparatively low earnings, women make a substantial contribution to their family's economic well-being. According to *U.S. Working Women . . .* , the family with more than one earner has become a prominent feature of American life, for, in nearly half of all husband-wife families in 1973, both the husband and wife were earners. Wives' earnings accounted for, on the average, 26 percent of the total family income in that year, and as much as 38 percent for wives who worked year round and full-time. Interestingly, children of working mothers typically are in higher-income families.

25. Women who work experience more headaches and backaches than women who stay home.

False.

Physicians have frequently advocated interesting employment for women who are the victims of minor headaches and backaches. Reports verify that in many cases these symptoms tend to disappear when the woman becomes gainfully involved. It has been suggested, therefore, that career participation may eliminate many of the minor physical problems that tend to be aggravated (or caused) by psychological tensions.

26. Your daughter's marriage is more likely to succeed if she leaves school to support her husband so that he can complete his education.

False.

Marriage partners should complete their advanced training or schooling and be able to face the world independently. Both husband and wife can admire and respect their mutual success and not "lean" on one to advance the other's opportunities. The best choice would be for young people to complete their education (minimally, through the completion of college) before marrying. If that is impossible, then each partner should assist the other through school so that they complete their education at approximately the same time.

Selected surveys place the divorce rate in the United States at approximately one of every three marriages and, for some categories and age brackets, one of every two. With odds like these, women must protect themselves against the possibility that their legal liaisons may become one of the less fortunate statistics. Letty Cottin Pogrebin is on target when stating that, ". . . when two persons focus on the enhancement of one person's worth, only that one person is storing away nuts for winters ahead. . . . If the upwardly mobile husband dies or the marriage ends in divorce, the wife's prospective employers don't tend to give much weight to the skills she developed while working for *his* career."[20] *U.S. Working Women* . . . notes that women with more education are likely to be in the higher-paying occupations than women with less schooling, will earn more money, and are less likely to be unemployed when desiring a job.

A man who loves his wife will want to protect her by having her develop marketable skills (through completion of her education), in the event that she may need to use them. Neither partner should "sacrifice" his or her education to enhance the other's opportunities; when a woman leaves school to support a man, he eventually feels guilty and resents his obligation to her, and she feels unappreciated and "used." These reactions are likely to *precipitate* the termination of the marriage.

27. Your daughter is more likely to attend college if you did.

True.

Daughters of educated mothers (and grandmothers) tend to aspire toward and obtain a college education themselves. In fact, the single most important item that determines the level of learning that a daughter is likely to seek is her *mother's education*. Of the 138 separate analysis tables included in Rita's doctoral dissertation concerned with the development of women's motivation toward professional aspirations, the mother's education and encouragement of her daughter's education yielded the most significant relationship.

28. Mother love is naturally stronger than marital love.
False.
Unfortunately, many mothers appear to develop a stronger, more devoted love for their children than they do for their husbands, but this is *not* a "natural" condition. It may be true that children are directly dependent and that this psychologically causes a mother to feel extremely responsible for her children, but "responsibility" is not equivalent to love. In addition, the logic of a mother love that is stronger than a marital love unravels when it is recognized that, ideally, marital love continues and remains enduringly mutual, whereas a child's love for a mother diminishes in favor of the child's own marital love and independence. Moreover, excessive mother love can be extremely harmful to both the child and the marriage. Excessive marital love (when reciprocated) can only be beneficial to all concerned; in fact, "excess" in marital love may be impossible to achieve.

29. A woman's behavior is more difficult to understand than a man's.
False.
Unless women are more complicated and more intelligent human beings than men, there is no reason to assume that they are capable of more complex behaviors. Although men and women use both logic and emotion in determining their actions, they do tend to depend on these qualities in different amounts according to repeated situations in our society. Possibly, this is why some women seem to understand the actions of other women easily, and some men seem to understand the actions of other men without difficulty. It also explains why each sex occasionally has difficulty in explaining the behavior of the other. Bright, insightful people often understand motivation and have no difficulty in explaining the actions of others—male or female.

30. A good mother loves all her children equally.
False.
A good mother is honest and secure in her own emotional reactions and recognizes that the special qualities of some of her children, irrespective of whether they are male or female, may tend to engender more or less love than do others. If she is wise, she will accept her reactions as normal and positive and continue to assure each child that she *does* love them equally (but differently). She need not, however, foster any guilt feelings concerning her own preference for one (or more) over the other(s).

31. It is safer to drive with a man than with a woman.
False.
There have been a number of studies that conclude that women commit fewer traffic violations and are involved in fewer accidents than men.

Statistics on violations and accidents that favor women are usually countered with these arguments (by males):

1. There are fewer women drivers.
2. Women drive during the "safe" hours when the roads are relatively clear.
3. Women do not drive as far or as long as men do.
4. Women are "more cautious" and "less aggressive" than men; therefore they do not take risks and thus drive more slowly.
5. These studies did not measure reaction time or other skills.

No matter which way one slices the data, women appear to be equal to or better than men when safe drivers are rated. Some insurance companies recognize these factors and charge lower rates for women in selected categories. Cursing and using one's car aggressively as a wedge in traffic does not aid in lowering the insurance rates (or blood pressure) for anyone and is considered one sign of emotional and psychological masochism.[21] As far as reaction time is concerned, it would seem that the women truck drivers, cab drivers, and bus drivers during World War II managed very well.

32. Women have no mechanical ability.

False.

There is no doubt that women have demonstrated their ability to acquire mechanical skills as easily as men. Again, the number and kinds of jobs held by women in this and other countries during World War II should have dispelled the female mechanical disability myth. It persists, however, and we all seem to take a measure of glee in the plight of the helpless woman confronted by a mechanical monster.

Examine your answers to the questionnaire and determine your own sex bias quotient for this inventory.

Recognize that the mirror of clichés reflects the generalized stereotypes and confused values that permeate our social structure. These frequently repeated misstatements serve to curb the motivation of many daughters and to restrict their educational and professional aspirations. It is these clichés about women that parents must help to eliminate from their daughter's environment.

THE DANGERS OF THE CLICHÉS

If you have three young daughters, at least one of them will one day be divorced and another will be widowed. The third will be mentally disturbed and require psychiatric assistance prior to her fortieth year, because she will be unable to maintain contact with reality in an era of rapidly changing morality and conflicting social and religious pressures. The causes are rooted in these self-perpetuating clichés and apathetic and misinformed parents.

The thirty-two clichés contribute to divorce in two ways: (1) they lull parents and their daughters into believing that women's chances for success in the professional world outside the home are minimal, and (2) they foster the fantasy that matrimony and motherhood will provide total fulfillment for most intelligent girls.

When faced with the dull routines of daily home and child care, most women are unprepared for and thus unable to alter the new restrictive life style they had chosen when younger—before they were sufficiently sophisticated and knowledgeable to select wisely. In addition, the clichés are focused only on the initial stages in some women's lives; society does not consider that age and experience gradually bring the maturing adult into direct confrontation with the need to move beyond survival and love needs. As a matter of fact, Abraham Maslow, in *Motivation and Psychology*, emphasizes that, once beyond the basic physiological, safety, and love requirements necessary for human existence, *all* human beings require ego enhancement through social recognition and eventually seek self-actualization—a process whereby individuals feel that they are contributing to society through creative, qualitative performance. We strongly believe that Maslow is correct and that intelligent people who succeed in obtaining security eventually are driven toward achieving in ways that move beyond the perfunctory tasks of daily living.

Although the clichés do not *cause* widowhood, they do deprive the surviving female head of the family of the skills that might easily assist her in providing for her children and herself economically. According to *U.S. Working Women . . .* , families headed by women account for a significant and growing share of all American homes. On average, of the 13 percent of women who head families, half are in the labor force, but proportionately more female than male family heads are below the poverty level.

Finally, a woman cannot believe in the clichés and develop self-esteem and pride. We are aware that a lie that is repeated often enough eventually is believed by many. A girl who is repeatedly exposed to the concepts that her species is highly emotional, often illogical, comparatively less intelligent, unable to make decisions, belongs in the home, must be superior to males in order to succeed, is less physically strong, is unattractive when intelligent, is a good woman when she devotes herself exclusively to her husband and children, is not likely to be willing to defy convention and society by aspiring to higher education and professional involvement. And yet, when she accepts the clichés and abides by them, she is inadvertently giving them credence, and simultaneously restricting her own options for happiness—factors which often contribute to mental illness.

Observe your daughter at play or "work," awake or asleep, in conversation or deep thought. She is a very special human being, a person whose identity and opportunity for growth, independence, success, happiness, and self-realization rests largely in your capable hands. You must decide whether you want to influence her future by releasing her from the restrictive clichés and attitudes that are transmitted through a negative culture as some kind of sacred gospel. You may question whether guiding her toward independence and professional involvement is really the best decision that can be made on her behalf. If these are your concerns, please consider the following projections.

NEGATIVE OUTCOMES FOR TRADITIONALLY FEMININE WOMEN

Without direct, knowledgeable, and encouraging parental guidance, daughters tend to absorb and reflect society's values. This suggests that they do not aspire toward advanced education and/or professional involvement. Eventually, they become dependent upon their husbands for personal identification ("My husband's an attorney!"), economic status (what they possess depends upon what he earns), and psychological sustenance ("I love you!")—support which many of today's males are no longer willing or able to provide for a long-term commitment.

During the years your grown daughter remains at home with her children (your grandchildren) to supervise their rearing and "make a home" for your son-in-law, *he* will be involved in the "real world"—an absorbing and demanding day-to-day commitment that gradually brings him into contact with new ideas, jobs, and people (many of whom are single, eager-to-attract-him females!). Your daughter, in the meantime, experiences *lowered I.Q.*,[22] restrictive nonintellectual activities, and a beginning sense of being "trapped" by boring homemaking responsibilities and associations with similarly narrow housewives. As she becomes increasingly shallow and resentful of her plight, she will become demanding of her husband's time and attention. As his interests and talents expand, he will recognize his increased desirability (both professionally and romantically) and will be flattered by many women with whom he comes into contact (and who no longer conform to outdated stereotypes of "femininity"). Your son-in-law will succumb to a "first" affair, and then another, and another—until, eventually, he, too, will feel "trapped" in a marriage that he will believe he has outgrown. In this situation it is only a question of time until strong animosity develops and a divorce is pending.

At this time in her life (when her children are growing and she has no marketable economic skills) your daughter will be faced with earning enough money to take care of herself and her children. If you believe that her (now) former husband will abide by their separation agreement and continue to support his family, as promised, speak to any experienced divorce attorney or Family Court judge and learn about the percentage of fathers who do not comply with child-support agreements (not to mention alimony!). Indeed, many husband-fathers "disappear" to another state or country.

Your daughter may become financially self-sufficient through a great deal of effort and ingenuity, but she will also become bitter and emotionally depressed. She may suggest (request) that she and her children (your grand-children) "come home" to YOU—either for financial assistance, so that you can watch her children while she works (and dates), or so that she can feel a type of security by returning to the nest.

Your grandchildren will survive the uprooting *if* your daughter is strong enough to assume BOTH roles—that of the mother *and* the father (many women do so successfully!). Your former son-in-law will probably remarry (usually a younger woman who is working), attain position and economic comfort (if not wealth), and will visit his children occasionally—when it is convenient for him.

The romantic dream of love everlasting and "forever" is no longer realistic for many young people, and to raise a daughter without preparation for life as it *is* can be cruel as well as neglectful.

THE ADVANTAGES OF INDEPENDENCE AND PROFESSIONAL INVOLVEMENT FOR DAUGHTERS

Independence is defined in the following ways:
- Not *subject* to the authority of another; autonomous; self-determining; free;
- Not affected or influenced in action, opinion, or in other ways by others (able to decide for one's self);
- Acting so as to manage one's own affairs; self-sufficient; self-reliant;
- Not *needing* financial support, help; self-supporting;
- Having a competency.

The single major factor that lowers the level of educational attainment of women appears to be our cultural view of the "feminine role." The feminine role or life style is counterproductive for academic achievement. It stresses a girl's need to attract a male who will marry and support her and for whom, in return, she will "keep house" and produce children. This concept requires the female to become as beautiful as is possible and to learn how to be a homemaker. It does not require that she perform well in school or develop skills so that she is capable of earning a living.

Related outgrowths of the feminine role is the underlying and rarely spoken belief that men are not as intelligent as women and that, as a result, they will be "threatened" by a girl's higher brain power. Girls who wish to have a man support them, therefore, do not belittle their spouses (or boyfriends) by demonstrating superior intellect; rather, they act "dumb" in comparison. They also refrain from obtaining "too much" education, so that they do not limit their chances by sharply reducing the number of men available to them, for since men need to feel superior, they obviously will not select a brighter woman. Finally, girls believe that if they are to achieve in school and in the economic world, they must be demonstrably more able than ever, in order to be successful.

Let us examine this feminine role and each of its subsets in order to demonstrate the advantages that independence and professional involvement hold for our daughters.

Marital Advantages of Independence and Professional Involvement

If a girl's primary goal is to marry someone from whom she can derive status and economic security, she certainly should focus on becoming a professional woman. Rita's extensive research study revealed that although women in the so-called masculine professions tend to marry later in life (either during professional school or after graduate school), 100 percent of the sample *were* married, and 40 percent of the dentists, 51 percent of the attorneys, and 58 percent of the physicians had married men in the same profession. Of greater interest might be the fact that these women *met* their future husbands while engaged in professional studies (16 percent during college, 29.4 percent while in professional or graduate school, and 44.3 percent after graduate school). These women, contrary to popular belief, did not forsake their own educations to help their men complete theirs; instead, both people earned degrees and professional status and then married.

The greater majority of these women dentists, physicians, and attorneys had between one and four children, and contrary to the opinions of many medical school admissions officers, *none* of these professionals remained in practice *for fewer than ten years* and almost 60 percent of them served their patients and clients for *between twenty and forty years*. Eighty-seven percent of this population believed that their professional involvement had either strengthened, enriched, or been entirely compatible with their marital lives. Nine percent insisted that no relationship whatsoever existed between the two.

Other studies of working women support these data, revealing that husbands of working wives tend to appreciate the financial benefits and the personal satisfaction that employment provides their wives,[23] and that the majority *value* their wives' professional interests and view them as having significance in family decision-making.[24] Employed women, themselves, frequently report more satisfaction with their marriages than do nonworking women[25] and, in addition, maternal labor force participation is not significantly related to a child's ability and performance in four-fifths of the comparisons made.[26] Indeed, Rita found that the children of the professional women in her study were college-oriented and essentially professions-bound. The only negativism evidenced toward working women by men was related by Genevieve Pichault, in her study of the husbands of wives who were not involved in the world of work, and by T. Neal Garland, when describing a small group of males whose income was less than that of their spouses.

Therefore, since professional women tend to meet and marry professional men who, for the most part, value their wives' contributions to society and the family, and since the children of these women professionals tend to reflect their parents' respect for education and to proceed toward advanced education themselves, professional involvement can only be considered advantageous to women interested in high socioeconomic marriages.

Economic Advantages of Independence and Professional Involvement

Both husbands and wives were earners in nearly half of the husband-wife families in the United States; in families where the wife was an earner, she most commonly contributed between 20 and 40 percent of the total family income. If equal roles for men and women were realized, it is projected that the material standard of living for families could increase substantially.[27]

Since American women have been living much longer than previously,[28] and longer than their male counterparts, and because so many endure boredom with their homemaking chores[29] and their lives after their children have grown, they will either enter or re-enter and work within the labor market for many years of their lives.

Furthermore, as the number of divorced women has increased, the number of female-headed families has also risen. Such families numbered over 7.2 *million* in 1975—13 percent of all families, and approximately a 73 percent increase since 1960![30] Correspondingly, the number of children in female-headed families grew from 4 million in 1960 to almost 7 million in 1970 and 10.5 million in 1975! More women are required and/or desire to be economically independent. If they must work, the professions offer women opportunities for obtaining higher incomes, self-determination and growth, prestige and status. Further, they are likely to meet men and women with similar interests and desires, because they are involved in the same field.

Psychological Advantages of Independence and Professionalism

The authors support the viability of Maslow's hierarchy of needs.[31] This general sociological model explains that people, throughout history or within a single lifetime, move through a series of levels that begins with basic needs for survival and moves toward self-actualization.

Specifically, Maslow describes humanity's quest as beginning with the necessities of food, clothing, and shelter—without which a person cannot survive. Once these maintenance items have been achieved, the next most important goal is safety—as personified by medical, police, fire, governmental, and/or insurance protection. Once the basic needs and safety have been insured, a person is able to give and accept love—through the development of personal relationships. When secure in the feeling of belongingness, the next objective may become the attainment of esteem or status. The final and ultimate height toward which individuals may reach (as described by Maslow) is that of self-actualization—a feeling of growth and achievement, as demonstrated by personal leadership, creativity, or accomplishment.

Friedan, too, emphatically insists that the human need to grow is basic and that interference with this growth will result in psychic trouble.[32] Significantly, she identifies art, science, politics, and the professions as the only fields which permit an able woman to achieve a combination of marriage, motherhood, identity in society, and the realization of her abilities. Involvement in these career areas enhances one's ego, permits the use of one's abilities through demonstrated achievement, leads to self-actualization, permits variations in geography, amount of time expended, continuation throughout pregnancy or child rearing, and is ". . . a continuous thread, kept alive [and keeping one alive!] by work and study and contacts in the field in any part of the country."[33] Unless our daughters are encouraged to break away from restrictive societal bonds, they will continue to manifest the debilitating neuroses generally associated with minority groups who are unsure of their own abilities because of their repeated exposures to a dominating "majority."

In his introduction to *Academic Women*, David Reisman cited the women students who prefer male teachers. J. D. Kulken and Russell and Phyllis Eisenman made reference to the Black patients who request Caucasian physicians.[34] Phyllis Chesler describes the oppression that drives women into psychotherapy because of their manifestations of a "slave psychology."[35] (She also cites studies of practicing clinicians that demonstrate that the majority *are male* and that they operate with *stereotypic attitudes toward women*.) To be explicit, self-deprecation may occur within any minority group to the extent that it embraces the values of the dominant (in this case, male) society.[36] What is most frightening is that (in terms of numbers of individuals) women in our society represent the *majority*—a majority taught to follow the directives of, to obtain their status and security from, and to serve the male minority. As parents, do you not recognize the psychological advantages of bringing up your daughters so that they function with the independence, confidence, poise, and self-appreciation of a majority group? If not, your daughter is in danger of acquiring a "minority psychosis," even though she is at least equal to males in every way and outnumbers and outlives them!

The problem has been placed before you. It neither has been exaggerated nor overdocumented; we have used valid and reliable research to support our beliefs.

Subsequent chapters will describe how to influence your daughters from birth through high school, so that they will choose independence, professional involvement, and success.

You hold the key. Open the doors to freedom for each of your precious daughters.

2.
What to Do
from Birth to Age Two:
The Precious Years

MY CHILD, MY DAUGHTER: PREPARING YOURSELF
TO RAISE A GIRL

Once you are committed to raising a daughter who is independent and capable of becoming professionally successful, concentrate on examining whether you, like many others, have harbored either conscious or unconscious preferences for a male child—particularly when considering your "first-born."

The roots of this type of sexual bigotry stem from social and economic customs; for example, males carry the family name, whereas females usually surrender this source of pride and assume their husband's. Since, in many societies, males are considered masculine when they procreate extensively, the more grandchildren that carry the family name, the more virile the father and grandfather appear to be among their peers. Girls, therefore, *reduce* this macho image, whereas boys enhance it.

Sons, too, are considered capable of earning a living and eventually contributing to the support of elderly patients. They are, therefore, an economic "investment." Because girls are expected to marry and be preoccupied with the raising of their own children and the caring of their husband and his "estate," girls are viewed as promising little in the way of security for parental old age. In addition, because many boys are more muscular than most girls, they offer an illusion of being able to protect their parents (someday); conversely, everyone "knows" that daughters need to be protected.

Mothers often express the feeling that they have pleased their husbands by delivering a son—almost as if they have produced someone to share his burdens and be his friend.[1] In contrast, most fathers articulate that their initial response to a new daughter is the realization that she must be protected and provided for.[2] Freely translated, someone who needs to be protected and provided for is a responsibility, and a responsibility is a burden.

Intelligent and sophisticated parents often acknowledge that their sole concern for a forthcoming child is that "it" be healthy. This is a mature attitude when it exists. Too often, however, such statements are made in the knowledge that the gender of a future child cannot be controlled and that, therefore, it is safer not to reveal a bias that may someday project a feeling that they did not receive their first choice.

If, in the depths of your heart, you really wanted a son but received a daughter, acknowledge the fact. Say to your spouse—or parents and/or in-laws—"I think I really did want a son. I thought that a son would . . . ," and complete the thought honestly. *Why* did you really want a son? Once stated, the secret no longer requires hiding or guilt and can be viewed objectively. You will probably add (perhaps to yourself), "I am so glad that this child is a daughter!"

If, after considering your past thoughts concerning your unborn child, you honestly believe that you had no preferences concerning its sex, you are a little ahead of the game. Others, however, can "catch up" quickly, for the qualms of once having wanted a son pass quickly, as a daughter begins to "warm" her way into your heart and life.

Fortify your emotional reactions with the knowledge that women may now choose to carry their surnames forward into their marriages by combining the two surnames through a hyphenated pairing, for example, Mrs. Jonathan Rhinebeck-Morganstern. In addition, children of either sex can become the strong friends and allies of their parents, depending on the relationship established between them. Finally, independent and professionally successful daughters are as able to provide economic assistance to needy parents as are independent and professionally successful sons. Obviously, dependent and non–income-producing children of either sex can be of little help.

A number of infant studies suggest that mothers treat their sons differently from their daughters beginning almost at birth. One longitudinal investigation[3] revealed that at three weeks of age, males were attended to, stimulated, imitated, and received affectionate contact from their mothers for twenty-seven minutes more, per eight hours, than females. Considering that infants slept from 25 to 75 percent of the time during the test periods, the comparative amounts of time available for learning experiences were important—particularly since relationships have been evidenced between the amount of stimulation youngsters receive and their future social learning and development. An inner preference for male babies, which might cause mothers to attend to and stimulate them more than female babies, may be overcome, at least outwardly, by the awareness that all infants require holding, snuggling, loving, talking to, movement, and positive stimulation, in addition to maintenance caring.

In general, however, female babies frequently are not given as much parental encouragement as boys in their early strivings for independence[4] and, consequently, do not develop the confidence and independence needed to cope with their environments. Many develop neither adequate skills nor self-assurance and become habitually dependent on others. Thus, from their earliest months, their achievement behaviors are motivated by survival needs and a desire to please. Moreover, perhaps *because* we treat girls differently from boys, the girls' high need for affiliation (a sense of belonging and approval) often blocks their achievement motives, and their performance is either sacrificed, or gained at the cost of high levels of anxiety.

At this point we ask only that you be aware of your inner feelings toward the sex of your youngster, so that you may consciously concentrate on doing those things for your daughter that will overcome the traditional child-raising patterns that gradually and insidiously strangulate individual uniqueness in favor of channelling everyone into expected sex "roles."

BEFORE THE GIRL-BABY ARRIVES

Prior to the birth of your child, consideration should be given to avoiding stereotyped sexual preferences in color, clothes, the environment in which your baby's first years will be spent, and the type of toys that you will provide initially.

Obviously, the pink or blue layette should be considered passé; those colors tend to encourage normally mature adults to coo at and flatter a girl-child in terms of beauty and to (man)handle a boy-child playfully and comment on his apparent strength or size. As innocent as such comments from passers-by might appear, they begin to accent the need for beauty and prettiness of clothes among girls and the respect for strength and power among boys. Beauty is an asset to all, and being strong and having power is *necessary* for all. The frequent approving comments (true or otherwise) to little girls concerning their looks or clothes eventually cause them to focus on these qualities as a means of gaining additional approval. The frequent approving comments (true or otherwise) to little boys concerning their size or strength eventually cause them to focus on becoming stronger and bigger to gain recognition. These comments (particularly because of the repetition and frequency) can be extremely harmful to children of both sexes and can be partially eliminated by the absence of sex-stereotyped colors in your child's environment.

Dressing your infant in green, yellow, brown, white, orange, or red undoubtedly will frustrate many well-meaning strangers who want to comment favorably about your baby but are at a loss as to what to say, because of their inability to identify its gender. That will be a positive step in the right direction, for one of your major goals should be to reduce (as much as possible) your child's exposure to sex-biased comments.

As you develop awareness of the number of people who become stumped and unable to verbalize approval of an infant without first knowing its sex, you will become impressed with the extent to which our mores have dictated how and what we say to little girls and boys—regardless of their actual personal characteristics. If you do not dress your infant in the traditional pink or blue colors, be prepared for the open question, "What is it?" and recognize the adjectives that have been used traditionally to describe girls (adorable, pretty, cute, beautiful, precious, gorgeous, or darling) and boys (handsome, strong, alert, powerful, active, intelligent, energetic, lively, healthy).

Our concern with avoiding "feminine" or "masculine" colors and word-descriptors is *not* to destroy a girl's femininity, but, rather, to avoid restricting her growth along solely stereotyped lines.

1. Girls who are constantly exposed to an emphasis on their physical being soon begin to devote most of their attention to their looks—at the expense of their minds and emotions.

2. Girls who are clothed in dresses are also expected to "behave like a lady" (implying nonparticipation in activity-oriented happenings and a sedateness that prevents the normal expression of personal growth patterns).

3. Girls who are dressed constantly in "feminine" clothing are restricted to emulating traditional "feminine" stances (precluding achievement in competitive sports, exploration, or skill development that do not lend themselves to the natural restrictions of dresses).

Your daughter will not become "masculine" or a "tomboy" because she wears red, white, or blue jeans. To the contrary, she may develop a very precise mental image of her own uniqueness and become reliant on her own good judgement, rather than on what either stylists or "everybody" (her peers) promote as suitable attire for women. Why? Because slacks protect the body from pain when exploring, thereby permitting more movement and activity and learning. Passivity does not enhance mental and physical development, and dresses promote noninvolvement in activities.

If you are thinking, "Part of the fun of having a daughter is being able to dress her in laces, bows, and frills!" you inadvertently are contributing toward producing a replica of the stereotypical girl—the "doll" that eventually becomes somebody's plaything. The real fun of having a daughter should be seeing her gain confidence and assurance and gradually become an independent person. When we surround her with traditionally "feminine" artifacts, we are subtly urging her to conform to the persistent "sugar and spice" image that society has created and maintained.

Color, clothing, and handling are but three of the subtle ways in which we convey to our daughters how they should conduct themselves, what they may or may not do, and what our expectations for them are. Such skillful manipulation is not to their benefit, for it produces dependence and conformity, rather than independence and the skill of weighing each situation on its own merits and of making decisions accordingly.

This is not to suggest that girls should not wear pretty dresses and dainty bows if these are becoming to her and the occasion. Choose clothing to compliment your child's body type and posture and the activity in which she will engage; eradicate from your mind preconceived notions that girls should conform to a particular type of dress. "Feminine" girls remain that way whether they are in overalls, jeans, slacks, shorts, dresses, gowns, or diapers, and "unfeminine" girls are not, in any way, made dainty by long gowns, ruffles, bows, or lacy fabrics. Purchase sensible, durable, washable clothing for your baby's layette and dress her as a "person," rather than as an ornament.

At most times, when your baby is not "on stage," dress her comfortably to permit free movement and relaxation. Overalls and slacks facilitate experimentation with standing, crawling, climbing, jumping, walking, running, and falling that teaches a child what she is and is not capable of doing at a given time. Such movements excite her imagination and gradually build confidence and a sense of power. Dresses will not protect her limbs when she rubs or brushes them against hard surfaces; friction and related abrasions inhibit further efforts and confidence in her ability to achieve. Part of the reason that boys become involved with sports activities at an early age is that their experiences with action-related movements have been positive, because of their clothing and because their parents (particularly their fathers) *expect* them to play "catch," baseball, football, and the like. Encourage your infant daughter to move (if she is so inclined), play on the floor or ground, explore, and try to do things. These activities will prepare her for additional action-oriented efforts that lead to skill development.

If you wouldn't place a hat on a son's head, don't require that your daughter wear one. If she pulls at specific garments because she is not comfortable in them, do not insist they remain on. Give her some latitude in selecting what she will wear at an early age and be aware of her reactions to what you choose. Without recognizing the consequences, we begin to require conformist, subservient behavior in daughters in infancy and grant much more freedom to sons, simply by accepting nonconformist behavior from the latter with less irritation.

WHEN SHE COMES HOME FROM THE HOSPITAL

Speaking and Handling

Babies are, of course, living creatures with physical senses—the ability to hear, see, touch and feel, smell, and taste. Most scientists doubt the efficacy of "talking" to plants, but no one would challenge the need to speak to babies and to take advantage of their other sensory contacts with the world.

Whenever you are with your baby, at any age, speak softly to her, using many of the same expressions repeatedly. For example, "Hi! I love you! I am so glad that we belong to each other!" Hold your baby whenever you can, hug her, pat her gently. All people—but particularly, young, growing children—want to be loved and accepted. We do not know exactly *when* a baby begins to sense warmth and affection (and it varies among children), but we do know that once children feel that they are loved and accepted for themselves (not on the basis of how they behave!), they begin to flourish and bloom. Some researchers now recommend "skin contact" between mother and child during the first twenty-four hours after birth. To infants, love is conveyed through caring, body closeness, and affectionate words. This does not imply that a child should be held continuously; but we do urge that, during an infant's waking hours, available loving adults should hold it, play with it, talk to it, feed and care for it, and provide all the positive stimulations that appear to make sense, without wearing out the parents or developing an overdependence by the baby on external stimulation.

There is no foolproof guideline to indicate exactly how much attention each child should receive each day; common sense must prevail. Be aware, however, that the more interaction that occurs between you and your daughter, the more alert, aware, and "ready" for skill development she is likely to become. Bear in mind, of course, that the birth process itself is a physically exhausting experience for babies and extensive sleeping by a newborn during the first postnatal weeks should not be interrupted. It is during your daughter's *waking* periods that she should be spoken to, held, and warmed by your affection.

During the first few weeks of your child's life, avoid sharp noises, jolts to the crib or bassinet, any sudden change in position, and extremely bright lights. These often cause irritation and irritability among infants. Remind visitors to keep their voices soft and pleasant and to hold your daughter securely (always providing head support). If you can control the situation, avoid having her handled by inexperienced people and children other than her own siblings. Babies are extremely sensitive and may be aware of (and made insecure by) inappropriate embraces.

Smiling

Burton L. White does not believe that infants, during their first six weeks of life, actually smile at their parents, although many parents insist that their children do. Since individual differences among children account for extreme diversity of behaviors, some may, and some may not. We do not consider whether or not a baby smiles during its earliest weeks to be of any consequence. What *is important* is that *you smile* at your baby.

Despite intensive medical studies, we cannot know what actually occurs in the mind of every child. It has been revealed that babies tend to imitate those who are in their immediate environment. Whenever your daughter becomes aware of people's faces, it is better that her focus is on pleasant expressions, rather than the reverse. Therefore, smile. Let her begin to associate warmth and physical comfort with the pleasant and acceptable manifestation of positive facial movements. As soon as she becomes sufficiently able to mimic, she will smile back. The earlier she becomes *aware* of how the people who care for her look at her, the earlier she will be able to begin to respond in a similar manner. That is the beginning of a stage in the learning process and provides both skill and affective (feeling) stimulation.

Reaching, Looking, and Holding

Somewhere between your daughter's first and third month, you will notice that she begins to look and stare at her hand(s). Eventually she will begin to reach out and grasp items, perhaps holding them for a while. At this stage, place objects directly into her hands. Offer these items to her if they fall. As she gets older, encourage the reaching out for a variety of different sizes, shapes, and/or textures, for this is a first step in the evolution of curiosity. It is worthwhile to provide different kinds of tactual experiences for the baby as she becomes able to respond; intelligence actually begins to develop from simple acts like grasping and glancing.

Comforting

You will hear various "grandmother experts" take issue with whether or not to lift and hold her or provide a pacifier for your crying baby. Parents who have and have not rocked (or lifted and held) and/or provided pacifiers for distressed youngsters report various results—sometimes positive and sometimes negative. We are of the belief that a baby's cries should be promptly attended to, because she will learn to rely on your consistent response to her basic needs and will develop feelings of security, rather than frustration.

It is reasonable to alleviate an infant's distress or to respond to it by comforting through any method that is effective. Babies do not cry for "attention." We do not always understand why they cry, but you will not "spoil" your daughter by responding to her quickly. Some children need to suck, others need to be "walked," others feel secure when they are rocked, some like to be spoken to or held, and others are perfectly fine when left alone. Respond to *your* baby as an individual and do not follow the narrowly defined, all-inclusive guidelines projected for everybody else's child by self-proclaimed know-it-alls. Every child is different. What works for one may not for another. Be sensitive to your baby, and if a pacifier is effective, use one. If it is not, try something else. Finally, do not be badgered into accepting someone else's practices; their children are different and require, perhaps, different approaches to satisfy their needs.

Suggested Toys for the Very Young Girl-Baby

We already have mentioned that once an infant can hold onto a rattle, several different sized and shaped samples should be available for diversity. These should always be clean, safe, color-fast, and without sharp areas. If the baby drops the rattle and does not appear to be seeking it, she is still too young to be concerned with this type of toy.

White suggests that two mobiles, one placed approximately twelve inches to the baby's right and the other the same distance to her left (never directly above her) might provide initial interest to your growing infant. He advocates homemade models that emphasize colorful faces, rather than commercially produced types that, he says, appeal to adults, rather than to infants. A slightly larger-than-life-sized crude replica of a mother's, father's, sibling's, and/or grandparent's face might serve adequately and, at the same time, please the baby's family. String a few "faces" from a protected wire clotheshanger, separating them with clip-on clothes pins and, certainly for the first few months, this will provide an interesting "toy" for the baby to observe (not hold).

When your daughter is approximately three to four months old, you might wish to bolt a steel "arm" to the side of the crib. From this arm suspend three or four large, brightly colored toys in different shapes and textures with semirigid plastic, so that it will not move much when she reaches for it. You might select one object in rubber, another in plastic, and a third in wood. Be certain that these are suspended from the arm securely, so that parts will not break or fall into the crib and ultimately endanger the baby. Many babies remain uninvolved with such toys until they are older, but eventually such a device will be of interest.

As your baby becomes able to "sit" in an infant seat, change her environment, so that she may observe different rooms or areas. Small mirrors are appealing to youngsters as they become increasingly alert, but these must be smooth, unbreakable, and without parts that are likely to break off. Playing soft music for some of the child's waking time may also stimulate interest and awareness, particularly since the sense of hearing is far more acute in babies than is the sense of sight.

HOMEMADE FAMILY MOBILE SUSPENDED OVER CRIB

String a few slightly larger than life-sized, colorful, cardboard representations of the faces of family members near—but out of your daughter's reach. Separate them with clip-on clothespins and suspend them from a protected wire clothes hanger.

Speech, movement, a change in scenery, music, simple toys, and people, in moderation, can provide stimulating experiences for your developing daughter. It is good to introduce the baby to a variety of toys and other safe objects early in her life. If she is unaware of them, no harm has been done; if she is aware, she will begin to watch, listen, and learn. If your youngster is no longer an infant, and if you did not provide experiences such as those that have been described, utilize the basic *principles* as soon as you become aware of their advantages. *Talk* to your youngster (at any age) and *listen* to her carefully; provide many interesting changes in her environment, beginning with opportunities to visit different parts of the room, different rooms, others' homes, other communities, other regions, and, if possible, other countries. Expose her to good music (whatever type *you* like!), different activities, and many positive kinds of people. The basic principle remains the same, regardless of the child's age—continue expanding her horizons and her awareness through her senses and increasing mobility.

Based on extensive study of the intellectual and emotional development of the very young child, White recommends a series of toys that could be introduced to a youngster at each developmental stage of her life. These are diagrammed for you, so that you may refer to the chart and experiment with the appropriateness of each item at approximately the time suggested. He urges that parents not succumb to purchasing expensive, commercially-produced toys and repeatedly states that manufacturers are unaware of *when* their sales items are usable and most appropriate for children. He further suggests that parents devise their own replicas, using safe paints and colors and securely bolted attachments.

If your youngster is aware of and responds to a given toy before most of the children of that age category, accept the fact that, in some ways, she has an advanced readiness. If she tends to respond to an item later than most, she will undoubtedly be more sensitive or ahead in another area. In other words, maturation and sensitivity do not run parallel for most children in the same way and at the same time. Individual differences in growth and responsiveness are so extreme that, in reality, there is no accurate "normal" age at which children tend to do certain things; there is only an "age range," and even that is broad, varied, and entirely inapplicable to some children.

For these reasons, we suggest that no harm is done when a child is exposed to an item before the books suggest that she should be "ready" for it; if she appears either to be unresponsive to or frustrated by the object, put it away and try a month later. Conversely, when children appear to be interested in a particular toy before the chart suggests they will be responsive to it, make the item available. So many unexplained factors contribute to a youngster's "readiness" that it virtually is futile to attempt to predict potential maturation to correspond to the availability of interest-provoking objects. Consider the desirability of variety and curiosity-provoking stimulants, and experiment with

TOYS FOR YOUR DAUGHTER'S DEVELOPMENTAL STAGES

alternatives when an item "strikes out." Which specific toy the child plays with, and *when,* is less important (providing that all items are safe and clean) than that the child is interested in varied items and begins to explore them and gradually uses them in different ways.

As your daughter begins to grow older, you will find that ordinary household items (pots, pans, rolling pins, hoses, wheel-barrows, trays, spools of thread, rope, shovels, blocks, or plants will promote more interest and creativity than store-bought, expensive, and intricate devices.

Try to tolerate the mess that results (in the interest of developing motor skill and sensory perceptiveness) and let your youngster pour water or filter sand through a strainer, in the bathtub or outdoors; paint with finger paints in a basement or a bathtub or on the kitchen floor covered with newspapers; run her hands through sand; hammer pegs into a board, and so on. We urge the availability of such activities for they extend interest and alertness, increase "intelligence" and experience, promote involvement and growth, and usually expand a youngster's confidence in herself and what she is capable of doing —vital characteristics of a young lady who will someday be independent and able to function in a professional world. The process should begin at an earlier age than is customarily suggested, and these activities are just as suitable for girls as they are for boys. We strongly believe that a direct relationship exists between an infant girl's exposure to a wide variety of objects and activities, as soon as she is ready for them, and her ability to function well in a diverse and intellectual environment in her later years.

Recent studies have begun to support the thesis that it is never too late to begin and that lost time can be made up. We agree with the first part of that concept and have observed that some children who were "behind" in their developmental readiness to move out into an unfamiliar world have been able to do so eventually. We believe, however, that the earlier you begin (providing your daughter has reached an appropriate readiness stage to correspond to the activities you are introducing), the earlier she will be receptive to each subsequent phase. Even if that were not true, the earlier you begin, the more experiences she will have at each level and the more concrete each understanding and skill will become.

These statements do not imply that children should be forced into playing with specific toys prior to their ability to enjoy and use such items. Our intention is to make people who are concerned with raising little girls aware that the introduction of new items and experiences are enhancing to growth. Reintroduction some time after initial disinterest will be equally effective.

STIMULATING INTEREST IN LEARNING FOR YOUR INFANT DAUGHTER

From Three-and-a-half to Five-and-a-half Months

Place a good (and safe) four- to five-inch *stainless steel* mirror approximately six to seven inches away from your daughter's eyes. Position this item over her crib, so that she can notice her own face from time to time. As she grows, she eventually will begin to recognize her face and realize that, as she changes position and expressions, her image will vary. One day, you will notice that she will begin to "make faces" at herself and will laugh at and recognize her ability to manipulate her features in very interesting ways.[5]

Locate or make an inexpensive crib gym that features a few simple items that your daughter may handle, strike, or pull. A kick-toy placed near the baby's feet but tied securely, so that she can kick it without displacing it, will also provide exercise and something to do. A large, vinyl covered surface strung between the crib uprights with strong elasticized rope (so that it returns to its resting position after the baby stops kicking or pushing) will be enjoyable, while simultaneously permitting her to develop her leg power.[6]

Finally, for this stage of infancy, invest in a good, not-likely-to-tip-over infant seat that can be used to provide a change in scenery for your daughter. Keep her near you while you work, entertain, or relax. It isn't that she needs company all the time; merely that the more stimulation she receives, the more alert she will become. It is true, of course, that *some* babies may not respond at all to stimuli at this age. If that should be true of your daughter, you have lost nothing but a bit of time and effort. Besides, providing her opportunities for growth early in her life will guarantee responses when she is ready. At the very least, you will have gained some time advantage and aided her toward progressing.[7]

From Five-and-a-half to Eight Months

During this stage, many young children begin to evidence a great deal of interest in dropping and/or throwing small objects downward when they are placed within reach. If you recognize that throwing downward is a measure of growth, you may not become irritated at having to pick up the things that baby throws away from her repeatedly.

Collect multicolored objects which cannot fit into her mouth. Permit her the grabbing-holding-elevating-releasing sequence several times and then, when *you* are tired, put the objects away. Do not even try to teach her, "No! No!" as a warning against dropping the items. Her fun (and growth) comes from the power that she develops in being able to experiment, control, and watch what happens to the articles that she drops. She is *not* trying to vex you by discarding the items, and she is not disinterested in them. This is a learning activity for her, precisely because she *is* interested in what happens to the things that she picks up and drops.

Sometimes, when you tire of this activity, permit a young child (your own or a neighbor's) to "play" with your daughter by returning the dropped objects to her. You will not only be helping your daughter, you will also be developing responsibility and a sense of self-worth in the child who oversees her dropping-pick-up-and-replacing activities.

When your daughter begins to crawl, place her in an area that is safe from danger, that is, no electric cords on which to pull, no valuable items which can be reached and broken, no steps on which to fall down, no sharp edges, or other hazards to her safety. A playpen can be helpful for the periods during which no one is free to supervise the baby's activities, but keeping her in a playpen all day will bore her, will prevent her muscles from developing to their potential, and will not provide much experience with leg extension.

In daylight hours it is easy to withdraw plugs from the electric sockets in a single room and move light, easy-to-push objects from the immediate area. Permit your daughter to explore and touch and examine things as she begins to propel herself about. Talk to her; if you have the patience, name some of the objects that she touches. She will not understand the meanings, but your voice will please her, and it has been suggested that talking to infants develops a sensitivity to sound and speech at an earlier age than in youngsters to whom adults do not speak much. Children who are spoken to a great deal tend to become more verbal and expressive than those who do not receive this kind of attention.

Once the area is safe, permit exploration to her heart's content. Do not protect her from experiencing the little falls and drops that inevitably become part of every child's life. Do not make a fetish of falls or bumps, for by doing so, you will be encouraging passivity and fear. When *you* are anxious, you are unwittingly teaching *her* to be anxious, and it has been theorized that anxiety is directly related to passivity and dependence. Furthermore, passivity-dependency may interfere with analytic thinking and some types of creativity.[8] You would not "carry on" if your son fell (at least you should not!); treat your daughter in exactly the same way you would a son. Be aware that *parental encouragement of non-sex-typed activities for girls may correlate with drive for intellectual achievement.*[9] You have another choice to make: Will you treat your daughter like a "person," rather than a frail, helpless, less-than-sturdy weakling and, thereby, permit her to grow up with a healthy sense of confidence concerning what she can and cannot do, or will you surrender to the traditional mode of overprotecting daughters from life's opportunities to learn through personal experiences?

When you choose the first alternative, you are stepping back (in a safe area) and permitting her to explore, measure her own abilities, experiment with textures, sizes, heights, strength, and have other valuable learning experiences. She will be *learning how to learn.* When you select the overprotective option, you are catering to your *own* needs, rather than your daughter's. It will be necessary to steel yourself against the cooing, comforting, and co-opting to which most little girls are exposed, but *she* will benefit from the attitudes and treatment which permit her to grow and to learn.

Once your daughter can move about a little, she will enjoy balls of various sizes that can be pushed and rolled and retrieved and pushed some more. A variety of differently sized, shaped, and textured items (none sharp or small enough to swallow) should be made available to her, perhaps on a blanket or mat placed on the floor. Add a few plastic containers (emptied from food items), and she will be occupied with learning how to put the objects into the containers, take them out, and pour them onto a surface. Her interest in exploring small items and in practicing small skills with them should be encouraged and praised. Change the items from day to day, adding new ones, replacing them, and returning formerly used ones.

This is also the period during which stacking toys may be of interest to your daughter. You can purchase the plastic cups that nest, rings that can be dropped onto a perpendicular pole, or boxes of varied shapes that fit inside each other. Discarded plastic bowls (the kind you might save from margarine or cheeses) or measuring spoons and a plastic jar can serve equally as well. In fact, as described previously, ordinary kitchen items and pots and pans are interesting, sufficiently varied, and attractive enough to sustain many a youngster's attention from this age through to the two- or three-year-old stage for some.

A walker may be appropriate if you have the space in which it can be used and if it is sturdy and not likely to tip over. It will permit your daughter to explore, but it will also permit her to get into places that you never intended she examine. If you do use a walker for her, beginning at about six or seven months, she may enjoy the freedom of movement it permits but will require your *constant* supervision while she is in it. *Never* walk away and leave a child alone in a walker, for the dangers that can arise are too numerous to list.

Restrictive devices, such as playpens, cribs, jump seats, highchairs, and play-and-feed tables have value, in that they protect the baby while you are unable to supervise her, but they stifle a child's movement and limit her intellectual development. True, eventually she will learn all the things about her environment that she might learn at an earlier stage if she were permitted to lie on a blanket on the floor and move when she is able to begin to crawl, but as each new learning is postponed into a later phase of her life, there is more and more to be covered, discovered, and uncovered. Realistically, place her in the safe restrictive areas when you *need* to do so, but spend at least two or three hours each day observing her as she lies in the center of a room that has been made "childproof" or safe for that given period and permit her to get a sense of her surroundings. As she begins to move about and explore, each new movement will add to her developing sense of independence and confidence and will, in the long run, serve her well.

When you are reasonably certain that your daughter can "speak" a word ("Mommy" or "Daddy"), express your pleasure! Tell her how wonderful she is and praise her effusively. Your voice and expressions will convey your pride and pleasure and, from this moment, every achievement should elicit a favorable response from you. You need not continually be demonstrative; do not overact or overdramatize. It is important, however, that you say, "You did that very well! I am proud of you!" or similar statements, so that she begins to develop a sense of pleasure in achievement. At this stage she will want to please you, and eventually she will want to please herself by acquiring new skills and talents.

Children sometimes demonstrate that they can follow simple instructions at this age, and they should be praised for any such performance. Waving goodbye, throwing a kiss, or giving something that has been requested are examples of such behaviors. Begin to *demonstrate* these actions and verbalize them yourself. If you leave, smile and say, "Good-bye," gesturing the wave at the same time. Children need varying amounts of time to learn to respond to this type of behavior, but eventually they do. When they do, reward them with well-earned praise, smiles, a hug, or other appropriate actions.

The first eight months of life are characterized as a period wherein the baby is attracted to many people. Somewhere before the baby's first birthday (perhaps as early as seven or eight months), she may become more selective and resist going to or being near people outside her intimate family sphere. *Do not ever force a child to be held against her will or to respond when she does not want to do so.* You must be more concerned about your daughter's psychological health than you are about either your parents', in-laws', or friends' feelings. A girl who is required to permit herself to be held, hugged, or handled against her wishes is subtly being told that someone else's wishes are more important than her own. You may demand that she comply with *your* wishes on matters of great importance, but save those times for issues of consequence. She is not a doll, a puppet, or a plaything. She is a person, entitled to receive affection or attention when she wants it and entitled to privacy when she wants that. Unless you know beforehand that your aspirations for her center on her becoming a courtesan, resist the inclination to be concerned about how other people react when your daughter does not want to be in their embrace, on their lap, or even kissed by them, and respect her reactions. You can be very sophisticated and accepting, and say, "Sarah does not feel like being held right now. We all feel that way sometimes! Won't you have a cup of coffee?" If that approach does not "sit right" with you, smile, show them this section of this book, and blame it on us! Time will verify the correctness of this approach for your daughter!

From Eight to Fourteen Months

Children between approximately eight and fourteen months are extremely curious and have an overpowering need to explore. White unequivocally insists that, "This urge is the motivating power underlying the acquisition of intelligence."[10] In endeavoring to respond to a child's needs and simultaneously maintain one's sanity, however, a mother is forced to cope with several apparent dichotomies.

On the one hand: (1) it is necessary for a child to crawl, explore, and experiment, or her intelligence will probably not reach its maximum potential; and (2) it is particularly necessary for a girl to have the crawling, exploration, and experimentation experiences, because it is highly desirable that she learn that she is *capable* of and enjoys achieving such wanted experiences before society "mythesizes" her into believing she should be passive, unathletic, and "ladylike."

In opposition to these first two points, (3) it is dangerous for a child to crawl anywhere without limitation; (4) it is unnerving to have to clean up after an exploring child has investigated the many nooks and crannies, doors and cabinets, and boxes and bags that exist in a home; (5) a crawling and exploring child can do a great deal of unintended damage; (6) a child cannot be safeguarded while she is exploring, unless her mother or a capable supervisor watches over her constantly and therefore this phase is a very time-consuming one; and (7) a mother's interests often are different from her baby's at this stage, and it is boring to follow constantly after an infant who needs and wants to examine everything in existence in her home.

At almost every turn, parents need to make decisions concerning how they will raise their daughters. On the one hand, child psychologists like Burton White tell us that this set of needs (to explore and crawl about) is the single most important stage of our children's movement toward intelligence. On the other hand, as intelligent adults, we must decide the amount of stress that we personally can tolerate. If you do not have the time to physically follow and observe your daughter for an extended period of time, permit her to explore for the amount of time that you *can* devote to her. Set aside an area in your home (a single room may have to do!) that is "child-proof" (as described earlier), fill it with many small (but too large to swallow!) multicolored, mul-tishaped, and multisized objects, and permit your daughter to investigate only in that special place. Add a few cardboard or plastic boxes into which she can crawl or a small minigym suitable for indoors. If you do not like to clean up after her, leave that section of your home "as is." Should you not be able to tolerate such disorder, provide her with fewer things with which to play, and you will thus have fewer items to pick up. If you have valuable items that can be destroyed or damaged, put them away until she is four or five and protect them by their absence.

Learning-to-learn skills can develop only when children are provided opportunities to experience doing things. Learning is an active process. The more activities you provide for your daughter, the more she will learn and the more adept she will become at learning.

There is no need to feel guilty if you cannot tolerate extensive disorder and/or do not have the time in which to supervise your daughter for lengthy periods during this stage. Do the most and the best you can. Knowing what is healthful for your child will fortify you, so that you can provide more of it more often. It is not necessary to drive yourself beyond the point of your endurance (whatever that point may be), because a tired parent is not an asset. Babies should be a pleasure for their parents—not a chore. If you are comfortable with a situation, you will be relaxed and pleasant with your child. If disorder and cleaning up afterward makes you tense, permit less of it. Consciously, however, encourage as much exploration, investigation, and activity as your daughter appears to desire and *you* find acceptable. In addition, talk to her as much as you can without tiring yourself. Keep your voice pleasant and low. Use familiar words often; for example, "This is a red box."

You may note that your daughter will become very interested in hinges and low doors at this stage. Kitchen and bathroom cabinet doors will be swung open and closed repeatedly. If you can, attach an inexpensive hinged door to a large box or construct one of cardboard, to reduce noise and danger to hands, and place many of "her" play items inside it. She will be kept busy and absorbed and will simultaneously avoid the hazards of emptying your cabinets and the contents of each can, bottle, or box inside. *A serious note of precaution:* Remove everything that might possibly be dangerous to your child's health from all lower cabinets and place them in a *locked upper* storage bin. Babies are curious about the taste of cleaning powder and everything that looks consumable *to them*—liquids of all kinds, anything that comes in small sizes (like pills), and many similar items commonly kept accessible in kitchens and bathrooms. Keep only safe items within the baby's reach—and be aware that during the next year, high places that appear to be above her reach may not be! She will climb, stretch, and gain entrance into closets and cabinets and must be protected against her own curiosity. Here are some simple precautions that are recommended for parents with children of this age:

1. Move all potentially hazardous substances (cleaning materials, sharp and breakable objects, or contraptions in which fingers or toes may be caught) to locked, sealed, or safely-beyond-her-reach storage places.

2. Fold up all electrical cords on hair dryers, razors, toasters, typewriters, radios, televisions, coffee pots, chandeliers, and the like, so that the objects to which they are attached cannot be pulled down (or up!). Cover unused electric outlets with blank plugs that fit into them, to prevent her from pushing items inside them.

3. Put away all unstable objects that can be moved or pushed easily, such as opened ironing boards (which should NEVER be left standing with irons on them!), unsteady chairs, tables, or carts, upright bicycles, skates, skis, sleds or similar sporting goods, and even heavy picture frames or potted plants—all of which can cause severe damage when pulled downward.

4. Check wooden furniture and railings for splinters and surface breaks.

5. Be certain that all paints within the baby's reach are lead-free.

6. Check all knobs to be certain that they do not come off easily (for many can be swallowed once they do!).

7. Place a latch on your medicine chest—or lock the bathroom door so that the baby cannot enter without you. Keep all medicines and pills beyond the baby's reach.

8. Keep the lids on toilets, washing machines, and dryers closed.

9. Be certain that unused appliances, such as refrigerators, freezers, washing machines, and dryers are disconnected and locked—or wedged open, so that they cannot be closed from the inside.

10. If you are going to be involved for a period of time during which you cannot supervise your daughter, place her inside a playpen or crib. Be wary of times when the phone rings and you do not think that the conversation will be extensive. Pick her up and take her with you to the telephone *before* you answer it. If the caller requires your attention, excuse yourself for a moment and take your daughter to a safe area where she will be confined. Do not ever leave her in the apartment or house alone—not even to get the mail or just to run across the hall.

11. Permit her to experiment with climbing up and down steps only under your supervision. The sooner she tries, the sooner she will be able to develop those skills—though being able to climb *down* takes longer to accomplish (at least a month or two more) than being able to climb up! Use a portable gate to obstruct steps or drops.

12. Babies often need protection from older siblings who resent their presence—and rightfully so! If your spouse, after a year or more of loving attentiveness and devotion, brought home a "playmate" for you—one that you neither requested nor wanted—and, in addition, he/she was affectionate toward that person, do you really think you would *love* the newcomer? If you were not physically, emotionally, and financially independent and therefore were unable to leave that terrible situation, you would undoubtedly try to hurt (immobilize or annihilate) the rival for your spouse's affections!

If you were told, "I love you just as much as before!", "I need your help in taking care of Anita [the other child]," you would fume and strike out, exactly as older siblings do. It is best to tell your older child(ren), "We both love you so much and have had so much happiness because of you, that we wanted to have another baby like you, so that all of us could have more pleasure together." Then *watch* the baby whenever the older child is around. Should you observe the older youngster hurting the baby, say, "I understand how you feel, but I must take care of Anita just the way I take care of you. I would not let anyone hurt you, and I cannot let anyone hurt her." Then divert the culprit by doing something nice with her/him!

13. Conversely, protect the older child *from* the baby. We do *not* believe in sharing one's personal items with others. We know that most parents

insist that toys and articles of clothing or equipment be shared among siblings; we do not agree. It is *not* "selfish" to refuse to give someone else something that belongs to you; it is self-protective. In a country that stresses the rights of personal property, it is amazing how many parents (and grandparents) get "hung up" on insisting that older children permit their younger siblings to "have" or "play with" their belongings. Children in each family vary. Some take good care of things, whereas others do not (and often cannot be trained to do so!). It is unfair to persuade a child to give a belonging (treasured or not) to someone else (either sibling, "friend," playmate, or adult). Since the responsibility for the item's maintenance is the owner's, she/he should be permitted to be its sole user.

Keep the baby out of the sibling's room, toys, clothing, food, and other personal property. Having learned to respect her older sister's or brother's privacy, she will be able to respect yours and, eventually, her own. Also, find some time for *each* child to be *alone with you* every day.

14. Finally, it is perfectly all right to set limits in your home. Your daughter may be told that she is not permitted to enter the bathroom alone—or any restricted area. She will not remember easily (for babies have very short attention and memory spans), but, eventually, she will understand that "No!" and a simultaneously negative movement of the head means that you do not want her to invade (go into) a special place. If you do say, "No!" *be consistent.* Only set limits when you fully intend that they be kept and, once they are established, insist that they be honored *all the time.*

From Fourteen to Twenty-four months

Children between the ages of fourteen and twenty-four months undergo a series of processes that build their language skills, enhance their already stimulated curiosity, increase their social abilities, and culminate in the foundations of their intelligence.

We have suggested that your daughter's curiosity should be given virtual free reign, within appropriate and practical limitations, and nurtured to build familiarity with her world and everything in it. This awareness will, in turn, build receptivity to further exploration that will expand from the physical to the mental and, eventually, to the conceptual.

We heretofore have not suggested purposefully "teaching" your child, for we have found that, when permitted to self-teach themselves through exploration and investigation, youngsters prior to a year (or so) become very receptive to learning. Besides, many parents overdo the "teaching" and either bore or "turn off" their children's interests in learning, because the babies are not yet at the stage where they *can* learn very much from others.

We have, however, suggested that parents speak with their children a great deal, mentioning the names of people and objects in simple, short sentences. We do suggest the use of records, stereos, and cassettes to bring music into the child's world, beginning with her first few months of life. Children's records of catchy songs—particularly those to which your youngster may clap or stamp—are also good introductory teaching techniques. These, however, may be turned off (either physically or mentally) when a child ceases to be interested in them. Some parents do not talk to their children enough, under the mistaken notion that the child is not interested. Let the youngster decide. Talk to her from the very beginning of her life. Whenever she loses interest, her attention will wander; then stop!

At this stage in your daughter's life she is ready to begin learning many things; but she may also be ready to enter into a negative phase (many youngsters do at about fourteen months). It is important that she does not sense that you want her to learn specific things and then turns a normal negativism into a refusal to learn. If she appears irritable, stop. If she gets fidgety, stop. If she refuses, obviously, stop! The second half of a child's second year is often one of orneriness, which may occur because nature is signalling that a youngster *needs* to become independent (partially) and that this is the first step in the process. Instead of fighting this transition, assist it in occurring naturally.

This is a good time to begin reading *short* stories that have familiar figures in them (such as babies, toys, or grandparents). If your daughter's attention wanders, stop! Teach her to play records by turning the record player on and off by herself. She will forget how, at first, but she will eventually remember. *Demonstrate* how she should do it and then help her to play it under your supervision. Let her try it by herself and praise her for remembering or being "gentle" with the arm of the player. Show her how to hold a record and how to place it carefully on the turntable. Do each task slowly, permitting her to copy you. Purchase an inexpensive child's record player or use someone's old one, so that you are not frustrated by her inaccurate efforts.

You also will find that during this period your daughter will be willing to engage in conversations. She will talk to you, describing such matters as what she is doing, what she wants, and where she wants to go. Encourage her to speak and praise her for doing so. "I like the way you explained that to me!" will probably cause her to "explain" many more things. Asking questions is another good way to get her to talk and, more important, to help her to begin to make decisions—a vital component of her developing independence. "What would you like to wear today?" may be giving her too great a range. Instead, ask, "Which of these two would you like to wear now?" or "Would you like to wear this red blouse or this yellow blouse?" (Permit her to wear her choice!) After she has selected the garment, if the opportunity presents itself, mention to someone who visits, "Patti selected that lovely blouse to wear! I like her choice!" (The basic concept is to encourage her to make initial simple choices and to praise her for them.) If she is disinterested in selecting her clothes, try toys, foods, or the time when she will nap or play.

At this age, many children become interested in water play. In the bathtub, permit your daughter to experiment with several different objects, some of which float and others which will sink. Show her the item and ask, "Will this float or will this sink?" Then let the object go. If it floats, laughingly say, "The little boat floats!" When something sinks, say, "The spoon sinks!" If she considers this procedure to be a game, continue it for a while and then repeat the same series another day. If she is bored or impatient, or merely wants to drop the items into the water herself, permit her to do that and *stop* the "teaching."

Your daughter will have visited the doctor many times, so instead of "playing house" (which you may certainly do!), play "a visit to the doctor." This game will serve to remind her of the things that happen when she visits the doctor and will help her to develop a sequence of events and also to name various items.

You probably will have taken her to a restaurant, and playing "restaurant" is also fun for her. Again, re-enacting any trip or visit reinforces her memory retention, creates a beginning familiarity with sequence, and extends vocabulary. You can also play "a visit to grandma," "going to the store," "speaking on the telephone," and any other out-of-the-house incidents with which she may be familiar. After you two have dramatized these events, subsequent experiences with them will sharpen her awareness of the incidents and increase her ability to retain in her mind the things that really happen.

Introduce your daughter to various-sized (but fairly small) balls, such as ping-pong balls, tennis balls, and handballs. On a hardwood floor they make interesting patterns and sounds, and children of this age frequently are fascinated by them.

This is also an appropriate time to introduce your daughter to a four-wheeled wagon. She will enjoy being pulled in it and will also enjoy pulling her possessions. You may notice that we did not suggest a doll carriage, and you may *want* to buy a doll carriage for your little girl. If you cannot resist, then do it, but recognize that you are contributing to the stereotypical image of each girl becoming a "mommy," rather than an independent professional woman who may *also* be a mother. Little boys grow up to become *fathers*, but it is not made the focal point of their existence. They will become professional men *first*, and husbands and fathers next. Little girls should be raised to think of themselves as professional women *first*, and wives and mothers next. Besides, when trying to alter a social stereotype, it is necessary to swing a little farther over toward the opposite side, rather than just to the middle *initially*, to fully overcome current inertia.

Pushing a toy or real baby carriage should not become the center, or even an important feature, of your daughter's existence. Pulling a cart (which is low and less dangerous if it tips) will lead her to investigate the wheels and axle and how they work; it will teach her a little about gravity and friction and about weights and counterforce (be careful of her fingers). She will learn about babies in due course (just as little boys, who are not mesmerized by the obligation of having babies, do!) but she will not instinctively learn about science and transportation. Try to control your inclination to surround her with the traditional restrictive items that suggest domesticity as her central life, and you will make her transition into the modern world broader and more successful than it is for those who play exclusively with mother-baby dolls and carriages.

Instead of buying a toy baby carriage for her, if you are creative and want to make her something, build a miniature, sturdy four-wheeled vehicle that she can help you construct and paint. Put her name on it in big, bold letters and help her to read it! Build a swing for her—though, of course, you can buy one, too. Building is fun, and telling her about it and showing her how to make it is emotionally and intellectually provocative for both of you. Build (or buy) a small slide or junior-sized gym equipment. She will learn to *do* many wonderful things with these items, and her mind will grow and simultaneously increase her interests, which, in turn, will motivate her and encourage her to try new things and build newer skills.

Purchase a plastic shovel and some multisized plastic pails; invest in a ten-pound bag of sand that can be poured into a container in which she can experiment with filling, pouring, turning over, packing, and building. An outdoor (or indoor) sandbox is fun for children of this age and will remain so for a few years at least. Again, the skills she will develop are immeasurable and will keep multiplying in direct proportion to the amount of encouragement and enthusiasm she receives from you as she experiences each new medium.

Build or buy some junior items, such as her own rocking chair, small cushions, a miniature swimming pool (and permit water play, measuring, "floating" test, and the like), a steel full-length mirror for her room, and a smooth board (about one foot wide) on which she can learn to balance and walk. She still will enjoy pots and pans of all sizes, plastic containers (especially if they can fit inside each other), and toys that represent familiar items, such as dogs, kittens, or ducks.

During this period she will begin to like plastic jars with covers that she can learn to put on and take off, plastic cars that can fit inside larger plastic trucks, stacking toys that can be placed, in sequence, onto a vertical pole or rod, and toy telephones (lightweight plastic). Telephone "conversations," as mentioned before, are wonderful ways for her to develop verbal ability, and, if close relatives and friends do not object, permit her to talk to them for a minute during usual calls.

Introduce dolls only if they represent adult figures or groups of figures. Try not to give her her own "baby." A baby doll is acceptable only for dramatizing the familiar episodes she has actually experienced, like a visit to the doctor.

Despite all these cautionary statements, someone invariably will purchase a doll for your daughter, either without realizing the end result or precisely *because* they know that you are endeavoring to provide her with a new set of environmental experiences and options. If she likes the doll, permit her to keep it without exhibiting any negative feelings, but do not lapse into cuddling it or encouraging her to do so. Treat it as any other object and direct attention toward other, more beneficial toys. In fact, you may wish to use this opportunity to hug your daughter and to have her hug you to demonstrate real affection for people—not things.

Toward the end of this stage, children begin to take a strong interest in simple books with fairly easy-to-turn pages that have pictures of items and types of people with whom they are familiar. The cloth books are sturdier than are those made of paper, but neither is very child-proof. Purchase only inexpensive books and try not to be concerned when the pages are torn, folded, roughed up, and twisted. One of the things that little children *thoroughly enjoy* is pulling, folding, crinkling, and twisting paper—and this is the major function usually served by baby's first dozen books. Read them to her, and if you have one at home, read them into a cassette tape recorder. When you are busy, she may be able to hear the tape recorder "read" the book, instead of you.

Our arbitrary divisions of infancy into groups of months are intended to serve as a guide, rather than a prescription. Children are very different from each other, and growth varies substantially among them. Youngsters excel in different ways—some are extremely verbal, others are athletic, others are sensitive and responsive, and still others are quiet but unusually cognitive and intelligent.

Children go through different "stages" at different times and in different ways; some "skip" various phases. Our suggestions for stimulating your daughter's interests and skill development during her first two years should be used intelligently, on the basis of *your* observations of her. Recommended play items may be attractive to her earlier than is suggested for "most" youngsters; some devices will continue to attract her long after many children become bored with them. Usually, when an item is suggested, its impact lasts through many months, depending upon the individual child's special talents and abilities.

No book can provide a perfect prescription for a child without having been written as a result of longitudinal (over a period of time) observations and examinations of that youngster. This book includes suggestions for raising your daughter so that she becomes highly motivated toward achievement and confident of her ability to succeed. Small or occasional deviations from the guidelines will not alter the basic outcomes, and variations that respond to your personal home situation may be necessary. Above all, remember that the activities and experiences often automatically provided to boys will aid your daughter's growth, as well.

You probably will not err if you provide your daughter with freedom for exploration (under supervision), encouragement for attempting new things, praise for accomplishments, and confidence in her ability to work things out for herself. This kind of home climate will develop in the child those qualities that will eventually lead toward independence and personal confidence. When combined with parental love, exercise, healthy food, fresh air and sunshine, your daughter at age two will be well on the road toward independence. Her next four years will largely determine whether she will select the route toward professionalism during her adult years.

3.
What to Do from Age Two to Five: The Years That Count Most

USING THE LARGER TOOLS OF LEARNING

The first two years of your daughter's life should be devoted to the exploration of her immediate environment and the development of the physical and mental skills required for self-initiated investigation. She should receive little (or no) exposure to the attitudes and manifestations of our sexist-oriented culture and she should be loved, encouraged, applauded, and praised for every effort toward achievement—whether verbal, gymnastic, dramatic, or intellectual.

From the beginning of her third year (or thereabouts), she may begin to appreciate very large, simple puzzles with just three or four pieces. Introduce only one picture puzzle at a time and wait until she has mastered that one and appears to enjoy putting the pieces together before you present her with the next one.

During this period of her life she will become able to ride a tricycle and will delight in her maneuverability with it. When she is near four, she may be able to control a small scooter. Whenever she manifests interest in devices of this type, permit her to attempt them. If she is not yet able, she will recognize the fact and be willing to wait. If she insists on repeatedly attempting to master a tricycle or other toy machine, encourage her to do so. Permit her to be the one who makes the decision as to *when* she begins to drive around on a given vehicle. Eventually she will be graduated to a bicycle. Again, have one available and let her decide when she will begin to try to use it.

One of our youngsters, having observed his older brother, decided at *four* that he, too, would ride a two-wheeler. No one in our neighborhood at that time had ever ridden a two-wheeler at the tender age of four. We said, "You're too young to ride a bicycle! Wait until you're older!" *He* said, "I am not too young! I can ride it now!" He practiced over and over for two weeks, falling, bruising, and pushing himself to try, right up to the limit of his endurance. At the end of his second week of effort, he *rode* that bike—and well! His self-image and confidence were escalated immeasurably. The experience aided his growth toward independence and self-reliance. He now *believes* that he can do almost anything he really wants to do—and he does!

Our daughter Rana, who is nine months Robert's senior, observed her younger brother ride the two-wheeler and decided that she, too, could ride one. It took her *less than two hours* to master the skills of balancing, steering, pedaling, and watching. She had less trouble, because she was older and physically "ready," but she might have waited longer, had she not seen her brother achieve. *Both* children benefited from his determination, and, to this day, they compete, so that neither falls behind the other very much.

OBSERVING MOTIVATIONAL DIFFERENCES

Children, even in the same family, invariably are very different from each other, and parents must observe each child closely, in order to aid each one to strive toward reaching maximum potential. For example, your daughter may resist new suggestions initially, and when left alone, eventually may pursue the activity. Or she may wish to discover for herself everything that it is at all possible to do in this world—to the extent where the activity need not at all be part of either your repertoire or anyone else's with whom she has had contact. This type of girl is likely to be fearless, persistent, determined, and capable of overcoming all obstacles. Then again, your daughter may not discover skills or activities by herself; she may accept new worlds to conquer only through "outsiders"—neighbors, schoolmates, or strangers. In this case, if you suggest she try something, she either may be uninterested, unable, "too busy," or negative. When that outsider suggests it, she may become able, confident, and enthusiastic. An alternative course may find her very dependent on you for stimulation and direction. These and other patterns may seem obvious to you in the quiet of the reading room. The difficulty arises when emotions and other problems distort your objectivity with respect to your daughter.

Begin to assess how your daughter becomes motivated toward new achievement through careful and objective observation. Some youngsters are "self-motivated;" they want to experience everything life offers and need only sufficient time. Some youngsters are "other" or "peer" oriented; they need the stimulation of one or more friends engaging in the venture with them. Other children are parent-, adult-, or "authority"-oriented; they need an older person to recommend, participate with, or supervise their efforts. When you begin to watch your child and look for clues that suggest who or what activates her toward trying new things, it will be easy for you to recognize what the major stimulus is. Once you diagnose the motivating force, use it to her advantage. Use the person or situation to encourage her to become involved in a variety of interesting activities, particularly sports, dance, music, and creative arts experiences.

STIMULATING INTEREST IN LEARNING FOR YOUR YOUNG DAUGHTER

From Two to Three Years

Drawing and Painting. At two, some children begin to enjoy large white sheets of paper and easy-to-roll-along crayons. We suggested finger paints as an exploratory medium for your daughter when she was younger (in the bathtub), and at this point in her development she will continue to enjoy this activity and her use of various art media will become more controlled. The colors she uses, the lines that she begins to make, and her feeling of movement and accomplishment are likely to delight her. Whenever your daughter shows you her creations, comment favorably without overdoing it or ask her to tell you what the picture shows. If she refuses, or prefers to return to her drawing, painting, or finger-painting, do not burden her with the explanations. If she enjoys describing the product, listen, smile, and say things that flatter her *ability*, such as, "I like the way you put those colors together!" or, "Your painting is so neat! You must have worked very carefully!" Short, sweet sentences are enough, unless she chooses to persist in the discussion.

Building Blocks. At about two years of age, or shortly thereafter, many children demonstrate that they are able to use blocks. Younger children, of course, handle wooden squares, but as often as not, they throw them and cannot discipline themselves to use them appropriately—as building units. Unless materials are used properly or creatively, they should not be available to little children, for thrown objects can cause damage to your home, to others, and to your youngster. Be certain, however, that whenever you introduce your daughter to a new device or medium, you *demonstrate* how it should be used and she then shows you that she knows how to use it properly. Praise her when she does it correctly.

Using New Toys. New toys should *never* be given to your preschool youngster if she has not had prior experience with them or similar devices, unless someone shows her how to use them. Children at this stage of their development are ready (usually) to be taught how to care for their possessions, how to use them, and how to return them to where they belong (or from where they were taken) when they have finished playing. Gradually, youngsters must assume the responsibility for taking good care of their toys and clothing, and at two years of age they are becoming ready to learn.

Windup toys (like the jack-in-the-box or musical boxes) begin to become appropriate for children sometime *after* the age of two. Although they have appeal for *adults,* this type of amusement does not appear to absorb youngsters very much until at least midway between the ages of two and three, and even then, many have difficulty in winding the devices and sometimes catch their fingers (and toes) in the moving parts. You will find that little children under three also often have difficulty with the plastic nut-and-bolt toys because they cannot screw the nuts on or off the bolts. There is no objection to having such playthings available after two, but (1) watch your daughter carefully as she uses them, (2) introduce her to the way in which the devices should be used and started, (3) observe her efforts to manipulate them by herself, and (4) store them for a later date if she appears disinterested. When a youngster seems to enjoy the windup mechanisms and merely needs experience in learning how to start them, patiently (and repeatedly, if necessary) *demonstrate* how to make them work. Permit her to try to work them, move her hands in the correct directions (if she will permit it!), and then give her time to develop the skill of turning the parts, so that the toy works. Learning to wind mechanisms is a worthwhile skill and should be encouraged, but it is important to avoid frustrating experiences whenever possible.

Many children, after having seen the toys wound, will continue to experiment on their own, over and over again, until after they have mastered the correct movement; others will avoid a device that they cannot work by themselves immediately. As stated previously, become sensitive to your own daughter's unique personality and respond to its individuality. If you recognize that she will continue trying to learn how to turn objects, in order to start a toy, provide her the opportunities in which she can teach herself, with practice (after you have shown her the correct process). When you note that she either becomes irritated with or withdraws from a situation in which she cannot succeed, keep a difficult-to-use toy out of sight and introduce it again two months later.

Role Playing. Your daughter's previous interest in "let's pretend" activities also will be extended at approximately two, and she will delight at playing roles and imagining visits that you discussed when she was younger, such as trips to grandparents, physicians, stores, friends, the post office, and vacations.

Visiting Local Agencies. Somewhere between two and three, she will be ready for her first visit to a fire station, the local police station, and the zoo. Miniature zoos or farms expressly designed for little tots are particularly good as an introduction to feeding and touching varied animals. Although many children under the age of two are taken to zoos, they often get very little from the experience, and they sometimes become frightened to the extent that negative consequences may develop.

Going to the Zoo.   Never urge that your youngster touch the animals. *You* touch them, feed them, and hold them if that is permitted. Be gentle, so that she *sees* how animals should be handled. If she reaches over to touch or take, explain how to hold them as you permit her to do so. Take her hand and gently let her feel the amount of pressure to exert on the animal. Then let her continue by herself. If she is not gentle, remind her, and, again, demonstrate. Continue showing her until she can touch the animals correctly. If, after several tries, she does not treat them nicely, she may not be ready to develop the control necessary. Consider the animal, and distract your daughter toward another experience. Try again two months later.

Watching Television.   Children between two and three often become very interested in television. Most parents encourage this; we do not. Children should *do* things, not just *watch* events happening. The most alert and accomplished adults are those who are participators, rather than observers. It is preferable for your daughter to be energetically involved in as many positive activities as possible during these very important, formative years. Television does have some advantages, in that it may increase your child's verbal ability or vocabulary, and it can bring the outside world to your living room. Also, a program like "Sesame Street" may introduce her to numerals and selected mathematical processes. "Sesame Street" is fine, if you are willing to turn the television set *off* when it is over. Aside from a handful of fine programs and its use as a "babysitter," television has few redeeming features and several drawbacks for children of any age:

1. Television becomes habit-forming; it can attract your daughter into automatically turning the dials to "see what's on." It distracts her from *thinking* of interesting things to *do.*

2. It is, as was mentioned before, a *passive* occupation; children should be *active,* so that they experience, "grow," develop new skills, and increase former ones. It can damage her future ability to read and to write.

3. For the most part, television is nonintellectual. It does not *require* that you *think,* and it is important that children think a great deal during this stage, so that thinking becomes a "way of life" on which they can depend.

Without the "boob-tube," children must *think* about what to do. They must make decisions; they must *act* on those decisions; they must locate whatever it is that interests them; they must *use* it or do something with it; they will need to cope with the consequences of what they do; they will want to discuss these or describe them; and they will have thoughts about what they did and ways to do it differently or better. We have virtually no evidence that television stimulates, requires thinking, causes learning (other than from a few select programs), or enhances a youngster's skills. Listening to a record that encourages singing along or clapping, or painting, or water play, or talking on the "telephone," or building a "house" with blocks will produce a substantially better learning situation than sitting before a television set and watching the antics of adults or cartoon characters or old films—*all of which literally can project misinformation or sexist and other negative stereotypes.*

It is important that programs are carefully previewed. Chapter 8 describes the ones that should be eliminated from consideration for your daughter's viewing because of the negative image they provide of women. When the comedy shows are scrutinized, and the dramas are screened to exclude violence, stereotyping, and idiocy, not very much is left. News broadcasts are informative for youngsters, but at this age (two and three) your child will not understand the vocabulary and will be exposed to many frightening images.

If *you* plan to watch television, certainly your daughter may observe with you, providing that you remain alert to negative story lines that impose stereotypical and/or misrepresentative attitudes toward women, people in general, places, or things. Should this type of situation occur, change channels or turn the set off. This may appear to be unnecessarily cautious to you, but it is easy for children to become imitative of unusual styles or caricatures. Should your daughter adopt the foolish mannerisms or speech of comedy-situation women or cartoon people, it will be difficult to eliminate such traits from her behavior.

Your daughter may not be harmed by observing a melodramatic "soap opera," but neither will she be improved, and exposure to many of the current programs offered on television is, at best, inappropriate to the development of young people and, at worst, potentially damaging. For an in-depth discussion of the *detriments* of television in this regard, please read Chapter 8.

DEVELOPING INDEPENDENCE

By the time your daughter has reached the age of two, she should have learned to find her way around her immediate environment (room, apartment, home, yard) and other familiar territory, such as the apartments or homes of people whom she visits frequently. This will have occurred because, as suggested in Chapter 2, she will have been permitted and encouraged to explore, satisfy her curiosity, and attempt many new feats. She will also have been praised for each accomplishment and should thus have been developing confidence in her ability to achieve.

It was suggested that after initially demonstrating the correct use of materials and devices, your daughter be permitted to further explore them alone and to use them in creative (but safe) ways. Having been exposed to many different kinds of materials and mechanisms, she will have begun to feel comfortable with a variety of toys, household items, and objects. It was also suggested that she gradually be trained to pick up the things with which she has been playing and that she replace each to its proper area or storage bin. Between two and three years of age, these organizational skills should become "second nature" to her, and she automatically should assume the responsibility for her own possessions.

Throughout her infancy, adults should serve as *resources* to either introduce an item or skill or to assist after a task has proven to be too difficult.[1] At first, your daughter will try a task and decide whether or not she is capable of completing it successfully. After age two or two-and-a-half, she will begin to mentally *estimate* her ability. Do not interfere in the thought process; permit her to make her own decisions. When she wants assistance, *show her how to do* what needs to be done and then wait patiently as she tries to do it. If additional help is needed, be available, but do not perform the necessary task for her. The more she does for herself, the sooner she will become able to tackle new and different feats and complete them successfully. A fine line exists, of course, between granting her the independence to learn to do something by herself and causing frustration by permitting too much responsibility too soon. Train yourself to observe your daughter carefully. If she remains intent on working out the process to make things happen in her own way, let her do so. If she becomes tense, offer to assist. If she refuses your help, permit her the freedom to keep trying. Many youngsters are unusually determined and obtain intense satisfaction from eventually working something out by themselves. Success of this type is one kind of self-actualizing experience for little children (and adults), and they should certainly be permitted to continue that course.

Caution grandparents about doing too much for little girls—things that they ought to be permitted to do for themselves. Carrying them when they can walk across a street while holding onto an adult's hand is one such instance; carrying their toys is another. Helping them to dress themselves when they are able to and want to do it themselves is a third. Feeding them when they are perfectly capable of feeding themselves is a fourth such dependency-reinforcing behavior. Permit your daughter to do everything that she wants to do by herself, providing that it is safe. You may supervise her actions and praise her for (1) wanting to do it, (2) doing it well, or (3) trying, but doing it *for* her will not increase her ability to become an independent person.

In addition to assisting your daughter with tasks that appear to be too difficult for her, encourage her to help *you*—and be certain that the things she does for and with you are not only domestic chores. It is perfectly all right for her to join you in measuring, mixing, and straining the ingredients with which to bake a cake or to help you clean, but she should also help you to build and repair items, care for plants or a garden, shop, engage in your hobbies and sports (painting, sculpting, tennis, swimming) and, minimally, observe you as you participate. Share some time in which you show her how to become proficient in the tasks that you enjoy. A three-year-old youngster will not play tennis well, of course, but she will begin to develop some of the coordination and interest, so that at four she will be prepared to practice and perfect the skills necessary to become a good player eventually.

When your daughter seeks your attention with tasks at which she is self-sufficient, she may be indicating that she wants more of *you*. From time to time, most people need affection and demonstrated manifestations of love. Perhaps children require that assurance even more than adults. If your daughter is able to do something for which she requests assistance, sit with her or hold her on your lap and say, "Let's try to do this together. Where shall we start?" Then, cooperatively complete the mission and remain with her for a while; if you can spare the time, stay longer. When you need to turn your attention to a chore of your own, suggest that she might like to accompany you and be near you while you are working at whatever requires your attention. Show her that you like to have her near.

In this regard, it is important to note that independence does not necessitate either being alone or being required to do most things by one's self. Independence suggests that one is *capable* of being self-sufficient, self-reliant, and self-determining. Further, this trait requires that one is capable of making decisions on personal beliefs and reasoning ability, rather than on the opinions and influence of others. Your daughter may be developing independence skills, but she may also need verification of your love and respect for her abilities and efforts. Several psychologists have suggested that physical skin contact between a mother and her newborn infant is vital to the sense of well-being of *both*. Certainly, a youngster of either sex should be affectionately held, hugged, caressed, kissed, and patted by both parents, and not just at birth, of course. Be careful, however, not to treat your daughter any differently from the way you would treat your son. *Both* sexes need to *feel* love through contact; both require an equal expression of physical affection. Individual children (male and female) vary in their liking of physical contact. Observe your daughter to identify her preferences and then accede to them. It is just as wrong to force unwanted affection upon another person as it is to deprive her of it. Respond to your daughter as an individual—according to *her expressed needs*, and not the generalized prescriptions incorporated into a text.

In addition to permitting your daughter to select the clothes that she wears and the items with which she chooses to play (mentioned previously), encourage her to speak on the telephone. Engaging in conversations, even for short periods, teaches her the amenities ("How are you, grandma? How is grandpa? What are you planning to do today?") and provides opportunities for her to express herself. The ability to articulate and verbalize well is considered to be the single most influential characteristic in determining the impression people make on others. Providing opportunities for your daughter to talk on the telephone is one way of helping her to use the language skills that she is developing.

To aid your daughter in developing excellent language skills, be certain to avoid teaching her an incorrect vocabulary that must, at some later date, be *unlearned* and replaced. Most adults recognize how difficult it is to substitute a good habit for a bad one; the analogy is identical. A nonword or "baby" word that is inappropriate for adult society is equally as inappropriate for your daughter. Generations of parents and grandparents persist in teaching their beloved children ridiculous words that are neither cute nor clever, requiring that valuable time be taken to eradicate the nonsensical vocabulary and then to teach new words. Reference here is made to words such as "choo-choo" (for train), "bottie" (for bottle), "wee-wee" (for urinate), "potty" (for toilet), "duty" (for defecate), "puddy-cat" (for kitten), "bow-wow" (for dog), and so on. It is educationally *unsound* to teach anything that is incorrect to anyone, particularly when it is acknowledged that what has been taught must be untaught.

Children of both sexes who are addressed through an adult vocabulary throughout their lives are more likely to find school reading and comprehension relatively easy skills for them to acquire. In addition, they will impress many adults (teachers) with their more extensive usage of the language than those children whose ability to communicate was severely hampered because of the limitations placed on *their* vocabulary through the use of nonsense words in their formative years.

PROVIDING OPPORTUNITIES FOR SELF-ACTUALIZING EXPERIENCES FROM THREE TO FIVE YEARS

The height of positive feelings that some people reach when they recognize that they have done their "best" has been described as a peak experience. That sense of supreme achievement is valuable at any age and serves to further develop self-confidence and positive self-image. The proverb, "Nothing succeeds like success," is accurate, and as your daughter realizes that she is able to perform well, she will be encouraged to grow and to strive toward new and sometimes more ambitious goals. This pattern appears to be related directly to motivation—a necessary ingredient of professional aspirations.

Most of us are convinced of the value of having our daughters become professional women, but for that to happen, they must *believe* that they are able to achieve, and they should have had many experiences demonstrating *to themselves* that they can succeed in endeavors of their choice. Therefore, consciously strive to create situations in which your very young daughter is able to learn to do things on her own and to obtain praise for her personal accomplishments.

At between two and three years of age, however, your daughter will begin to become interested in playing with other children. When that happens, you will be faced with the decision of whether to continue on the non-sexist and successful path we have sketched for you, or whether you will buckle to social expectations. For it is at this point that two socially difficult phenomena will be encountered: the cultural views of (1) sharing and (2) competition.

Sharing

Many parents insist that their children share their belongings with the other children with whom they come into contact. A friend visits and brings along her four-year-old youngster who wants (naturally) your daughter's cherished possessions. You are embarrassed by your daughter's refusal to permit the visitor access to her toys. Because of your own background, you conjure up images of selfishness, self-centeredness, and stubbornness; the pressure mounts. What are you going to do?

Since you want your daughter to assume the responsibility for taking care of her things, she must be permitted to decide *how* they should be used and maintained. Most people do not exercise the same care with someone else's possessions that they do with their own (*if* they do take care of their own), and it is unreasonable to expect that another child will treat her belongings as well as your daughter (who loves the possessions and who has been trained to handle them carefully). It is *not* selfish for her to dislike having another child use her treasured items; it may even be negative to permit such usage. Nor is it self-centered to prefer to maintain one's belongings in safety away from others; it is protective and caring. Your daughter should not be cajoled into permitting the unwanted exchange, for it is wise to let her know that her wishes concerning her possessions are respected. If she insists on maintaining the separation of toys, she may be viewed (by some) as being stubborn, but her insistence could just as easily be called "determination"—a vital prerequisite to success.

Of course, you must be consistent. If she does not care to share with others, they may elect not to share with her, and she must be taught to recognize that that decision is *their* prerogative. Even if your daughters *does* share (some children are naturally very "giving," while others win approval by sharing), others need not necessarily reciprocate. Respecting someone else's wishes is part of the maturation process, too.

To prevent a difficult situation from occurring at all, why not keep a group of appropriate toys set apart from all others in your home? These "visiting day specials" can be stored out of sight and brought out only at times when guests are present. In that way, the children will have interesting items to explore and play with, which will be a treat for both without infringing on the possessiveness of either. Should the two (or more) youngsters want the same "visiting day special," they either may choose to take turns for specific time intervals, or they may play with it simultaneously; if the problem cannot be resolved, the toy should be withheld from both.

Competing

Competition is the second concern of parents when youngsters begin to play with peers. Some people are disturbed by the concept of encouraging a competitive spirit in children and believe that somehow it is always harmful. In our view, this is an unjustified perception of a necessary and often vital characteristic. Self-competition, of course, is the best type to support, as when your daughter tries to outdo her own previous record, such as in the skill with which she reads, catches a ball, creates a new painting, or begins to write. Realistically, however, how can a youngster be expected to involve herself in a field that is held in high esteem unless she has evidence that she is capable of succeeding? Moreover, every child (and adult) should excel in at least one area. Your daughter's self-image, confidence, self-reliance and determination will grow enormously if she can gain superiority in even a single endeavor.

Competition in sports is viewed as healthy, as is competition toward excellence in any undertaking. Our cultural orientation toward individual achievement, independence, and responsibility *requires* that individuals compete, in order to acknowledge superiority. It may be sad to lose a race, but it is even sadder to refrain from entering into the meet. People improve on the basis of their continuing efforts, and along with the growth of your youngster's awareness of personal ability in the third year of life, she will develop an ever-increasing tendency to seek approval for activities or achievements successfully completed. White states that this tendency can be relatively well-established by three years of age,[2] and it is important to recognize that you will need to respond to it.

Your daughter may comment proudly on a new skill that she has mastered—for example, the ability to ride a tricycle—and demonstrate (through statements) her need for recognition, perhaps in comparison with others. Whereas you should not praise her for deeds that are unworthy, you *should* flatter her for deserved accomplishments. Too many parents downgrade their child's successes by responding, "Well, yes, you did learn to ride earlier than your friends, but they can do something that you cannot." Presumably, this statement is intended to keep the youngster's ego in tow and to prevent the child from developing feelings of superiority in relationship to peers.

Perhaps the concept is appalling to an egalitarian-oriented person, but *it is your daughter's feeling and expectation that she will be able to achieve and to succeed that contributes so effectively to her willingness to approach new tasks* without trauma or debilitating anxiety. Early exploration of the environment and self-directed experimentation with multiple materials is recommended, in order to provide your daughter with the knowledge that she could *make things happen* with various items by expending her own effort. Knowing that she is *able* to do some of the things that she *wants* to do enhances her confidence. Confidence engenders additional emotional strength and determination to reach higher and to try something new and a bit more difficult. Frequent attempts at increasingly difficult tasks—*particularly when accompanied by success and recognition*—lead toward the mental set: "I can do it!" Those are beautiful words when used by your daughter and are followed by success and the inevitable smile of self-pleasure.

It is necessary to *feel* that success is possible and to "project" the final result before attempting something beyond one's normal "reach." Therefore, if your daughter is to strive toward becoming a professional woman eventually, it is important to build her confidence and ability to project success.

In the initial stages of confidence-building, competing against her own previous accomplishments ("I *did* reach that closet!" or "I *did* get all the rings onto the hook!") is excellent; eventually, however, she will need to recognize that she is capable when compared with other children of her age: "How marvelous that you can ride that tricycle when you're only three (four) years old!" or, "That's a beautiful drawing! I'm surprised that you can draw so well at your age!" Again, do not praise without justification, but when something is done well, recognize the quality and congratulate your daughter, the doer.

"In the best sense of the term, a competitive person is very much interested in achieving, in doing things well, and in having [her] output compare favorably with others."[3] When your child *takes the risk* of competing against others, it is verification that she is feeling comfortable about her ability to achieve. Encourage participation in games that require a "winner" or two. When she wins, say something like, "You played very well." If she loses, say, "You played nicely, but no one wins all the time" or, "We win some and lose some. We'll try again, soon."

If you can find the time, organize some ballgames for your daughter and other children beyond the age of three. As one example, a group can form a circle, with one youngster at a time standing in the center. A lightweight volleyball or "kickball" may be used, with the object being for the ones in the circle to throw the ball at the one in the center. Be certain that the rules are *clearly understood.* No one may throw the ball above the child's knees. If the youngster is hit above the knees, the thrower has one point *reduced* from her/his score, and the child in the center has one point *added* to her score. When the thrower's ball hits *below* the knees, the thrower has a point added, and the one in the center has a point reduced. If the thrower misses, or the player in the middle skips out of the way in time, a point is added to the "target" participant, and one point is subtracted from the thrower. The ball may hit the target "on the fly" or on "one bounce." You should have a warmup or trial round to be certain that the distance for throwing is not so close that a child may be hurt or so far that it is not possible for the throwers to reach the target. Each child in the outer circle has one chance, in turn, to throw the ball during each round. Start out with three rounds per game. Adjust the number of rounds and games and distance according to the participants' desires and interests. You should not insist on detailed "rules of the game" beyond the ability of the participants to follow, but they should be challenged to follow and interpret procedures to the growing limits of their potential. Your daughter's powers of observation, self-control, problem-solving, and application will be enhanced through structured games.

If you can obtain some large (20″ x 20″) newsprint or easel pad paper and fasten it upright to a nearby wall, you can keep the score in full sight. Print each child's name in large letters in a column on the left-hand side of the paper. Use a heavy crayon or a large felt pen. Then add points (one by one) next to the appropriate name. When it is a "plus" point, write "1+"; when the point is to be subtracted (for having thrown the ball so that it strikes above the knees), write "1−." In this way, the participants will become familiar with seeing their names in print and will begin to develop the concept of addition and subtraction. Total each child's number of points at the end.

When the children no longer care to play, say to the winner, "You really threw the ball well!" or "You really knew how to avoid being hit by the ball." To the "losers," you might say, "It is important to concentrate on throwing the ball *below* the knees. Next time you will be able to throw it better!"

This type of competition can be beneficial and can lead to increased skill development and motivation. Vary the games to include catching, knocking down bowling pins, tossing rings on pegs, throwing balls into baskets or through old tires or hoops, or tossing objects into pails.

When there are two or more youngsters in the same family, and one has better skills in a specific area than do the others, praise each child for *her* (or his) skills. It is important that children (and adults) realize that different people do have different strengths, and that the way to "win" in life is to *capitalize on one's strengths.* Indeed, your daughter (and most people) *learn more* from their strengths and successes than from their weaknesses and failures.

As your daughter reaches four years of age, some group participation in things that she can do well will increase her sense of ability and involvement. If she is athletically inclined, arrange for her to play in baseball games, mini-basketball games, miniature golf as part of a team (or with the family), and other sports. If she is artistic, invite a group of youngsters to a "painter's party," where all may draw, paint, sculpt, and otherwise express themselves artistically, as part of an "exhibit." If she sings, acts, or dances, invite a group to join in "having a show" in which each can have a few minutes "on stage," performing for you and, perhaps, other parents. Whatever her interests and skills, occasionally provide for small group get-togethers wherein she can observe and compare her own talents with others. She will begin to recognize the areas in which she excels and also may develop new interests and skills based on her observance of what others can do.

As your daughter builds her competitive confidence through expanded experiences, she will be sufficiently self-protective to avoid areas in which she cannot compete and which hold no attraction for her. Therefore, *if your daughter is reluctant to compete, do not pressure her*. Moreover, some children excel easily but do not enjoy competing or direct involvement with others.

Learning about the Arts

From the time your daughter is approximately three years of age (and certainly by age four), take her with you to art museums, concerts, the theater, and any other center where she can be exposed to creative arts. It is best to visit such places because *you* are interested and to take her along, but even if these activities do not entice you, take her so that she becomes aware of them. It is fun to visit an art gallery with a child, so long as you remember that she will not be absorbed for a long period of time (perhaps only fifteen minutes in the beginning) and that she may not appreciate the experience until she becomes more familiar with that environment.

If you introduce her to each new center for short amounts of time (unless she wants to remain longer!) and express your appreciation for specific items, your daughter gradually will become relaxed in going to new places and eventually will begin to enjoy the art form(s) to which she has been introduced.

When taking her to the theater or to concerts, you should be prepared to see only part of the performance during the first few times—particularly if she is between three and five years of age. Young people's shows, where fairy tales and children's classics are dramatized, are excellent introductions to the theater, and outdoor concerts often are appealing to children, particularly if they feature energetic dances.

Maslow, in listing the "peak experiences" of achieving adults, commented that the various art forms had provided exhilarating moments for many. Sometimes, when a youngster is introduced to the arts, an interest in becoming involved as a participant is sparked. The ability to paint, dance, play an instrument, sing, act, or sculpt may be a latent talent that your daughter might have but may never develop unless she has the opportunity to become aware that the art exists and that she might like to try her hand at it. *Exposing* a youngster to various creative arts and then providing opportunities for her to engage in them obviously is *positive*. Selecting an art form for a child and/or *insisting* that she become proficient in it, however, is *negative*. Your daughter should be able to choose how she will channel her energies, and the arts, as with any endeavor, are only one group of alternatives.

Developing Intellectual Skills

People also have experienced moments of extreme pleasure and satisfaction or pride when they recognize that they have been particularly intelligent or intellectually creative. Providing opportunities in which your daughter can develop intellectual skills at an early age will sharpen her abilities and promote her growth.

Anticipating Consequences.   One of the skills that will facilitate your daughter's mental growth is the ability to anticipate consequences.[4] In adults, we call such a trait the knack of projecting outcomes or mental alertness to the future, but it is really a specific talent that many people do not develop, because their attention has not been directed toward this important cognitive planning and decision-making skill, and they have received no training toward that goal.

For example, as we see juice being poured rapidly into a small glass, we say, "Be careful, or the glass will overflow!" We urge that children remain aware of the amount of water going into the tub, because it, too, may overflow. We say, "Do not leave the lights on when you walk out of the room, or you will be wasting electricity!" Young children hear us say, "Turn the radio off when you are finished, or the battery will wear out!" and "Don't turn the crank too much, or it will overwind, and the toy won't work."

But *hearing* us warn about the consequences of a behavior is only one way to develop the skill of anticipating. Youngsters should be required to consider the outcomes of their behaviors without being told; in fact, if we continue to forewarn them, we are eliminating their need to think of the possible consequences on their own.

The "appropriate" time in which to focus on developing anticipation skills varies among children, but it is fairly safe to begin somewhere between your daughter's second and third birthday—depending upon her maturity and willingness to learn. Increase her opportunities to anticipate consequences between three and five.

Assuming that throughout the first two years of her life you have pointed out the need to be aware that one thing may/will follow another (as cited in the examples above), you might begin by stating the first part of a sentence and permitting your daughter to add the consequence section. For example, you might suggest that you two play a "game": you will tell her the beginning of a short story, and she will tell you the end. The following are examples that might be used:

Anticipating Consequences
1. Sometimes, when a baby is hungry, it _____.
2. If we don't wash our hands after painting, they will _____.
-or-
3. What could happen if we have paint on our hands and do not wash it off?
4. What could happen if we leave the toys outside when we come into the house?
5. What could happen if we overwind a toy?
6. What might happen if we were walking down steps and did not look in front of us?

At an advanced level, you might try:

7. A lady was baking a cake. Her telephone rang, and she went to answer it. She talked on the phone for a long time and forgot all about the cake in the oven. What do you think happened to the cake?

Since each problem may be answered correctly by more than one response, any intelligent or plausible reply is acceptable. After a while, when your daughter suggests one possible consequence of a described action, you might praise her and ask her to think of another answer to the question. Do not tire her, and always praise her for being able to think of correct replies. If she does not enjoy this type of mental coaxing, do not continue it, but try again, a few months later.

Using Imagination. Exciting your daughter's imagination through storytelling and dramatizations is another way in which to develop her intellectual abilities. Read to her as much as she will tolerate, and after she has become familiar with it, ask her to tell *you* the story by looking at the pictures. Ask her to "make up a story," or create one together by looking at an interesting painting, cartoon, or photograph.

Counting and Comparing. Do not "overdo" an attempt to introduce her to counting, but when a picture portrays two of a kind, say something about the two figures, such as, "These must be the two houses in the story," or, "Those two trees seem to be very tall!" Eventually, she will begin to recognize sets of two, three, and four and will associate them with previous groups with which she has become familiar. Begin to ask her to compare sizes, colors, distance, groups—which is larger? darker? closer? more numerous?

Building Creativity. When your daughter is about four or five, ask her questions that require her to put herself into someone else's place. For example, "If you were the doctor in the story, what would you have done?" This is not an easy skill, and you must be sensitive to the ease or difficulty with which she is able to answer. If she cannot imagine what she would do in another's place, suggest what you might do in that situation; then, try again at another time. Eventually, after hearing your ideas, she will begin to understand how to imagine how she might react in situations that are, as yet, unreal to her.

Solving Problems. If you were to tell her about a little girl who went to visit her grandmother but forgot her toothbrush, you might ask, "What do you think the little girl did about brushing her teeth?" Problem-solving is difficult for a child of four, and she may need to think for a while. If she cannot respond, ask, "What would *you* have done if you were visiting Grandma and had forgotten your brush? What are some things that you *could* do?"

Projecting Behavior of Others. Should you come across colorful pictures of individual children engaged in various activities, you could ask, "What do you think the little girl in this picture might do next?" Pause, and wait patiently. If no response is forthcoming, try, "If you were that little girl, what would *you* want to do next?" Again, if your daughter is not ready to put herself into someone else's place, suggest what *you* might do, and then terminate that conversation.

Never place your daughter into repeated situations when she is incapable of responding. Children mature at different rates, and each is capable of achieving nicely in one or more areas at a given time, but most require additional experience and time to begin to function proficiently with a variety of skills. Do not make her feel as if she is incapable in any area; when she cannot perform, give her the grace period that is necessary for her to develop and mature.

Should your daughter be able to place herself in another youngster's shoes, praise her and say, "Understanding what someone else might be thinking is very difficult! You are so smart (or intelligent)!" Let her experience your recognition and approval through a smile, a hug, or a sharing of the feat with your spouse or other adult.

Analyzing Motives.   There are many valid reasons for your daughter to develop the skills needed to understand how and why others behave in various situations. All contribute to your daughter's growth toward self-actualization.

1. The ability to consider and understand what others might be thinking (and why) is an intellectual skill that will sharpen her reasoning ability and help her to focus on people and situations, thus increasing her ability to think, plan, and solve problems.

2. This skill will permit your daughter to be self-protective in situations that may be potentially harmful. For example, when our own daughter was approximately four, she and two older brothers were taken to New York City to see *The Fantasticks* in Greenwich Village. When we returned to the public garage in which we had parked our car, a maintenance man went into the rear section of the under-a-building parking lot to retrieve the vehicle. Our daughter followed behind him for a way, but when he reached for her hand and said, "Come, I'll drive you back to your mother!" she repeatedly screamed so loudly that our entire group was alerted and reached her in a matter of seconds. When she was calmed, she gave us at least four reasons why she screamed—all of them valid from her point of view. In this instance, she was not acting out of fear, but, rather, out of the ability to project what a strange man might be thinking.

3. Being able to anticipate someone else's thoughts is an excellent attribute in all competitive ventures and will give your daughter a distinct advantage as she seeks success in the professions.

4. It can stimulate the imagination and potentially lead toward many types of creative experiences, such as writing, acting, interpretation, or painting.

Learning by Example.   You can begin to build your daughter's proficiency in analyzing behavior if you make the effort to demonstrate *your* ability with this skill when she is present. For example, if someone has been curt, and you are describing the related incident in your daughter's presence, you might suggest, "He may have been feeling ill, or perhaps he spoke that way because he is unhappy with his job." Suggesting reasons for people's behavior—and particularly *alternative* reasons—will help your daughter to grow in this area.

Learning through Interaction. In addition, you should ask her to suggest the motivation for someone's behavior from stories you read to her or real situations that occur. Try to be realistic without being cynical. For example, a little boy may want her to play in a game and say that he's doing it because he "likes her." In truth, he may be motivated to ask her because:

1. The group is short one player;
2. He knows he's a better player and wants her for the other side;
3. He has to prove to himself that he's better than a girl;
4. His mother forced him to be nice to the neighbors;
5. She's really a good player, and he wants her for the game;
6. He really does like her.

Help her to understand the alternatives through questions, suggestions, storytelling, analogies, and so on. Encourage her to offer possibilities and praise her when she provides one or more correct possible option(s). Again, if she's not ready for this type of mental gymnastics, wait two or three months and try again. Often the intellecutal seeds you plant will sprout in bunches!

Overcoming Self-Defeating Mechanisms. Dyer[5] describes the self-defeating emotional characteristics that deprive individuals of fulfillment and self-actualizing lives. Among the traits he cites are:

1. the need for others' approval (therefore, one does not do what others will frown upon);

2. permitting past traditions, incidents, or situations to restrict one's own progress (therefore, one conforms to traditional role models or blames lack of progress or success on unfortunate childhood experiences or on other people);

3. guilt or worry (we do not engage in specific activities or select specific directions, because we feel guilty about the selections or are worried about the outcomes, rather than providing for various eventualities);

4. fear of the unknown (one cannot anticipate what higher education or professional involvement will require or exact from us, so we avoid entering into a sphere with which we are not familiar);

5. the need to conform to convention ("everybody's getting married," and that's the way "it's spozed to be," so why "fight the tide"?);

6. the frustration experienced at the lack of justice (they make it more difficult for girls to succeed in a profession, so why fight the system? You can't win!);

7. procrastination ("I'm not ready for graduate school right now! I'll marry Jim and perhaps go back later—after he's been graduated . . .");

8. anger ("I'm so angry with the grades they gave me that I can't face another teacher just yet!"); and others.

This clinical psychologist explains in detail how each of the above characteristics can destroy a human being's determination to succeed in life—in terms of one's own goals and aspirations. He also suggests that understanding the reasons behind institutional demands on citizens permits each of us to *choose* the behaviors we exhibit and the life style in which we engage—preventing us from succumbing to patterns designed for "everyone" (the masses) by society, religion, government, the schools, and other bureaucratic agencies.

One of his major premises is that people who can overcome these negative traits, or "erroneous zones," through their own insights into the intentions of others and themselves, will be free from self-destructive behavior.[6] When your daughter becomes able to understand what other people (and, eventually, institutions) want, and why, she will not need emotionally to fit neatly into predetermined roles or job descriptions. She will not limit her educational horizons by considering only entry levels, and she will not limit her aspirations toward lower-level positions with limited financial reward. To build her perceptiveness into a valuable skill, it is suggested that you continually pose to her the type of simple projective problems described earlier in this section whenever she's ready and interested. Increase the complexity of your questions as she grows older and more able.

Setting Self-Actualizing Goals. Many authors have written about emotional health, self-actualization, and fulfillment. There is a close parallel among the characteristics found in "healthy" people by Dyer in *Your Erroneous Zones,* by Maslow in his description of "self-actualizing" adults,[7] and in the New York University research study reporting on outstanding American women professionals in medicine, law, dentistry, and administration.[8] Each of these writings emphasizes that women who live satisfying and fulfilling lives do *not* match stereotypical role models of "femininity." In contrast, they are self-determining, independent, personally oriented (but with strong positive values), highly creative and non-conforming, have diverse interests and are comfortable doing many different things, are capable of enjoying previously untried activities, and are enthusiastic about life and want to get all they can out of it.

Emotionally well, self-actualizing people do not groan, mumble, sigh, complain, or accept setbacks; they cope with problems as they arise and "make the best of" situations. They do not pretend joy and do not have the need to impress others with their ability to "reach heights," obtain recognition, or be successful. Instead, they *enjoy* whatever they make happen and reach out toward the next experience. If situations need to be altered or eradicated, they work toward that goal and enjoy the process. They can admit to making mistakes but consciously try to avoid repetition of them. They do not become angry—they *ignore* anger-provoking people and situations.

These people are energetic, idealistic, persistent, ambitious, intellectual, outgoing, highly individualistic, and loving (of self, too). They solve problems, have a great need of privacy, and are extremely active. They appreciate and enjoy nature, interesting (to them) people, new places, and varied experiences. They have especially deep ties with rather few individuals; their circle of friends is small, but those within it are well-loved. They have a sense of humor and are able to discriminate between means and ends and good and evil. They often need privacy and solitude; self-meditation is productive.

The activities that are suggested for raising your daughter from birth through approximately five years of age are designed to begin the development of these positive characteristics. Your parental awareness of the value of these traits will aid you in encouraging them in your daughter and will reduce your requirements for her to conform to long-outdated societal expectations.

ENCOURAGING INDIVIDUALITY WHILE DISCOURAGING OVERINDULGENCE

Whereas you are urged to permit your daughter to mature as an individual, encouraging her interests, exposing her to a variety of highly creative and scientific experiences, and tolerating her needs to explore, self-learn, express, and experiment, you are also urged to require that she behave "like a responsible person"—with standards similar to those you would expect of another adult. Such behavior is not difficult to achieve if *you treat her* in exactly the same way you would treat another person whom you both like and respect. If you react to her with calm dignity and caring, she will treat you and others in the same way. If politeness, reason, and consideration are granted to her, the likelihood is that she will grant it to others.

During the first five years of your daughter's life, the most important people who will mold her personality, character, and behavior will be the *role models with whom she lives.* If her parents are gracious and charming, she will be, too. If they read a great deal and pursue intellectual activities, so will she. If they speak correctly, using a full and sophisticated vocabulary, she will emerge with similar skills. If ever in your own life you wished that you were better than you are, *now* is the time to become that way—for *whatever you are,* you will be influencing your daughter to become a replica of yourself. If she sees that you are growing and learning, so will she.

A child that is raised in the accepting environment that has been described earlier will do well—until she comes into contact with other children who have been raised differently. Because she will have been trained to be observant, to estimate what others are thinking, and to work things out for herself, it will not take long for her to realize that other, less mature girls cry easily, throw temper tantrums, behave coyly to obtain what they want, manipulate, and become affectionate on demand. She will become aware of such tactics somewhere between the age of three and four.

This is another time in her life when you must be very strong. You should *never* give in to tears or temper-tantrums, regardless of the circumstances. You may hold her and say something to the effect that, "I understand that you want that watch," or, "I know you are angry, but you must calm down and talk about it with me." Do not try to speak over her noises, and, if it is possible, walk away until she stops and is ready to be held or diverted into a more positive activity.

Do not encourage coyness, manipulation, or outer manifestations of affection because others desire it of your daughter; in fact, protect her right to give kisses and hugs when she *wants* to. *You* must also be careful not to be coy, manipulative, or free and easy with your own attentions in your daughter's presence, for she will emulate many of your characteristics before you realize that she is either old enough or sufficiently capable of doing so.

Be firm whenever you discipline your daughter—but be reasonable, too. The years when children were expected to do what their parents demanded, merely because their parents demanded it of them, are behind us, and there is no point in becoming involved in philosophical discussions of the merits or disadvantages of either approach. It is enough to state that children should be treated with the same kind of respect, consideration, and kindness that adults desire and that, in the long run, such treatment is more likely to result in their becoming respectful, considerate, and kind human beings.

TEACHING YOUR PRESCHOOL DAUGHTER AT HOME

Many parents are willing to devote the necessary time and energy to teaching their preschool children at home, and there are a number of excellent books that can guide you in this effort.[9] If you intend to devote yourself to this worthwhile and often productive activity, remember that each child matures and learns at a rate and in a manner that is drastically different from that of other children and that activities prescribed in selected readings may be more or less appropriate for different children at different times.

When you attempt to teach as suggested in a specific set of materials, be sensitive to and observant of your daughter's reactions. Continue with the activities to which she responds favorably; avoid the tasks that appear to frustrate her or the ones with which she experiences difficulty. Most children are capable of learning anything if they are taught the item at a time in their lives when they are "ready" to learn it and if given enough time in which to learn it with ease.[10]

Among the books recommended are several that describe arts and crafts, mathematics and reading, science and social-studies-oriented experiences. Borrow as many of these resources as your library has available and choose from them the activities that you believe will be of interest to your daughter and which appear to be appropriate for her at her stage of development.

Nooks, Crannies, and Corners, although intended for redesigning an early childhood or elementary school classroom, includes clever ideas that are adaptable for your daughter's bedroom, your basement or playroom, or an outdoor porch area if you have one. You might experiment with one nook or corner and establish it as a learning center in which mind-extending activities are available for your daughter and a friend or two of hers. You might sequence or color-code the materials (as suggested on page 136 of that book) and observe the ease with which the various tasks are accomplished, in order to determine the level of activities to be designed for future use.

Three critical conditions must exist if you are to attempt to teach your daughter skills, facts, and concepts that will facilitate her intellectual growth:

1. You must enjoy teaching, so that the pleasure you feel is communicated to your daughter and, in turn, makes her learning experience pleasurable.

2. You must be patient and supportive, so that she does not feel pressured to achieve or inadequate when she cannot. This requires the recognition that at some times she will be willing to work with you for an hour or more; at other times, for only ten minutes; and at other times, perhaps not at all. You must remember that items that she cannot remember at one time will be easily retained by her at another time. You must also be aware that children learn in different ways and under differing conditions and that, if need be, you will be required *to adapt your teaching method to her learning style.*

3. Your daughter must be *willing* to learn. Do not coerce or cajole her into working with you, and *never* bribe her to learn. When she is really ready to begin a formalized learning process, she will approach you. If you pressure her before she is able to concentrate on specific studies, you may alienate her.

Your youngster is ready to learn when *she* approaches *you* and asks questions. She is also willing to learn when you approach her and she remains with you and pursues the activity with interest and concentration. Many children at age four are anxious to begin learning how to read—particularly when older siblings are reading. Begin whenever she is willing and pause whenever she indicates she wants to stop.

Use the suggested books on activities for the young child to obtain suggestions.

SELECTING A SCHOOL FOR YOUR PRESCHOOL DAUGHTER

There are many types of schools for three- and four-year-olds, including day nurseries, child-care centers, private nursery schools and kindergartens, church-sponsored and school-affiliated preschool groups, parent-cooperatives, and backyard play groups.[11] The one you select for your daughter will depend essentially on its location and proximity to your home, its cost, and the kind of children that attend it.

When deciding whether or not your daughter should attend a preschool of any type, consider several factors:

1. Do you need to be away from your home—or her—for part of a day? If so, is there a better alternative than a preschool?

2. Does she have opportunities in which to play with other children in your own neighborhood? If so, are those youngsters suitable for her?

3. Will she profit more from attendance at a preschool than from being with you? Will you profit more from being with her or from sending her to a preschool?

These years (between birth and five) are the most important ones in your daughter's life and, if possible, should be under your direct care for at least part of every day. This does not suggest that you cannot be gainfully employed or participate in activities of either a voluntary or interest nature, so long as you devote part of every day to being with your daughter and the *quality* of the time spent together is excellent. Ideally, you should be working as a professional or contributing voluntarily to society at least part-time. You should continue to learn, grow, and aspire to greater achievements for yourself and your daughter. You may even wish to pursue your professional interests at home by establishing an office or workroom there. Let your daughter see you at work; talk to her about it; share your experiences with her. Be certain, however, to schedule time with her if you leave her to go to work. If you need to be away, arrange for an adult to be with her, to see that she is safe and secure.

Reservations arise concerning a girl's attendance at preschools on several counts: In extensive observations of three- to six-year-old children, White found many who were intellectually precocious, able to converse fluently, able to do simple arithmetic, and equipped with information far in excess of that of most children of a similar age category, but who were quite unhappy and uncomfortable in dealing with children and adults other than those of their immediate family.[12] Nursery school for self-oriented and content youngsters is an error.

White also warns against unsupervised play groups which can, on a daily or weekly basis, exert insidious psychological pressures on children.[13] Nursery schools encourage peer-group interactions, in the mistaken belief that "playing with other children" is good for all youngsters. Some children learn best from adults, some from their peers, and others from working things out by themselves.[14] Preschool faculty permit small groups to play together, with only cursory awareness of the conversation or behaviors among them. Often, a submissive child is intimidated by an aggressive or directive youngster and is not capable of resisting. Extended interactions of this nature can result in reduced self-image, frustration, and destructive feelings toward others, par-ticularly in your daughter if she has been stimulated to achieve closer to her full potential than the other children she may meet at the nursery school.

Another common activity of preschool centers is small (or large) group instruction, such as story reading. Such experiences are often irritating to youngsters who are used to being read to by their parents. On a one-to-one basis, your daughter sits close to you, examines the pages and pictures as you read to her, asks questions, responds to your questions, takes "breaks" when she needs to, and can even "read" the words she recognizes to you. In a small group, the children sit in a circle around the reader. Most cannot view the pictures. When the pictures are held up for examination the time in which the children are permitted to really *look* at them is too short an interval to allow adequate eye-focusing and absorption of the concepts. Questions and answers usually are limited to the few aggressive ones who speak up first without either embarrassment or hesitation. The children may have heard the story previously, may not find it interesting, or may not be able to remain silent and seated for the amount of time required of them.

Old-fashioned educators will assure you that it "is good" for children to learn to conform to pre-established standards of conduct and to learn to be part of a group. They are incorrect. Rules and regulations should be established with the advice and consent of the governed (even preschoolers!), and being "part of a group" requires the surrender of part of one's self. The conformity required of little children in traditional elementary schools often crushes their creativity. their individuality, and their ability to make decisions on their own. It is an unnecessary part of the bureaucracy called "school" and continues only because the majority of educators lack the modern skills of individualizing instruction. Introducing large group instruction and group rigidity to preschoolers is an outrageous and almost cruel infringement of their right to grow and to explore and to create.

Assuming, however, that your daughter needs to be provided opportunities to meet and play with other children or to be positively channeled during a period in which you cannot be with her, what should you look for when deciding on a nursery school for her?

What to Look for in Preschool Institutions
Rather than questioning employed administrators or personnel, ask for an opportunity to visit the schools in which you may be interested. Note whether sufficient resources and materials are present on many varied levels (since all

preschoolers are not intellectually equal!). Observe whether the children who pair off or team together conduct their activities essentially without supervision or whether adults move among them at all times—going from group to group, interacting, discussing, directing and responding to questions. Obviously, the latter is preferred.

Note whether "milk and cookie" or "snack" time occurs for all the youngsters simultaneously or whether children are permitted to help themselves as they need or want to. Observe the instructional periods. Are children taught in a group most of the time? Are youngsters pretested, so that their level of functional ability is known to the teacher? Are records maintained of each child's entering skills, levels, and growth on a periodic basis?

Does the teacher schedule or find time to speak to each youngster, one at a time, several times during each session? Does she praise children for their efforts but *teach* them to improve as she examines their work? Are the things that are being taught *beyond* your daughter's present repertoire of knowledge? Or will she need to sit through repetitious or boring experiences that she already has mastered?

Are many activities self-directed? Or just a few? Are many activities group-oriented? Or just a few? Does the teacher "call on" one child at a time—and by name? How much discussion of an intellectual nature actually occurs?

Since some children learn by listening, while others learn by seeing, and still others learn through touching or experiencing, are items of an instructional nature taught through two or more senses? Are adjustments made for the energetic child and the one who requires a great deal of rest? Or do all the children take their "naps" at the same time during the session and for the same amount of time?

Stereotypical Sexist Practices at the Preschool Level

The advisability of attendance at preschool institutions assumes a greater risk, when one considers the outdated emphasis engendered in most primary curriculums which focus on the family being a father, a mother, and two children—in an era where one of three (and sometimes one of every *two*) marriages in the United States terminates in divorce.

One preschooler, whose father is an investment broker and whose mother is a pediatrician, responded to her teacher's query concerning her father's employment with: "My daddy just makes money, but my mommy makes all the sick babies better!" Her enthusiasm was squelched with reproaches for "not realizing the importance" of her father's contribution to society.

Preschool and primary teachers, perhaps more than most, accentuate the role-model expectations of our outdated society. Teachers frequently ask tots, "What does your daddy do?" and assume that mothers "stay home." They also ask, "What will you do when you grow up?" of boys and encourage girls to "dress up" in the "Wendy Corner" or "doll house." They read stories to their charges that reflect sex biases and schedule the boys for woodwork and the girls for sewing. In reality, these "teachers" are unaware of the prejudice they are reinforcing and honestly would deny their influence and intent. Nevertheless, unless you want your daughter to become susceptible to running the gender gauntlet, interview the personnel with whom she will be meeting on a daily basis and explain your views concerning the availability of all activities and tasks to girls, as well as boys. State that sports activities should include all children enrolled in the program, as should cooking, arts, crafts, science, and all other ventures.

If you decide to send your daughter to a preschool program, (1) dress her in overalls or slacks, so that she is not eliminated from gymnastics and sports because of a lack of clothing protection, and (2) visit the school occasionally, if possible on unannounced occasions, and watch the daily procedures. Finally, unless her nursery school is one of those exceptional places of learning where your daughter is exposed to new and interesting experiences and children, she may be better off at home where she will be free to continue her sequential growth toward independence and problem-solving under your concerned supervision.

4.
How to
Promote Success
During Her School Years

**TRANSLATING RESEARCH INTO PRACTICAL
METHODS FOR RAISING DAUGHTERS**

The first part of this book was intended to serve as a guideline for raising very young children from birth through their preschool years. Experts such as Spock, White, Gordon, Gesell, Ilg, and Ginott have written extensively in this area, and much of their advice is sound and based on research and continuing observations. A major problem for females, in our view, is that these child-rearing professionals do not differentiate between the practices that are recommended for boys and those that are appropriate for girls—except in the most perfunctory or stereotypical fashion.

Spock, for example, in *Baby and Child Care* (third edition, 1968) finally became aware of his own sexist style and, at that late date, explained that "he" meant girls, as well as boys. In his more recent revision, he tried to eliminate sexist language but did not differentiate between preparing girls and boys for their adult roles and contributions.

The point is that separate advice for raising girls is absolutely essential to their future equality as adult women, because, under current child-rearing practices, girls are reared differently, and prepared for different roles, roles that provide them with less status, less economic security, and less personal self-fulfillment than boys.

Our major concern, therefore, is to identify those specific procedures and conditions that will help parents to raise their daughters in a manner that provides them with options to become professional and successful in their own right, options that would permit each daughter a choice of life style, rather than exclusively "boxing her into" a traditional homemaker role.

That need is clear. Researchers such as Maslow, Friedan, and Mager[1] have verified that people without choices experience reduced motivation and achievement. Other studies, quoted extensively in Chapter 1, indicate that the restrictions of a homemaker-mother role cause many women neurological and psychological distress, that women who do not achieve education beyond the high school level experience reduced I.Q.'s over a succeeding ten-year period, that a majority of all women are actively involved in the labor market today (but primarily in nonprofessional jobs), and that the divorce rate in the United States has so accelerated that women had better be prepared to become economically independent through their own earning-power.

A logical way to begin the search for ways to raise successful professional daughters would be to interview outstanding women who reached "the top," despite the odds. Could they recall what inspired them? Did they engage in certain kinds of experiences? Could specific patterns in their lives be recognized and applied to the upbringing of other girls?

Rita's New York University doctoral dissertation[2] studied a select group of eminent American women who were professionally involved in the fields of dentistry, law, medicine, and educational or nursing administration, to discover if there were differences or essential similarities between specific environmental, experiential, human-impact and time-sequence factors to which the participants had been exposed and by which they believe they were motivated toward professional attainment and subsequent involvement.

The findings revealed that "there were no significant differences among the motivating factors identified by the respondents"—or, in other words, that these professional women who had attained educational levels beyond the norm for most girls, who had become professional, and thus economically independent, and, who, in addition, had achieved recognition and status in fields that essentially are male-dominated, were motivated by similar (if not identical) factors.

The studies revealed five key steps that appeared to have led these women toward independence and professional success. Thus, the central motivating ingredients and the practical applications and procedures described in this book are derived from the consciously recalled experiences of independent and outstanding[3] professional women: attorneys, dentists, doctors, and educational and nursing administrators of institutions of higher education and hospitals.

Since the respondents involved in the study provided information concerning their experiences from their elementary school through adult years, it was necessary to translate the five key steps into the practical applications for preschool children noted in the first part of this book. At this point, however, each of the five steps can be itemized for your examination and immediate application to your daughter's life experiences as she moves into the elementary school and continues, hopefully, into graduate institutions of higher education.

One interesting side-note: When the New York University study was undertaken, several of the supervising graduate professors and doctoral students theorized that the findings would reveal that those women who had achieved professional involvement and success in their fields would be "old maids"—unmarried spinsters who, for the lack of a marital relationship and motherhood objective, had devoted their lives toward career and economic success. In addition to other surprising information, the study revealed that the majority of these outstanding women were married, and most of the attorneys, dentists, and doctors had one or more children.[4] In addition, a positive benefit derived from their professional aspirations was that 40 percent of the women dentists were married to dentists; 51 percent of the women attorneys had married lawyers; and 58 percent of the women doctors had wed physicians.[5] The projection of these data would seem to indicate that by aiding your daughter to *become* a professional, you are subtly increasing her opportunities to meet and marry a professional man with interests and abilities similar to her own.

Furthermore, this type of "counterpart" marriage apparently has a fine chance for longevity and happiness, for, among the women in the study, none of the dentists, less than 6 percent of the attorneys, and only 6.5 percent of the physicians had divorced[6]—a figure far below the national "norm," which is estimated at somewhere between 30 and 50 percent, depending on the group, geographic location, and age at the time of marriage.

FIVE STEPS TOWARD INDEPENDENCE AND PROFESSIONAL SUCCESS

If your daughter is already in school, and you cannot "begin at the beginning," do not be concerned. It is a distinct advantage to begin as early as possible, but the elementary school years can be extremely important for the type of training suggested, and the middle and high school years can also influence your daughter's decisions to a great extent. You may also find that contributing to *her* growth may enhance *your own* opportunities for self-realization!

The practical applications of the five key steps are described here to serve as a base for ages six to eighteen, the years during which your daughter is in school. During this period of extensive intellectual growth, she also will be developing *"affectively"*; she will become acutely *aware* of the feelings and values of the peers and adults with whom she comes into contact. At some point between the ages of six and eighteen, she will become *willing to examine* a value system that will determine her entire future. What you do at home should help her to *select with discrimination* the path(s) of life on which she will walk. She will react to your influence by either accepting or rejecting the suggestions you offer; if you follow the five steps that lead to the professional involvement and success of the New York University research population, your daughter will, more likely than not, internalize your training and establish *your values* as *her preference.* Once this process occurs, her *commitment will become a conviction.* She will then further *identify, organize, conceptualize, weigh,* and *regulate* the alternatives that are available to her. She will also *judge* the decision(s) she has made, *revise* them where appropriate, *internalize* her aspirations, and then *consistently* move in the direction(s) she has chosen. Eventually, she will be *characterized* by the values she has selected to be her own.[7] The initial stage of this process must be introduced by her parents; the later stage must be worked through on her own. This is the process that all women experience as they make their life decisions. If you can incorporate the guidelines of the five key steps into your daily interactions with your daughter, there is a very strong likelihood that she will choose to become a professional woman as one of the major roles of her life.

Step 1: Encourage Your Daughter to Obtain as Much Education as Possible
From the time she begins to understand language, concentrate on the development of a love of learning. Build her self-image by praising her achievements in positive and glowing terms frequently, wholeheartedly, and unwaveringly. Encourage her toward the goal just beyond the one she reached last week (or month), but do not insist. Speak of, "When you go to college . . ." and start a bank account where coins and gift money are "matched" (by you) when saved "for college." It is this emphasis on and appreciation of the value of education, the educated, and educational institutions that will be one of the major means of motivating her toward intellectual growth and, ultimately, toward educational achievement.

Encouragement toward learning, education, and achievement should begin in infancy, as previously noted. It is launched by consciously praising those who exhibit an interest, curiosity, or desire to learn and by surrounding your daughter (and yourself) with the instruments of learning—books, magazines, radio, selected television programs, records, cassettes, pencils and paper, crayons, paint, clay, mechanical objects, puzzles, climbing and gymnastic apparatus, construction kits, and so on, as soon as she exhibits interest in and ability to use any or all of them.

A two-year-old who "builds a house" by pulling together an assortment of pillows, blankets, and small furniture items should be praised for her creativity—not admonished because of the disarray that results. Saying, "What a beautiful house you designed! When you go to college you will learn how to build them of steel and glass!" is *not* silly! The child feels a sense of satisfaction at having formed a shelter (of sorts). This act of achievement will be combined with your praise and the suggestion that, at some future time, she will learn how to make "bigger and better" creations. The combined sense of achievement and parental praise will be associated pleasantly with the word "college" (regardless of the fact that the word has no meaning for the youngster *at the moment*), and "college" will gradually become a desirable place to her.

Learning and receptivity toward new ideas and activities is also expanded and emphasized by exposing your daughter to a combination of cultural events in which *you* actively participate, such as the theater, movies, concerts, exhibits, museums, sports, visits, travel, and reading. The sooner your daughter accompanies you to such varied and stimulating activities, the sooner she will begin to appreciate and enjoy them. Remember, as described earlier in this section, your daughter first must be exposed to each of these exciting options and become *aware* of them. If she is too young or too immature to be aware and to be *willing* to pay attention, she is not yet "ready" for the experience. Wait a month or so, and try again.

Many people do not "take to" new things easily; sometimes several visits to a specific event is necessary before receptivity develops. Occasionally, returning to an activity can facilitate its acceptance, but where obvious rejection is apparent, permit lengthy periods (perhaps a year) to intervene.

Engage in cooperative projects with your daughter through activities that incorporate learning experiences to which she has been exposed. For example, simulate a court case (after visiting a few trials or hearings) and encourage your daughter to assume the role of an attorney or judge. Introduce her to photography and develop a "script" that explains your neighborhood, a visit, or a hobby through words and pictures. Design a new urban center with blocks of cardboard and let your daughter be the "chief architect."

In addition to the potential for eventual success in this "man's world," it is important that you and your daughter pursue a common enterprise and share the joy of achievement and production together. These projects should be enjoyable (developing film, learning to ice skate, building a desk for her room, building a bird house), and she should be praised for her work enthusiastically. Be certain to guard against either "overdoing" the praise (it should be justified and real) or becoming competitive with your daughter; your primary objective is to focus positive attention on *her* achievements and to provide her with a sense of *earned* success in varied endeavors. These activities and actions will build her confidence and ego strength, to say nothing of the many skills she will develop!

Simultaneously, your young girl must become aware of your level of expectation for her intellectual growth and constantly increasing achievement. If you believe that females need no more than a college education, chances are that all your daughter will demand of herself is that she obtain a baccalaureate degree, or less. If, however, you expect her to reach her own maximum potential—on whatever level that will be—she will probably strive toward achieving that goal, whether it be a doctoral degree or a business of her own.

Some child-rearing experts have suggested that it may be dangerous to demand more of your child than she (or he) possibly can achieve. Danger exists at either end of the scale, but the tragedy of our time is not the youngster who strives beyond her potential but, rather, the overwhelming number of daughters who do not strive at all. These young girls frequently take "the path of least resistance" and never experience the joys and satisfactions of self-actualization. Many of these unmotivated youngsters submerge their frustrations or inadequacies in drugs, blame their parents or "The Establishment," complain about the irrelevance of their lives, and cease "growing," in the sense that they never realize their maximum potential. This pattern results in an enormous loss of human ability—skills that might have aided in the struggle against cancer, heart disease, or birth defects, that could have reduced pollution, poverty, or human blight, or that might have designed new methods for harnessing energy or for revising our outdated judiciary system.

Step 2: Become as Well Educated as You Can Be
Throughout these chapters, our reference to "you" is directed at any adult responsible for raising a young girl today—although our primary focus has been on mothers and fathers. Step 2, however, is aimed primarily at mothers.

The single most important item that determines the level of learning that a daughter seeks is her *mother's education*. Of the 138 separate analysis tables included in the New York University study concerned with the development of women's motivation toward professional aspirations, the mother's education and encouragement of her daughter's education yielded the most significant relationship.[8]

The research supports the conclusion that mothers who achieve a high school level of education will encourage their daughters to acquire *at least as much and usually more* than they did. These findings, translated into meaningful action patterns, appear to indicate that a mother should consider herself *obligated* to improve her own mind continually—whether through formal or informal education—to serve as a positive role model for her daughter.

At the beginning of Step 2 we mentioned that this section is primarily focused on the mother of each little girl. The research evidence draws direct and significant relationships between a mother's education and her daughter's achievement, but it is likely, too, that other relatives exert at least *some* influence over a girl's aspirations. It is likely that a father enrolled in a college course during his daughter's awareness years will increase her receptivity toward study. A grandmother who registers for a cooking or embroidery series, or a grandfather who volunteers to teach some disadvantaged children how to read may equally enhance a little girl's outlook toward increased education. All of these acts sponsor the concept that learning is important and never-ending.

Should any member of the family be involved in studies of any type, taking your daughter along once in a while, either as observer or as participant, can produce an important learning experience for her. In fact, having her teach younger children any skill that she has acquired will also serve as a positive reinforcement, both of the skill and the learning act itself.

Mothers who recognize that they have limited their own educational opportunities and who can find some time should consider seriously "going back to school." Talking about your plans with your daughter, permitting her to share in your excitement (and concerns), allowing her to see you studying and learning will all assist her toward in egrating the need for advanced education with her own planned life style.

The mother who is *always* "at home with her children" probably does them less good (and may do them more harm!) than the one who breaks away a couple of times each week to pursue a course in whatever it is she "always wanted to take." And, if you have not already done so, now is the time to complete your undergraduate education or obtain that advanced degree that will add to your own sense of accomplishment or ability to be economically independent.

Step 3. Develop Your Daughter's Professional Aspirations: Help Her to See Herself as a Professional Person

Introduce your daughter to a wide variety of professional women. Plan specific contacts with many successful females, to establish role models she might wish to emulate and to demonstrate the reality of women's accomplishments. Begin early—at age two or three!

As noted earlier, use the services of a female pediatrician and buy your child a doctor's kit instead of a nurse's costume, an erector set instead of dolls and dresses, a counting-bead frame instead of play make-up, a blackboard and chalk to "play school" instead of an embroidery card. Have her teeth checked by a woman dentist. Guide her toward block construction, coloring and painting, and kits to put together model houses, airplanes, rockets, and cars. If you are afraid of "curtailing her childhood," ask her to examine her doll with her miniature stethoscope after a visit to the female pediatrician; then compare the exuberance and learning of that play experience with what she derived from other activities, such as washing or ironing a doll's clothes.

When your daughter approaches seven or eight, take her with you to a court of law where a woman judge is presiding. Let her see female doctors, engineers, and other professionals at work, and when she becomes a teenager, encourage her to interview some of them.

When she is still a preschooler, take her with you when you vote or when you register for a course at the local college or university. Introduce her to a woman professor after class. You need not indicate that these professional people are of the feminine gender. Merely provide the *contact* without drawing excessive (or any) attention to sex. Your young girl should be exposed to professional women as a matter of course. She should think of these women as *people,* and not as unusual women. The sex of a female professional should be no more obvious to your daughter than the male elementary school teacher is to your son.

Express very positive attitudes toward working mothers: do not disparage them. Do not intimate that the children of these women are either neglected or potential delinquents. If they *are,* the fact that their mothers are working does not necessarily contribute to the cause. Most judges in children's courts will testify to the number of grievously delinquent children brought before them every day who live in homes where both parents are "devoted" to the child and where the mother is *not* working.

Research studies conducted during the past ten years consistently yield *no* traceable negative effects stemming from maternal employment. Children of working mothers are no more likely than children of nonworking mothers to be underachieving, delinquent, or neurotic. Personality disturbances occur when either parent (or both) is (are) negative, rejecting, lacking in warmth or affection, or when they neglect, overprotect, or overmanage their children. In fact, Maccoby reported that "The brighter girls tend to be the ones who have not been tied closely to their mothers' apron strings, but have been allowed and encouraged to fend for themselves." [9]

Mothers who bind their daughters to them, instead of fostering their initiative and independence, create dependent young women—and no amount of education will sever the bondage between a dependent young woman and her *need* to find a male who will care for her. Unfortunately, inner security and self-fulfillment cannot be obtained through others.

Conversely, children of intellectually or artistically involved and stimulated mothers tend to wish to emulate them, and they appear to establish a level of expectation for *themselves* that parallels their observations of their mothers. In addition, children seem to want to fulfill the expectations of the mother who is, herself, involved with personal interests—*particularly when those interests appear to be making a contribution to society.* It may be that children become as proud of their accomplished parents as their parents are of their successful children.

Step 4: Be Firm in Your Convictions but Simultaneously Respect Those of Your Daughter

If you hope to help your daughter to become independent, confident of her ability, and able to cope with an ever-expanding series of experiences, you will need to be consistent in your approaches to everyday problems so that she can begin to gauge how to behave *without* your direction; you will need to be firm about the rules and regulations that have been established (with her consent); and you will need to be fair about determining alternatives and making decisions that affect her.

It is difficult to explain *how* to be consistent, firm, fair, and, simultaneously, flexible, but that, too, is necessary, for rules and regulations often require change, and it is important to *hear* her logic when she complains about an agreed-upon standard that no longer is valuable or valid for her.

Perhaps the following guidelines will be of assistance:

1. Whenever a problem arises, discuss it together and try cooperatively to decide how to eliminate it. Establish rules together and explain that you expect her to abide by them;

2. On occasions when she forgets, remind her kindly and patiently; it will be many years before she remembers accurately and religiously the many things she is required to do.

3. If she forgets consistently, discuss ways to help her remember. Assist her with "reminders," whether verbal, illustrated, or pantomimed. Make a game of helping her to recall her promises.

4. If she complains about the requirements, discuss possible changes and try to reach a common agreement. Pretend that you are involved with an older person who is limited mentally. In that situation you would not be abusive or impatient. Try to treat your daughter with the same respect that you would a senile aged person. This suggestion is made only because parents often chastise their children and, without realizing it, wound them psychologically by challenging their self-confidence. Children forget, often and repeatedly. Perhaps because they are learning so many new things every day, it becomes difficult for them to concentrate on unrelated obligations. Do not disparage her because of her forgetfulness; help her to overcome what may be a tendency to resist concentrating.

Research among successful women verifies that in cases where parental discipline had been firm but reasonable, the majority of youngsters developed sufficient ability and independence to become outstanding professionals.[10] The *least successful* method of discipline (8 percent) was found among the group whose discipline had been viewed as "lenient."[11]

If your child is to become successful, she should be taught at an early age that you will not be swayed by whining, cajoling, nagging, or coyness. At the same time, she should recognize that you respect her as a human being who has dignity and rights. Crying because of a desire to be held as an infant is not to be confused with crying because she cannot play with a given item. Hold and hug your daughter with affection—but do not surrender *your* prerogatives as a parent because of her determination.

Step 5: Help Your Daughter to Develop a Code of Values So That She Will Want to Become a Contributing Member of Society

A well-defined set of social values that includes contributing to others will help your daughter to develop professional interests. When asked *why* they selected their specific career fields, the largest number of professional respondents listed reasons such as:

- Meaningful work;
- An opportunity to be helpful to others or to be useful to society;
- Pride in accomplishment;
- An opportunity to work with people, rather than things;
- Living and working in the world of ideas; and
- A chance to exercise leadership.[12]

These statements reflect a personal value system that was developed early in the lives of the outstanding women in the motivational research study. Specific career choices of almost 19 percent of these professionals developed *before* they were twelve years of age. In addition, 53 percent had decided upon their professional fields *before* they entered college.[13]

Therefore, very early in your daughter's life, make her aware that you believe that it is positive to help people, to be kind, to make things better, to care for animals, to help the needy, to do something for others, and to do things well. As she grows older, she will realize that contributing to the community welfare and being helpful to society is good, positive, worthwhile, desirable, and necessary, in your view.

The development of a public conscience and respect for law and order is part of this total approach. Do not discuss the ways in which you may have avoided paying a traffic ticket, taxes, or loans. Do not condone or show apathy toward political dishonesty, graft, chicanery, or breaking of the law. Little things like returning books to the public library and caring for someone else's property are essential to the development of a personal code of ethics by your daughter. If you want her to live a happy and meaningful life, show her by your own actions the standards and values by which you live.

LEARNING ABOUT HER LEARNING STYLE

The study of successful professional women and follow-up by the authors focuses on the importance of your daughter's love of learning, continuing and extensive education, and professional aspirations. These characteristics, when coupled with your own continuing education and encouragement, are central to your daughter's eventual success. In addition to these strong emphases on positive attitudes toward and commitment to continual education, it is essential that you identify as much as you can about the way your daughter tends to learn. Once you have diagnosed her most effective "learning style," you will be able to plan and manipulate her environment and materials to promote maximum, pleasant results.

Selected aspects of how students learn have been undergoing study for more than three quarters of a century! Only in recent years, however, has it been possible to employ some of the more sophisticated research techniques available in measuring instructional methods and outcomes. In this regard, the various elements that comprise a person's learning style were investigated and synthesized from the literature of educational, industrial, psychological, and sociological research. After nearly a decade of study, observation, and testing with thousands of students from primary grades through university graduate school levels, we have developed a description of the unique characteristics of individual learning styles that applies to all students—youngsters and adults. More important, we have designed a "Learning Style Questionnaire" that you can use to diagnose exactly how your daughter learns.

The description of what learning style actually is and the questionnaire with instructions for its use follow. This valid and reliable instrument may be used to interview your daughter and should be followed by observations and a re-interview to confirm her original responses. If your daughter is less than eight years of age, you may have to simplify some of the questions and rely more on your observations than on her perceptions of how she prefers to learn.

The questionnaire included in this book has been validated and deemed reliable for students in grades 3–12. It may be used for younger children but should be supplemented, as suggested, by your repeated observations of how she performs during her learning experiences. If you administer the instrument to youngsters in the elementary, middle or junior high school grades, test for only one or two elements at one sitting. There is no need to acquire all the information at one time, and fatigue may cause irritation and resultant incorrect answers.

THE ELEMENTS OF LEARNING STYLE

Most adults recognize that people are so individual that they learn, recall, interpret, and use information in ways that are very different from each other. In addition, each person responds uniquely and in varying amounts to her/his (a) immediate environment, (b) own emotionality, (c) sociological needs, and (d) physical requirements.

Learning style, therefore, is the manner in which at least eighteen different elements from four basic stimuli affect a person's ability to absorb and retain. The combinations and variations among these elements suggest that few people learn in exactly the same way, just as few people think exactly alike.

Environmental Elements of Learning Style
The environmental elements that affect how much your daughter is able to achieve at a given time include *sound, light, temperature,* and *design.*

Sound. Some people can block out surrounding noises and function effectively in spite of them. Others can adjust to selected sounds, depending on the task. A larger group appears to require virtual silence if the learning to be accomplished requires concentration or is difficult for them. Another group appears to be unable to study or concentrate without discussing the materials to be learned; this group, in effect, *requires* sound.

Light. The way in which a room is illuminated also appears to affect the learning process. Whereas some people can function with ease only when the environment is well-lit, the same degree of lighting is considered excessive by some and insufficient by others. If lighting is incorrect for your daughter, it can prevent concentration, either by overstimulating her or by lulling her into drowsiness.

Temperature. Temperature is an element that yields easily observable differences in learning ability as the degree of heat varies. Some require a warm environment before they can study; others find that the same amount of warmth that relaxes certain people actually makes them uncomfortable. Your daughter may be able to function well only in a cool area, whereas other girls become "nervous" at the same degree of temperature.

Design. The way in which an environment is designed also produces differences in the amount of learning that your daughter is able to achieve. Certain students indicate that they require a formal study area that includes a desk or table and a chair—such as might be found in a library or a kitchen. Others report that they "cannot sit" in a highly structured area for any length of time and continue to concentrate; these people require a relaxed setting and find that they can continue to work for longer intervals when the furniture and surroundings are informal. This very informality, however, usually causes drowsiness or daydreaming in the group requiring the more structured design. You may even find that your daughter functions best on a carpeted floor. Encourage the design that works best.

Emotional Elements of Learning Style
The emotional elements that affect how much a student is able to achieve at a given time include *motivation, persistence, responsibility,* and the individual's need for *structure* or flexibility.

Motivation. If you have been a source of stimulation, guidance, poise, and love, as described earlier, motivation should be natural to your daughter. Look for an unquenchable zeal to learn, to ask questions, to want to go and do and to respond with interest and excitement to new situations. As you observe and diagnose your daughter, be certain to give her many opportunities to (1) make choices, (2) self-test and evaluate herself, (3) establish social-learning groups with other children and adults, and (4) vary the way she functions, to complement her learning style. For example, if she is an "auditory" learner who likes to learn alone, supply her with many tapes, records, "talking" books, and other visual materials with accompanying recordings. These four guidelines will aid in sustaining her motivation.

Persistence. Some children cannot stay with a task or assignment for an extended period of time; others will pursue current objectives until they are completed. The length and type of learning tasks you offer your daughter should depend on your observations, her responses, and your perceived diagnosis of her persistence levels. Allow flexibility within time ranges, try tasks of different lengths, assess her attitude toward and interest in different objectives. Interact with her and allow her to elect topics of interest, methods of learning, time intervals, and potential rewards.

Responsibility. Many children will follow through on almost any task, job, or learning requirement; they always can be trusted to complete their work to the best of their ability. To ensure your daughter's developing sense of responsibility, be certain that she clearly understands (1) what she should achieve, (2) how she may complete the task, (3) the time interval suggested (with minimum and maximum limits), (4) how she may check her own progress and test the final results, and (5) how she can show you that she has achieved her objectives when the assignment has been completed. You should serve as her combined "teacher," consultant, and "supervisor." It is critical to build a joint expectation for progress toward completion of tasks through reminders of "deadlines," progress reports and conferences, and cooperative assessment of her work. As she functions with increased confidence, expand and lengthen her learning activities, make them a bit more difficult, and permit her to work more independently.

Structure. Frequent supervision, reminders, specific schedules, and detailed explanations probably will not be necessary as your daughter builds high personal levels of motivation, persistence, and responsibility. Provide her with many opportunities to solve problems by herself. Making correct decisions, determining alternative approaches, and coping with obstacles will enhance her self-reliance. Allow her to obtain assistance from you, other adults, or friends, but constantly encourage her to "find the answers" or solve the problem by herself if she can. Ask her to show you the results and to do as much as she can, first. Help her to learn how to plan her own work and to set her own deadlines. Do not frustrate her but hold high expectations for her independence and self-sufficiency.

Sociological Elements of Learning Style
Students react differently to their peers, adults, and the learning process itself. Some prefer to study alone and can achieve more in this manner than when working directly with either other youngsters or adults. Some students require direct and virtually continual interaction with an "authority figure," whether it be you, her teachers, an expert, an outside resource, or a paraprofessional. There are, however, children who become "uptight" or intimidated by adults;

they find they can learn more easily when working with a friend or two, or even in a small group. This is true of many students and is often manifested by an inclination to work within a committee structure or on task forces.

Take advantage of your diagnosis of her sociological preferences in this regard. Allow her to work alone and independently if she prefers that mode and achieves successfully in that way. Do not be negative about her "lack of friends" if she likes to work alone. Work with her closely if she prefers you as a partner in her endeavors, but build her confidence and self-reliance. Invite her peers to the house if she studies better with another youngster.

Establish social patterns of learning which best suit her. The goal for any of these alternatives, however, is independence—independence which will permit her to make all of the choices that are best for her during the years that she moves toward becoming a professional adult.

Physical Elements of Learning Style
To a major extent your daughter is not a free agent; she is controlled to some degree by her physical needs. Only the strongly motivated learner can achieve when her physical requirements are at variance with the learning system in use.

Perceptual Strengths. Some people learn well through hearing; for these, a lecture, a discussion, a record, or a cassette will facilitate achievement. Some must experience visually what should be learned. Both groups comprise only a portion of the student community, and sometimes their abilities to advance academically through the use of auditory or visual strategies are mutually exclusive; sometimes they are complementary or reinforcing.

Other students experience great difficulty when trying to learn without a tactual (touching, feeling) or kinesthetic (whole body activity) involvement. This is often true of youngsters who do not learn to read through either a phonics or word recognition approach. When exposed to tactual or kinesthetic methods however, they frequently overcome the difficulties they had when taught through auditory or visual techniques. Using a multisensory approach to teaching your daughter often will overcome learning problems that she may be experiencing if you (or others) usually explain things to her by talking.

Touching, feeling, and doing with her entire body (such as developing an understanding of weight and measurement through baking or constructing) should be included in many learning activities. She should explore through all of her senses and learn with you which combinations are best for her.

Intake. Another physical problem that confronts some children is the need for *"intake"* at regular intervals. Whether this is a physical need to replace the energy being expended by concentration or a means of releasing nervous tension, some students frequently need to eat, drink, chew gum, or even bite on objects while engaged in the learning process. If your daughter requires food while working, provide nutritious items such as carrots, celery, nuts, raisins, fruit, green peppers, raw cauliflower, and so on, in small amounts near where she is working. You may discover that your daughter can't eat or drink until after she completes a task. In this event, sit with her afterward and react positively to her description of her achievements as she eats or nibbles.

Time. The *time* when a person is most alert and, therefore, best able to absorb learning varies with the individual. Some students work most effectively early in the morning, others excel later in the day, and still others are proverbial "night owls." If timing is an important learning style factor for your daughter, try to work out schedules that enhance her best learning and doing patterns.

Mobility. Finally, the physical need for *mobility* (evidenced in many youngsters) may easily inhibit learning efforts. Your daughter may not be able to remain in her seat or in a restricted environment for long periods of time. She may be at ease in a chair or in a single position for thirty or forty minutes or for even longer periods of time. If she fits the latter category, she may find the noise and movement of those who require mobility disconcerting. Be aware of her need to move, walk, return, and shift positions as she concentrates if this is an important aspect of her learning style.

USING THE LEARNING STYLE QUESTIONNAIRE

Learning styles can be diagnosed, and recent research studies have demonstrated that (1) students can identify their own learning styles, (2) students score higher on tests, have better attitudes, and are more efficient when taught in a style that matches the ways in which they believe they learn best, and (3) it is advantageous to teach and test students in their preferred styles.

The questionnaire which follows has been tested with several thousand students from grades 3 through 12 during the past decade. It is valid and reliable; that is, you will find it accurate with respect to what it is supposed to measure and consistent for similar children.

Interview and observe your daughter and complete the Learning Style Profile at the end of the instrument. Then plan with her to organize an area in your home, so that she may learn in ways that are consonant with her learning style.

Use the revealed diagnostic data to teach her in the ways that she learns most easily and share her Learning Style Profile with her teachers throughout her school career. It is a good idea to retest your daughter annually to be certain that substantial changes do not occur in her learning style. We have found that, where an element is *important* to an individual (a high score is yielded), that element does not tend to change. It is possible, however, that time, experience, increased maturity, and certain motivating factors may contribute to the development of different environmental, sociological, and physical preferences.

Administering the Questionnaire
Your youngster may be given this questionnaire in writing, on tape, or orally. All of the "true" and "false" questions should be answered. There are questions that, if thought about in detail, would cause many modifications, limitations, and exceptions in responses. Children should be encouraged to give immediate reactions to each question on a "feeling" basis. The entire questionnaire need not be completed in only one sitting, but may be responded to at intervals that are convenient to both your daughter and you.

In cases where girls do not read fluently, or where they have experienced learning difficulties, it is valuable to administer this instrument through a personal interview. The one-to-one relationship that develops as the parent questions the youngster about her preferences often provides new insights into the child's thinking that may not be afforded otherwise.

Scoring and Interpreting Your Daughter's Answers
When the questionnaire has been completed, all of the "true" and "false" answers in each category should be checked against the Consistency Key and added. The total number of each category's set of responses should then be placed above the line on top of the numeral under either "true" or "false" in that category's column under the section called "Totals."

By following these directions, you will form a series of fractions by (1) adding the number of your daughter's responses in each column that agrees with the numbers in the Consistency Key and (2) writing that total as a numerator above the denominator in each correct column. The strength of the fraction (its closeness to being a whole number) determines whether or not that element is important to your daughter. For example, $7/7$ or $6/7$ implies that an element is a vital factor in your daughter's learning style. A fraction of $5/7$ or $4/7$ suggests that, under certain conditions and at various times, your daughter can accommodate to different aspects (either positive or negative) of that element. Below $4/7$ indicates that either the element is not part of her learning style or, when balanced by a high fraction at the opposite extreme, that it responds to her style negatively. A preponderance of answers in any one column, or pair of columns in a category, will indicate the probable type of learning style for that element.

When answers are divided among several columns in one element, the indication may be that there is no predisposition toward any one category. That element, therefore, may not be a factor in your daughter's learning style. In some cases, answers that are divided among several categories in an element may indicate that she has no major preferences and can function effectively under a number of varied situations, such as during many hours of the day or with peers, adults, and alone.

Comments based on the highest ratios in each category should be noted on the Learning Style Profile form found at the end of the questionnaire and should be used to individualize your daughter's program when she attends school. Each child, and certainly those with learning problems, should be diagnosed to identify her learning style, particularly since the research verifies that students are able to identify how they learn.

SAMPLE SCORING EXERCISE

These two samples will aid you in understanding how to score and interpret each section.

	Sample A Responses		Sample B Responses	
Sound	*True*	*False*	*True*	*False*
1. I study best when it is quiet.	X			X
2. I can work with a little noise.	X		X	
3. I can block out noise when I work.		X	X	
4. Noise usually keeps me from concentrating.	X			X
5. Most of the time I like to work with soft music.	X			X
6. I can work with any kind of music.		X		X
7. I often like to work with rock music playing.		X	X	
8. Music makes it difficult for me to work.	X			X
9. I can work if people talk quietly.		X	X	
10. I can study when people talk.		X	X	
11. I can block out most sound when I study.		X	X	
12. It's difficult to block out TV when I work.	X			X
13. Noise bothers me when I am studying.	X			X

CONSISTENCY KEY (FOR THE PARENT)

The consistency scoring key is reproduced here with the responses matched against those in the scoring key. For example the young girl in Sample A responded with a check in all six numbers listed under the true column in the scoring key (1, 2, 4, 8, 12, 13). This total of six is then placed in the numerator (top) part of the fraction and yields $^6/_6$. Examples are given for all columns in Sample A and B.

Sample A

Needs Silent or Quiet Areas		Sound Is Acceptable	
True	False	True	False
1. X	3. X	2. X	1. ___
2. X	5. ___	3. ___	4. ___
4. X	6. X	5. ___	8. ___
8. X	7. X	6. ___	12. ___
12. X	9. X	7. ___	13. ___
13. X	10. X	9. ___	
	11. X	10. ___	
		11. ___	

Totals

6	6	1	0

Sample B

Needs Silent or Quiet Areas		Sound Is Acceptable	
True	False	True	False
1. ___	3. ___	2. X	1. X
2. X	5. X	3. X	4. X
4. ___	6. ___	5. ___	8. X
8. ___	7. ___	6. ___	12. X
12. ___	9. ___	7. X	13. X
13. ___	10. ___	9. X	
	11. ___	10. X	
		11. X	

Totals

1	1	6	5

Total Scores

Needs Quiet		Sound Is Acceptable	
True	False	True	False
$^6/_6$	$^6/_7$	$^1/_8$	$^0/_5$

The preponderance of high scores indicates a need for quiet.

Total Scores

Needs Quiet		Sound Is Acceptable	
True	False	True	False
$^1/_6$	$^1/_7$	$^6/_8$	$^5/_5$

The very high scores under "Sound Is Acceptable" may indicate that sound is either desirable or tolerable.

The young girl in Sample A should be given a quiet place to study, read, or complete any work requiring concentration and thinking. Quiet music is the only sound she can tolerate while learning. Interruptions, noise, conversation or rock music from another room will disturb her ability to work. Note the high scores $^6/_6$ and $^6/_7$ for "Needs Quiet" and the low scores for "Sound Is Acceptable", $^1/_8$ and $^0/_5$.

The youngster in Sample B has almost the reverse preference with respect to sound. Her high scores for "Sound Is Acceptable", $^6/_8$ and $^5/_5$, and low scores for "Needs Quiet", $^1/_6$ and $^1/_7$, indicate that sound is not only acceptable, it is likely to be desirable. It may seen odd to you, but the daughter in this case may work very well with music or TV blaring. Indeed, *quiet* may be disturbing to her. It is likely that she concentrates by blocking out the silence which many people find disconcerting.

Our own daughter concentrates well with the television on. We wondered about this but discovered that she really doesn't "watch" the set. We often have observed her working with her back to the screen. She needs sound in her learning environment.

Obviously, it is the results that count. If your daughter completes her work successfully with sound, it may be that she requires sound as a key element in her learning style.

Should your daughter exhibit mixed scores, $5/6$, $1/7$, $2/8$, $4/5$, or an even distribution, $3/6$, $4/7$, $4/8$, and $3/5$, sound is probably not a factor for her.

LEARNING STYLE QUESTIONNAIRE[14]

Name_____Date:_____

Directions: (To your daughter—Answer *True* or *False* to each of the following questions.

I. Environmental Stimuli

    A. *Sound*   *True*   *False*

		True	False
1.	I study best when it is quiet.	___	___
2.	I can work with a little noise.	___	___
3.	I can block out noise when I work.	___	___
4.	Noise usually keeps me from concentrating.	___	___
5.	Most of the time I like to work with soft music.	___	___
6.	I can work with any kind of music.	___	___
7.	I often like to work with rock music playing.	___	___
8.	Music makes it difficult for me to work.	___	___
9.	I can work if people talk quietly.	___	___
10.	I can study when people talk.	___	___
11.	I can block out most sound when I study.	___	___
12.	It's difficult to block out TV when I work.	___	___
13.	Noise bothers me when I am studying.	___	___

Totals: (To be completed by the parent)   ___   ___

Needs Quiet		Sound Is Acceptable	
True	*False*	*True*	*False*
___	___	___	___
6	7	8	5

Consistency Key: (For the parent)

Needs Silent or Quiet Areas		Sound Is Acceptable or Desirable	
True	*False*	*True*	*False*
1			1
2		2	
	3	3	
4			4
	5	5	
	6	6	
	7	7	
8			8
	9	9	
	10	10	
	11	11	
12			12
13			13

Directions: Total the number of trues and falses for each column. Fill in the top half of the fraction. Follow these instructions for all categories.

B. *Light*

	True	False
1. I like studying with lots of light.	___	___
2. I study best when the lights are low.	___	___
3. I like to read outdoors.	___	___
4. I can study for a short time if the lights are low.	___	___
5. When I study I put all the lights on.	___	___
6. I often read in dim light.	___	___
7. I usually study under a shaded lamp, while the rest of the room is dim.	___	___

Totals:

Requires a Great Deal of Light	Requires Low Light	Light Not a Factor	
True	*True*	*True*	*False*
4	3	6	6

Consistency Key:
Requires a Great
Deal of Light   Requires Low Light   Light Not a Factor

True	*True*	
1	2	Light is probably
3	6	not a factor if six
4	7	or seven questions
5		are marked either
		all true or all false.

C. Temperature	True	False
1. I can concentrate if I'm warm.	___	___
2. I can concentrate if I'm cold.	___	___
3. I usually feel colder than most people.	___	___
4. I usually feel warmer than most people.	___	___
5. I like the summer.	___	___
6. When it's cold outside I like to stay in.	___	___
7. When it's hot outside I like to stay in.	___	___
8. When it's hot outside I go out to play.	___	___
9. When it's cold outside I go out to play.	___	___
10. I find extreme heat or cold uncomfortable.	___	___
11. I like the winter.	___	___

Totals:

Needs Cool Environment *True*	Needs Warm Environment *True*	Temperature Not a Factor *True*
___	___	___
5	5	5

Consistency Key:

Needs Cool Environment	Needs Warm Environment	Only Temperature Extremes Are a Factor
True	*True*	*True*
2	1	3-4
4	3	6-7
7	5	10
9	6	
11	8	

(Divided or paired [3 and 4; 6 and 7] answers may indicate that temperature is not a factor.)

D. *Design*

	True	False
1. When I study I like to sit on the floor.	——	——
2. When I study I like to sit on a soft chair or couch.	——	——
3. When I study I feel sleepy unless I sit on a hard chair.	——	——
4. I find it difficult to study at school.	——	——
5. I finish all my homework at home.	——	——
6. I always study for tests at home.	——	——
7. I finish all my homework in school.	——	——
8. I find it difficult to concentrate on my studies at home.	——	——
9. I work best in a library.	——	——
10. I can study almost anywhere.	——	——
11. I like to study in bed.	——	——
12. I like to study on carpeting or rugs.	——	——
13. I can study on the floor, in a chair, on a couch, and at my desk.	——	——
14. I often study in the bathroom.	——	——

Totals:

Requires Formal Design *True*	Required Informal Design *True*	Design Not Important *True*
——	——	——
4	9	2

Consistency Key:

Requires Formality	Requires Informality	Design Not Important
True	*True*	*True*
3	1	10
7	2	13
8	4	
9	5	
	6	
	10	
	11	
	12	
	14	

II. *Emotional Stimuli*

A. *Motivation Toward School Work*

	True	False
1. I feel good when I do well in school.	——	——
2. I feel good making my mother or father proud of me when I do well in school.	——	——

	True	False
3. My teacher feels good when I do well in school.	___	___
4. Grown-ups are pleased if I bring home good reports.	___	___
5. Grown-ups are pleased when I do well in school.	___	___
6. I like making someone feel proud of me.	___	___
7. I am embarrassed when my grades are poor.	___	___
8. It is more important to me to do well in things that happen out of school than in my school work.	___	___
9. I like making my teacher proud of me.	___	___
10. Nobody really cares if I do well in school.	___	___
11. My teacher cares about me.	___	___
12. My mother cares about my grades.	___	___
13. My father cares about my grades.	___	___
14. My teacher cares about my grades.	___	___
15. Somebody cares about my grades in school.	___	___
16. I want to get good grades for me!	___	___
17. I am happy when I do well in school.	___	___
18. I feel bad and work less when my grades are bad.	___	___
19. I feel happy and proud when my marks are good.	___	___
20. There are many things I like doing better than going to school.	___	___
21. I love to learn new things.	___	___
22. A good education will help me to get a good job.	___	___

Totals:

Self-Motivated True	Adult-Motivated True	Teacher-Motivated True	Unmotivated True
6	8	7	4

Consistency Key:

Self-Motivated True	Adult-Motivated True	Teacher-Motivated True	Relatively Less School- Motivated True
1	2	3	8
16	4	6	10
17	5	7	18
19	6	9	20
21	7	11	
22	12	14	
	13	15	
	15		

B. *Persistence*

	True	False
1. I try to finish what I start.	___	___
2. I usually finish what I start.	___	___
3. I sometimes lose interest in things I began to do and then stop doing them.	___	___
4. I rarely finish things that I start.	___	___
5. I usually remember to finish my homework.	___	___
6. I often have to be reminded to do my homework.	___	___
7. I often forget to do or finish my homework.	___	___
8. I often get tired of doing things and want to start something new.	___	___
9. I usually like to finish things that I start.	___	___
10. My teacher is always telling me to finish what I'm supposed to do.	___	___
11. My parent(s) remind me to finish things I have been told to do.	___	___
12. Other grown-ups tell me to finish things that I have started.	___	___
13. Somebody's always reminding me to do something!	___	___
14. I often get tired of doing things.	___	___
15. I often want help in finishing things.	___	___
16. I like getting things done!	___	___
17. I like to get things done, so I can start something new.	___	___
18. I remember on my own to get things done.	___	___

Totals

Persistent *True*	Not Persistent *True*
7	11

Consistency Key:

Persistent	Not Persistent
True	*True*
1	3
2	4
5	6
9	8

Persistent	Not Persistent
True	*True*
16	10
17	11
18	12
	13
	14
	15

C. *Responsibility*

	True	False
1. I think I am responsible.	____	____
2. People tell me that I am responsible.	____	____
3. I always do what I promise to do.	____	____
4. People say that I do what I said I would do.	____	____
5. I do keep my promises most of the time.	____	____
6. I have to be reminded over and over again to do the things I've been told to do.	____	____
7. If my teacher tells me to do something, I try to do it.	____	____
8. I keep forgetting to do the things I've been told to do.	____	____
9. I remember to do what I'm told.	____	____
10. People keep reminding me to do things.	____	____
11. I like doing what I'm supposed to do.	____	____
12. Promises have to be kept.	____	____
13. I have to be reminded often to do something.	____	____

Totals:

Responsible	Not Very Responsible
True	*True*
____	____
9	4

Consistency Key:

Responsible	Not Very Responsible
True	*True*
1	6
2	8
3	10

Responsible	Not Very Responsible
True	*True*
4	13
5	
7	
9	
11	
12	

D. *Structure*

	True	False
1. I like to be told exactly what to do.	——	——
2. I like to be able to do things in my own way.	——	——
3. I like to be given choices of how I can do things.	——	——
4. I like to be able to work things out for myself.	——	——
5. I like other people to tell me how to do things.	——	——
6. I do better if I know my work is going to be checked.	——	——
7. I do the best I can whether or not the teacher will check my work.	——	——
8. I hate working hard on something that isn't checked by the teacher.	——	——
9. I like to be given clear directions when starting new projects.	——	——

Totals:

Needs Structure	Needs Little Structure
True	*True*
——	——
5	5

Consistency Key:

Needs Structure	Needs Little Structure
True	*True*
1	2
5	3
6	4
8	7
9	8

(Four or five answers in both columns may indicate that structure or the lack of it is not necessarily a factor.)

III. *Sociological Stimuli*

	True	False
A. *When I really have a lot of studying to do:*		
1. I like to work alone.	___	___
2. I like to work with my good friend.	___	___
3. I like to work with a couple of my friends.	___	___
4. I like to work in a group of five or six classmates.	___	___
5. I like to work with an adult.	___	___
6. I like to work with a friend but to have an adult nearby.	___	___
7. I like to work with a couple of friends but have an adult nearby.	___	___
8. I like adults nearby when I'm working alone or with a friend.	___	___
9. I like adults to stay away until my friends and I complete our work.	___	___
B. *The thing I like doing best, I do:*		
1. alone.	___	___
2. with one friend.	___	___
3. with a couple of friends.	___	___
4. with a group of friends.	___	___
5. with a grown-up.	___	___
6. with several grown-ups.	___	___
7. with friends and grown-ups.	___	___
8. with a member of my family who is not a grown-up.	___	___

Totals: Prefers Learning, Working, Studying, or Doing

Alone	One Peer	Two Peers	Several Peers	With Adults	Combined
True	*True*	*True*	*True*	*True*	*True*
3	4	3	3	3	4

Consistency Key: Prefers Learning, Working, Studying, or Doing

Alone	One Peer	Two Peers	Several Peers	With Adults	Combined
True	*True*	*True*	*True*	*True*	*True*
A1	A2	A3	A4	A5	A6
A8	B2	B3	B4	B5	B7
B1	A8	A9	A9	B6	A7
	B8				A8

IV. *Physical*

	True	False

A. *Perceptual Preferences*

1. If I have to learn something new, I like to learn about it by:
   a. reading a book. ____ ____
   b. hearing a record. ____ ____
   c. hearing a tape. ____ ____
   d. seeing a filmstrip. ____ ____
   e. seeing and hearing a movie. ____ ____
   f. looking at pictures and having someone explain them. ____ ____
   g. hearing my teacher tell me. ____ ____
   h. playing games. ____ ____
   i. going someplace and seeing for myself. ____ ____
   j. having someone show me. ____ ____

2. The things I remember best are the things
   a. my teacher tells me. ____ ____
   b. someone other than my teacher tells me. ____ ____
   c. someone shows me. ____ ____
   d. I learned about on trips. ____ ____
   e. I read. ____ ____
   f. I heard on records. ____ ____
   g. I heard on the radio. ____ ____
   h. I saw on television. ____ ____
   i. I wrote stories about. ____ ____
   j. I saw in a movie. ____ ____
   k. I tried or worked on. ____ ____
   l. my friends and I talked about. ____ ____

3. I really like to
   a. read books, magazines, or newspapers. ____ ____
   b. see movies. ____ ____
   c. listen to records. ____ ____
   d. make tapes on a tape recorder. ____ ____
   e. draw. ____ ____
   f. look at pictures. ____ ____
   g. play games. ____ ____
   h. talk to people. ____ ____
   i. listen to people talk. ____ ____
   j. listen to the radio. ____ ____
   k. watch television. ____ ____
   l. go on trips. ____ ____
   m. learn new things. ____ ____

	True	False
n. study with friends.	___	___
o. build things.	___	___
p. do experiments.	___	___
q. take pictures or movies.	___	___
r. use typewriters, computers, calculators, or other machines.	___	___
s. go to the library.	___	___
t. trace things in sand.	___	___
u. mold things with my hands.	___	___

Totals:

Auditory *True*	Visual *True*	Tactile *True*	Kinesthetic *True*
___	___	___	___
16	16	6	9

Consistency Key:

Auditory	Visual	Tactile	Kinesthetic
True	*True*	*True*	*True*
1b	1a	1h	1i
1c	1d	2i	2d
1e	1e	3e	2k
1f	1f	3o	3g
1g	1h	3t	3d
2a	1j	3u	3l
2b	2c		3p
2f	2e		3q
2g	2h		3r
2h	2i		
2l	2j		
3c	3a		
3h	3f		
3i	3b		
3j	3k		
3n	3s		

B. *Intake*

	True	False
1. I like to eat or drink or chew while I study.	___	___
2. I dislike eating or drinking or chewing while I study.	___	___

	True	False
3. While I'm studying I like to		
a. eat.	___	___
b. drink.	___	___
c. chew gum.	___	___
d. nibble on snacks.	___	___
e. suck on candy.	___	___
4. I can eat, drink, or chew only after I finish studying.	___	___
5. I usually eat or drink when I'm nervous or upset.	___	___
6. I hardly ever eat when I'm nervous or upset.	___	___
7. I could study better if I could eat while I'm learning.	___	___
8. While I'm learning, eating something would distract me.	___	___
9. I often catch myself chewing on a pencil as I study.	___	___

Totals: ___   ___

Requires Intake	Does Not Require Intake
True	*True*
9	4

Consistency Key:

Requires Intake	Does Not Require Intake
True	*True*
1	2
3a, 3b, 3c, 3d, 3e	4
5	6
7	8
9	

C. *Time*

	True	False
1. I hate to get up in the morning.	___	___
2. I hate to go to sleep at night.	___	___
3. I could sleep all morning.	___	___
4. I stay awake for a long time after I get into bed.	___	___
5. I feel wide awake after 10:00 in the morning.	___	___
6. If I stay up very late at night I get too sleepy to remember anything.	___	___

	True	False
7. I feel sleepy after lunch.	___	___
8. When I have homework to do, I like to get up early in the morning to do it.	___	___
9. When I can, I do my homework in the afternoon.	___	___
10. I usually start my homework after dinner.	___	___
11. I could stay up all night.	___	___
12. I wish school would start near lunch time.	___	___
13. I wish I could stay home during the day and go to school at night.	___	___
14. I like going to school in the morning.	___	___
15. I can remember things when I study them:		
a. in the morning.	___	___
b. at lunchtime.	___	___
c. in the afternoon.	___	___
d. before dinner.	___	___
e. after dinner.	___	___
f. late at night.	___	___

Totals: Functions Best

Early Morning		Late Morning		Afternoon		Evening	
True	*False*	*True*	*False*	*True*	*False*	*True*	*False*
3	7	3	7	6	5	8	3

Consistency Key: Preferred Functioning Time

Early Morning		Late Morning		Afternoon		Evening	
True	*False*	*True*	*False*	*True*	*False*	*True*	*False*
8	1	5	3	3	7	2	6
14	3	12	8	5	8	4	8
15a	5	15b	9	9	11	5	14
	10		10	12	13	10	
	11		11	15c	14	11	
	12		13	15d		13	
	13		14			15e	
						15f	

(A fairly equal distribution among all four categories usually indicates that the time of day or night is not an important factor.)

D. *Mobility*

	True	False
1. When I study I often get up to do something (like take a drink or get a cookie) then return to work.	___	___

	True	False
2. When I study I stay with it until I am finished and then I get up.	___	___
3. It's difficult for me to sit in one place for a long time.	___	___
4. I often change my position when I work.	___	___
5. I can sit in one place for a long time.	___	___
6. I constantly change position in my chair.	___	___
7. I can work best for short amounts of time with breaks in between.	___	___
8. I like getting my work done and over with.	___	___
9. I like to work a little, stop, return to the work, stop, return to it again, and so forth.	___	___
10. I like to stick to a job and finish it in one sitting if I can.	___	___
11. I leave most jobs for the last minute and then have to work on them from beginning to end.	___	___
12. I do most of my jobs a little at a time and eventually get them done.	___	___
13. I enjoy doing something over and over again when I know how to do it well.	___	___
14. I like familiar friends and places.	___	___
15. New jobs and subjects make me nervous.	___	___

Totals:

	True	False
	___	___

Needs Mobility *True*	Does Not Need Mobility *True*
___	___
7	8

Consistency Key:

Needs Mobility	Does Not Need Mobility
True	*True*
1	2
3	5
4	8
6	10
7	11
9	13
12	14
	15

LEARNING STYLE PROFILE*

Name _____Date_____

Comments Based on Highest Ratios Noted on Questionnaire
  I. *Environmental*
     Sound _____
     Light_____
     Temperature _____
     Design _____
 II. *Emotional*
     Motivation _____
     Persistence_____
     Responsibility _____
     Structure _____
III. *Sociological*
     Appears to Work Best With:
     1._____
     2._____
     3._____
 IV. *Physical*
     Perceptual Preferences _____
     Nutritional Intake_____
     Time _____
     Mobility _____

     The following Learning Style Profile is a composite taken from the
school records of real fourth-grade students, only the names are fictitious. If
Ruth were your daughter, would you know how to adjust her home-learning
environment to help her to achieve as well as possible? In addition, would you
know how to help her teacher to help Ruth learn?

*In 1975 Dr. Gary Price, Associate Professor, Department of Counseling, University of Kansas,
Lawrence, Kansas, conducted a content analysis of each of the questionnaire items and isolated
those that achieved 90 percent consistency, or better. A shortened form, the Learning Style
Inventory (LSI), then was developed and, since that time, cooperative research has been conducted with teachers and their students in many school systems in several states. Students answer a
series of questions concerned with their environmental, sociological, and physical preferences and
the way(s) in which they believe they behave in certain situations. Their responses are submitted to
computer analysis which yields an itemization of those learning style elements that are important
for each individual youngster. A manual provides a guideline for the kind of school prescription that
probably would be effective for that child. Alternatives are suggested if the specific element
indicates more than one resource or method.

LEARNING STYLE PROFILE

Name: Ruth M.   Teacher: B. Gold   School: Howard Elementary

Grade: Nongraded, 4–6   Counselor: L.T.P.   Date: October 16, 1976

Comments based on highest ratios noted on questionnaire responses.

I. *Environmental*

Sound: Sound does not seem to be a factor, though she tends to speak loudly.

Light: She is sensitive to excessive light and avoids it.

Temperature: She dislikes heat.

Design: She can't seem to sit at her desk; prefers sprawling.

II. *Emotional*

Motivation: She works well when interested.

Persistence: She is persistent when she is interested.

Responsibility: She does follow through. She is confident that she is able to do her work well and does to the best of her ability. She can be given long-term assignments when she likes what she is doing. She feels pressured when she knows completion is expected of her, and she is not interested or motivated.

III. *Sociological*

Works well alone when interested; requires another classmate to work with in order to complete assignments that don't motivate her. Rarely needs teacher, except for assistance with difficult problems.

IV. *Physical*

Perceptual Preferences: Visually-oriented; does not retain well through listening; tactual [touching] is her secondary perceptual strength.

Nutritional Intake: She could eat all day; nibbles constantly—particularly when working on "required" tasks that are not of major interest to her; she calms down when involved with studies that motivate her.

Time: Interest, rather than time of day, is the factor of importance.

Mobility: Cannot sit still; moves constantly; works everywhere.

In your analysis, note that Ruth (1) speaks loudly, (2) is sensitive to excessive light, (3) dislikes heat, (4) "can't . . . sit," (5) does not retain well through listening, and (6) eats continually. There are perfectly healthy children who share these same characteristics, but, as a parent, you might want to have Ruth checked by a physician, just to be certain that the loud speech and inability to learn through hearing does not reflect poor hearing. You would certainly have her eyes checked to determine whether sunglasses would make her feel more comfortable on sunny days.

At home, if Ruth were your daughter, you would set aside a softly lit, cool, carpeted area where she could lie on the floor or lean against cushions when she studies or reads. You might have a bowl of sliced carrots or celery available for her as snacks. Understanding her need for mobility, you would permit her several "breaks" wherein she could relax or move to another area during or between the studying periods.

Since Ruth works well and will be persistent when interested, the schoolwork that she is required to complete will be no problem when it is something that she *wants* to learn. When she is *not* interested in the topic or assignment, you might suggest that she invite a friend to your home, so that they may do the work together. Ruth's profile indicates that she is usually responsible; therefore, when she seeks your assistance, give it willingly until she understands what needs to be done.

In school, Ruth's teacher would do well to use many of the same strategies. Ruth's seat should be placed away from the light and heat and should be near a classmate with whom she gets along, so that the two may work together on tasks which are not motivating to her. She should be encouraged to learn through books, transparencies, filmstrips, films, pictures, and other visual resources. Since her secondary perceptual strength is tactual, games, task cards, and manipulative materials would also benefit her. Ideally, new knowledges and skills should be *introduced* to her through visual resources and reinforced through tactual ones.

If her class is either individualized or an open classroom, she will be permitted the mobility she needs at certain times. If it is traditional, the teacher may permit her to work in the rear of the room in a learning station or interest center, so that Ruth may move but not disturb her peers.

Identifying your daughter's learning style is a very important step toward enhancing her academic growth, for it facilitates learning, both at home and at school. In attempting to obtain a true picture of your daughter's total learning style, rely on your conversations, observations, and insights concerning her everyday actions. These, in addition to the results of the Learning Style Questionnaire, will help you to understand the ways in which she tends to learn most easily.

To illustrate, one day we found our daughter Rana reading aloud on the lawn in the front of our home. When asked what she was doing, she replied, "I can only remember what I read when I *hear* the words." Since she had no one to read to, and because she had heard that flowers "grow" when spoken to, she had decided to "read to the flowers," in order to have a reason for reading aloud.

Rana was correct about how she retains information. Although she reads well, she does not remember details that she sees in print unless she can also hear them. If she can use a cassette to learn information, she learns easily; when she must rely on books, either she or someone else must read them aloud to her.

One day, when she was in the eighth grade, one of her teachers directed the class to read a passage in a text and to then explain it in writing. As she read, she moved her lips and spoke the words. Her teacher told her to read silently. She explained that she had difficulty understanding what she was reading unless she *heard* the words, and asked if she might sit outside the room in the hall to read the information before she began to write the answers. He responded in a derogatory manner, suggesting that if she could not understand a book without reading it aloud she ought to obtain remedial assistance. The teacher did not understand that many youngsters are auditory, rather than visual learners, and that many are the reverse. Despite his unintentional disparagement, Rana's understanding and acceptance of her own learning style has helped her to study and learn through ways in which she can be successful. Had she not been aware, she might have had many problems as a student.

5.
What to Do Just before and during the Critical Elementary School Years: Ages Five to Eleven

A GREAT HEADSTART DOES NOT ALWAYS SECURE THE RACE

For the first time in her life, your daughter will have a decisive advantage over most boys of her own age! Regardless of the *causes* of the extensive research findings,[1] girls generally are better prepared for kindergarten and elementary school experiences than are their male counterparts!

Girls are more physically and mentally developed at birth; they also tend to mature earlier. As a result, they arrive for kindergarten with better speech, better eye-hand coordination, and better control over their finger and wrist movements. This early advantage permits girls to achieve certain academic skills more easily than boys, because these physiological proficiencies are necessary for learning how to read and to write.[2] In these two essential experiences, therefore, girls outperform boys in virtually every elementary school.[3]

Chapter 1 described many of the reasons that highly achieving, academically successful girls refrain from continuing their education beyond high school—and the destructive effect that withdrawal from continuing education has on their intellectual attitudes,[4] their future lives,[5] and their ability to become self-actualizing adults.[6] Although the discouragement from competitive academic achievement occurs essentially during adolescence, parents can take specific steps during the elementary years to blunt the effect of this

112

society's "appropriate sex role" mythology that bombards girls from birth and affects the majority of them somewhere between the ages of eleven and sixteen.

Precisely because they *are* more mature than boys in their own age group and have had comparatively positive learning experiences, most girls are both interested in and delighted at the prospect of "going to school." This accepting attitude and their advanced physiological skills, which permit successful beginning reading and writing achievement, give girls a head start that causes many boys psychological ego damage and justified feelings of inferiority.

If our educational institutions were organized to promote the best interests of our children, all youngsters would be tested to determine their mental and emotional readiness for entry (and continuing) experiences and then grouped by matched abilities or taught in an individualized program, which would provide for their true "maximum growth." Instead, all children —the gifted and the intellectually disabled, the athletic and the physically handicapped, the artistic and the scientific, the precocious and the retarded —are admitted at exactly the same time in their lives (the September after they have reached their fifth birthday), exposed to exactly the same experiences in exactly the same way, and evaluated on the basis of their comparative achievements.

Our schools continue many incorrect practices, but nothing is quite so outrageous as their equal treatment of unequals. Under the pretext of providing socially broadening experiences for children by bringing them into contact with many different types of youngsters, they force most children to recognize that they are either intellectually (and otherwise) superior *or* inferior to others. This system can have many negative outcomes for your daughter:

1. The youngster who realizes that she is superior to her classmates but is required to master identical skills—and does so with ease—need not motivate herself to achieve better than she already has, for she retains status and recognition by merely coasting along.

2. The youngster who realizes that she is inferior to her classmates becomes frustrated at her inability to compete favorably. Her self-image is wounded, and a defeatist syndrome begins to emerge, so that the child may never "catch up." Once a student "falls behind" in group learning, it is difficult, if not impossible, to achieve at a rate that is fast enough to compensate for and eradicate previous inequities.

3. People tend to like other people who are intellectually similar to themselves. Grouping children of unlike abilities does not promote their friendships, except in rare cases; as a matter of fact, our combined experiences of more than fifty years in the schools, with students at all levels, tend to suggest that: (a) friends are selected on the basis of their similarities, *not* their differences; (b) youngsters who are required to interact with others who are different from themselves intellectually or in terms of maturity tend to *develop* prejudices against those people; (c) mixing children of dissimilar academic

ability in the same class tends to *decrease* the learning rate of both the brighter and the less able students; and (d) teachers generally find it more difficult to work with mixed groups than they do with homogeneously grouped students.

Why, then, do the schools continue heterogeneous (mixed) grouping of children with vastly different ability levels in the same class?

1. Many teachers do not know how to teach each child individually, despite the fact that research[7] demonstrates that it is a more effective method than group instruction for most youngsters.

2. A distorted sense of liberalism suggests that the mixing of children of unlike mental ability and readiness will produce greater understanding and empathy among them.

3. All bureaucracies resist change.

4. The educational system is experiencing many problems and set-backs toward which it must direct its attention. It is, therefore, more concerned with survival than with improving the schools during the seventies and eighties.

These negative practices, however, tend to be much more harsh on boys than on girls. For example, surveys indicate that four times as many boys are referred to remedial reading clinics as girls,[8] and can you imagine the impact on boys (who are pressured toward career involvement and achievement almost from *birth*) when they realize that most of the girls in their classes are achieving better, faster, and with greater ease than they? Societal mores damage women in their young adult and middle years, but they are devastating to elementary (and often junior high and middle school) boys.

EXTENDING YOUR DAUGHTER'S INDEPENDENCE AND NURTURING HER ACADEMIC ACHIEVEMENT

Parents often become intimidated by teachers, lose their confidence in their judgment about their own child, and assume that, once a youngster enters into the school, they can cease teaching her at home. If you rely on the school to provide your daughter's major intellectual development, she is likely not to achieve to her full potential. Try to recall the eager learner that your daughter was during her preschool years and continue to duplicate the home environment for learning that nourished her so well in the beginning.

If you have not already done so, establish a nook or cranny somewhere in your home where, based on the information yielded by the Learning Style Questionnaire, your daughter can study, do her homework, read or meditate. Prepare her for successful academic achievement in school by playing games with her that will teach the items that most teachers expect a youngster to master during the first years in school. Remember that "success breeds success," so be certain to teach a curriculum for which she is ready and with which she can cope nicely.

Designing Learning Circles
A Learning Circle is a fun way for children to review many worthwhile skills. For example, you can teach the formation or recognition of new words, mathematics concepts, historical data, and almost any kind of skill development through them. Why not try making one or two Learning Circles, to see whether or not your daughter responds favorably to them? If she does, let her assist you in creating more.

If your daughter tells you that she has been learning to add in school, begin with a Learning Circle that will provide opportunities for her to practice the completion of different "number fact" problems. You will need the following items:

Materials:
Two pieces of colored oaktag, heavy construction paper, or poster board.
One wire coat hanger.
Black, thin-line, felt pens.
Approximately eight clip-on clothes-pins (the colored, plastic type are pretty and do not break easily).
Masking tape or metal glue.
Clear or lightly colored transparent Contact paper.
Optional: Old magazines that may be cut up to either color-code or picture-code the mathematics examples and their answers.

Directions:
1. Cut two rounds, eighteen inches in diameter, for each Learning Circle.
2. Divide each circle into approximately eight sections.
3. In each of the eight sections, print (using a black felt pen) an addition problem that is simple enough for your daughter to compute.
4. Print the answer to one of the math problems on the tip-end (rather than the squeeze-end) of a clothespin. Follow suit for each of the seven remaining problems and clothespins.
5. Turn the second circle so that its eight sections become its back. Place the front of the second circle against the back of the first circle (spoon-in-spoon fashion). Either color-code or picture-code each correct answer the same as its problem. Do this by placing an identically shaped and colored symbol *underneath* the clothespin that matches the problem and inside the section of the second circle (bottom one) that will be pasted directly beneath the problem.
6. Cover both circles with the clear Contact paper.
7. Glue the two circles together with a wire hanger securely fastened

between them. The Learning Circle will remain in excellent condition when covered with the clear Contact paper, despite extensive use, and it may be stored easily by hanging on a doorknob, a hook or a hardware arm.

8. Show your daughter how to use, locate, and share the Learning Circle (and to return it to its storage place after use).

Using Learning Circles
Store the Learning Circle in a convenient place in your home—preferably in or near where your daughter usually studies or works. When she has the time or inclination to use this resource, explain how.

First remove the clothespins from their storage niche, either on the lower half of the wire hanger or in an oaktag pocket attached to the back of the Learning Circle. Have her mix the clothespins and then try to match the answer on each to the related question or problem on the chart.

When the clothespins have been matched to what she believes is the correct section of the chart, show her how to turn the entire chart over (onto its back) to see whether the color-coded or picture-coded symbols match. The design of the underside of the clothespin should be identical to and directly above the same design on the back of the second circle to permit self-correcting. When the two symbols match, her answer is correct; when they do not, the matching answer may be found by comparing the paired colors or pictures.

Another instructional resource is the Learning Strip, an elongated version of the Learning Circle. It can be made by dividing a long piece of oaktag, construction paper, or poster board into eight or ten sections and printing a different number in each box. Tape the wire hanger to the top of the back of the board. Place different numbers (within your daughter's range of addition facts) on each of the clothespins.

If she is learning to recognize numbers, a simple match will do. If she wants to learn to add different numbers, on the *back* of each section neatly print the number combinations that complement the addition of all of the numbers on each clothespin that may be added to the number on the front. For example, if the number 3 is placed in the first section on the front of the Learning Strip, and if the numbers 1, 2, 3, 4, 5, 6, 7 or 8 each appear on a different clothespin, then on the *back* of the section of the Learning Strip that has number 3 on top, print the following:

3+1=4	3+5=8
3+2=5	3+6=9
3+3=6	3+7=10
3+4=7	3+8=11

Follow suit for each of the strips, providing the correct answer by printing all of the correct number combinations added to the number on the front of the chart. In this case, you would not need to color- or picture-code the answers, for they will be evident.

Learning Circles or Strips are excellent resources for either introducing or reinforcing an endless number of facts or skills that your daughter may be required to learn. For example:

1. In each of the sections on the front of the resource, place the letter combinations: *an, and, at, ear, en, end, in,* and *on.* (Any word roots may be substituted.) Place a different alphabetical letter on the top of each clothespin. By placing one clothespin at a time in front of each of the sections on the Circle, your daughter may be able to form new words and read them. If she is just beginning first grade, she may need you to work with her, to be certain that the words she forms are correct. When she is able, perhaps toward the end of that year, write all the possible words that may be formed by adding a single letter or group of letters to the basic letters on the chart. Do this on three-by-five index cards, which you should store in a pocket on the back of the chart.

2. Print the names of each of eight different geometric shapes on the chart and paste pictures of the shapes onto the clothespins. Your daughter will learn to recognize, *spell* and *write* the names before most of her peers!

3. Print new vocabulary on the chart and paste pictures of the words onto the clothespins. By matching the pictures to the words she will become familiar with the formation and letter combinations and will begin to read them—first on the chart and then in a text.

If you do not care to keep the Learning Circles, you need not use the contact paper and can discard the resource as it becomes worn. Or, if you prefer, divide the chart into eight sections, put contact paper on the chart itself, and then temporarily attach different combinations onto it with an easily removable substance, such as masking tape. Place a pocket on the back of the chart, and you will be able to store a variety of letters, numbers, or shapes that may be used with the same resource.

By using self-instructional or self-correcting materials, your daughter will gradually become increasingly independent. Initially, during her early childhood, she was permitted to explore, investigate, and learn what interested *her.* As she grew older, you taught her things that *you* wanted her to learn. In school the teacher will be stressing facts and concepts that *she* believes are important. Gradually, your daughter will need to be able to master requirements that others deem to be necessary—but by herself. By using Learning Circles or Learning Strips, you will be introducing your daughter to the process of learning what she needs to know, without direct assistance from others. This activity will increase her independence, and if she learns well, will facilitate her academic achievement in later years, when she will be expected to learn on her own.

Teaching through a Variety of Instructional Resources
As described in the review of the eighteen elements of learning style in Chapter 4, youngsters learn through different senses, depending on their individual perceptual preferences or strengths. When teaching your daughter important skills, such as mathematical concepts, word recognition, reading, spelling, or writing, consciously use more than one sense to help her to "internalize" what she learns.

When we teach by telling (either personally or on tape), we are appealing to a child's *auditory* (or listening) ability; when we teach by showing, we concentrate on the *visual* (or seeing) sense; when we teach through touching methods, we appeal to the *tactual*; and when we teach by doing (providing real experiences, such as teaching inches and feet by building a wagon) we are emphasizing a kinesthetic (whole body involvement) approach.

Materials that facilitate a tactual approach include clay, sandpaper, fabrics of varied textures, such as felt, velvet, or buckram (you can cut up old clothing that will no longer be worn), sand, water, finger paints, or uncooked macaroni. For example, if you wished to help your daughter to learn to spell a very difficult word, you might use any or all of the following activities, depending upon her preferences and how long it would take for her to master the word.

1. Say the word. Explain its meaning. Give her an example of how it might be used in a sentence. Ask her to say the word and to use it in a sentence. When she can do that, spell the word for her.

2. Print the word in black on a white sheet of paper. Repeat the spelling and point to each of the letters as you say them. Ask her to look at the spelling and to try to memorize the letters in correct sequence. Ask her to try to spell the word without looking at it.

3. Ask her to write the word by copying the letters that you wrote. If she can copy the letters accurately, ask her to spell the word again without looking. If correct, praise her. If not, show her the word written by you and point out the error(s).

4. Purchase a small bag of sand in the hardware store and empty its contents into an aluminum pan. Encourage your daughter to trace the letters of the word in the sand. Permit her to look at the printed word as she "writes" the letters. Then see if she can write the letters without looking at the word. If she can, ask her to spell the word without looking and without writing.

5. Ask her to dip her finger into a plastic cup of water and to write the word on a blackboard or chalkboard slate without looking.

6. Cut the small letters of the alphabet out of heavy sandpaper. Make duplicates of letters that are used often. Place all the letters into an empty shoe box and ask your daughter to find the letters in the spelling word *without looking* (strictly by feeling each of the letters and discarding those that are not in

the word). When she has found all the letters, ask her to place them into the correct sequence, so that the word is spelled correctly.

7. Cut the small letters of the alphabet out of old fabric. Place them into an unused shoebox. Follow the procedure suggested for using sandpaper letters.

8. Press different-colored strips of clay into a pan. Ask your daughter to write the word in the clay with a toothpick.

9. Keep a jar of uncooked macaroni available for spelling. If you have the "alphabet macaroni," ask your daughter to find each of the letters in the word and to glue them onto a cardboard. She will then have a three-dimensional spelling list. If you have the more common forms of macaroni, print the word in large letters on a sheet of writing paper (8½" x 11") or shirt cardboard and let her paste the food bits onto the letters so that they, too, form the word.

10. She can also trace the word in salt, in colored or white sugar, or use finger paints to write it.

All of these activities will not be necessary at one time. They are suggested to provide you with alternatives. Your daughter may learn to spell a word by merely hearing it, writing it once or twice, or concentrating on memorizing its letters. If not, offer her a choice of a few of these activities and continue experimenting with these options until she has mastered the spelling. Unless she indicates special preferences, use different activities for different words, so that she does not become bored.

These suggestions may be used to teach numbers, letters, mathematical computations, geometric shapes, and other items, in addition to spelling and writing.

The Value of Teaching Your Daughter at Home during the Beginning Elementary Years
Although, at the beginning of this chapter, we acknowledged that girls usually achieve more easily than boys do in school, we would like to stress the ways in which you can help your daughter to become an *outstanding* student, an essential goal for each of the following reasons.

Although girls do achieve more easily than boys in elementary school, this is the only time in their early years when they have an advantage. It is important, therefore, to capitalize on this opportunity and to use it to help them to get very far ahead. It isn't that they will be competing with these same males in later life; what happens, though, is that, somewhere between the fifth and ninth grades, girls become very aware of the societal perception of femininity —shyness, passivity, quietness, conformity, and subservience to the opposite sex. At the same time, they become aware of their own sexuality and are attracted to boys. Thus, in order to be appealing and ultimately to attract the opposite sex, they begin to assume the characteristics that supposedly increase their desirability, including permitting boys to believe that males are intellectually superior. This effort is accompanied by a disinclination to "outdo" the boys in class in upper elementary and the junior high years.

It would be advantageous, therefore, to have your daughter become so outstanding in school that she will (a) *feel* very superior to the boys in her classes, and thus not find them attractive, (b) be a "threat" to their weak egos and therefore not encourage their pursuit of her, or (c) become so absorbed in her studies that, at that stage of her life, she will remain temporarily neutral toward either her own or their sexuality.

Do not be concerned about the outcomes of this strategy. If the plan succeeds, there will be no loss to your daughter, because (a) if she really is intellectually superior to her age peers, she will profit from interaction with older boys—which will not occur until her high school years, giving her extra, vital time in which to develop her mind; (b) it is not important that boys between the ages of ten and fifteen find her attractive (and perhaps divert her attention from school); it is preferable that she wait until after completing college before she considers the opposite sex seriously; (c) she will be developing "social graces" through her interactions with faculty, girlfriends, your and her friends, relatives, and classmates, and she will not suffer the adolescent tensions that occur when sexual concerns are forced on her prematurely; and, (d) the primary foci of her life at this stage should be to become an excellent student and to develop skills in those areas of the arts, hobbies, or sports that she finds interesting.

Obviously, *all* girls do not learn easily—but it is important that they *do* learn and begin to think of themselves as able achievers. Therefore, if your daughter experiences any difficulty in school, you should know how to help her and to be equipped to eradicate any minor learning deficiencies that occur before they are escalated into major ones.

By using multisensory resources, such as the Learning Circles, Learning Strips, sand, water, clay, paint, and other suggested materials, it will be easy for you to assist your daughter to understand or remember items that her teacher considers important.

A girl who enters school with a fairly extensive vocabulary, is able to read, recognizes and can add simple numbers, and can write her name, address, and a few words will be "an instant success," for teachers are like Madison Avenue executives who are impressed with the outer semblance of well-packaged items. More winning than the specific skill that your daughter has mastered is the reputation she will establish as a youngster who is *able*. Most teachers *love* to teach achieving children; they make a teacher's task easy, pleasant, rewarding, and worthwhile. These children are seen by instructors as the "future leaders" of our country, and they "deserve" (and get) special attention and more individual guidance than most. If your daughter is equipped to enter into the primary elementary grades "prepared" to outshine her peers academically, she will become her teacher's "favorite" and, almost automatically, will have earned her very special place in the sun for the entire year!

Psychologically, when a schoolchild *feels* that she is *liked* and held in esteem by her teacher, she is more likely to (a) perceive herself in a favorable manner, (b) achieve well academically, and (c) demonstrate positive classroom behavior.[9] Thus, preparing your daughter for school prior to her entrance is one certain way of her gaining her teacher's approval and thus building your daughter's chances for a successful educational experience.

Today's children are exposed to books, pictures, comics, radio (while riding in the family car), television, cassettes, and records almost from infancy. As a result, they are so attuned to communications through multimedia that most are *ready* and eager to read long before they enter into formal schooling. Despite our criticisms of the poor *quality* and *sexism* of television, this medium has demonstrated that youngsters of four and five can learn to read words with which they become familiar in commercials and then can recognize and read those words in supermarkets and on an endless number of products.

In recent years the consequences of failing to learn to read adequately have become very apparent to parents, citizens in general, educators, public officials, and legislators. The difficulties of teaching a large class of children to read are so great that the average child learns rather slowly. In addition, most teachers, despite their rhetoric to the contrary, use essentially only one basic reading method to teach the entire class. Chapter 4 explained that each youngster enjoys a very individual "learning style"; since teachers gear their lessons toward the group, the kind of variety that would be certain to facilitate each child's ability to read is rarely available.

Furthermore, most teachers introduce youngsters to reading through a "phonics" approach, which is a sound decoding system that is effective with auditory learners (children who can *hear* the differences among sounds that represent the various alphabetical letters and combinations of letters). For youngsters with *visual* sensitivity, a "word-recognition" approach would be an effective method for teaching reading. When youngsters do not learn easily, either through the phonics or word-recognition techniques, they should be taught to read through *tactual* methods, such as the ones suggested to you earlier in this chapter. Few children would resist learning to read if the variety of approaches just listed were available to them, but the teacher who uses several different methods is a rare gem and a highly skilled professional!

You need not be an expert (*or* a professional) to teach your daughter to read.

Begin a few months before your daughter's fifth birthday, by printing her name in non-capitalized (except for the first) letters on many things that she owns. Use a black felt-tipped pen or thinline felt marker.* At the same age, and for the next few months, sew name tags into her clothing and draw her attention to her name.

From the moment she appears to be interested (during infancy!) and will remain with you to listen, *read* to her. Read *everything*—short stories and books of interest to her and books and newspaper articles of interest to you. Read aloud, slowly (but not too slowly, for you want to maintain her interest) and dramatically. Read to yourself silently and allow her to see you enjoying the leisure of the moment, relaxed with your book. Take her to the local library for story hours and permit her to (a) select a book from the preschool section for you to read to her and (b) observe *you* browsing for readings that will be of interest to you.

When your daughter is five, make signs that you can post all over her room (or the house) proclaiming in large letters: "Joanne's bedroom," "Joanne's bed," "Joanne's rocker," "Joanne's wagon," and so on. Read them to her. When the signs have been posted for two weeks or so, ask her to read one or more. If she can, praise her—but do nothing more at that time. The next day, change the signs—so that the one for her bed is placed on her door (for example), and the one for her door is placed on the rocker. Say nothing, but observe her to see whether she notices the change. If she does, praise her effusively and explain that you tried to play a game with her, but that, because she is so bright, she "won"! Exchange another pair of signs during the next day and continue the process until she can read every sign well and can return it to its correct location.

If, perchance, your daughter did *not* notice the changed signs on the first day, ask her to look around the room and to try to tell which sign is in the wrong place. Again, if she can, praise her and follow the suggestions for continuing the sign recognitions in different parts of the room. If she cannot, *tell* and *show* her which signs were changed, read them with her, point out the shapes of the letters, add a drawing that will represent what the words on the sign mean, and replace the two signs to their original, correct place. A day later, change the same two signs and go through the entire process again. Every time she recognizes the signs that have been changed, replace them and change two different signs. On some days, change two new signs and two signs that she previously recognized as having been changed. When she can read every sign in her room, begin with the signs throughout your home, and then outside, and in your car. Eventually, mismatch the signs in your home with the ones in your car, and when she can recognize those and read them, elongate the signs to include more words, such as: "This is Joanne's bedroom. It is Joanne's room." Use the same words many times on different placards. For example:

---

*Because some children are able to learn to read prior to this age, you might wish to experiment with these methods a little sooner if your daughter appears to be interested or ready.

"This is Joanne's bed. It is comfortable." (Do not be afraid of using long words; many children learn those faster than shorter ones!)

"This is Joanne's rocker. It is comfortable."

"This is Joanne's rug. It is comfortable."

"This is Mother's rug. Mother's rug is comfortable."

Each time you print and post a new sign (introducing no more than two each day), show it to her, read it to her, ask her to repeat it to you, and ask her to tack or tape it onto its correct location.

Make a Learning Circle using many of the nouns that you repeatedly printed on her signs. Paste pictures of the items onto the clothespins. Ask her to match correctly the clothespins with the printed word that the pictures represent.

Ask her to *write* one of the often-used printed words on her signs. Give her opportunities to write the same word with a pencil on paper, in sand, with finger paint, in clay, with water, and in salt. If you believe that she is becoming very familiar with its letters, you might try letting her find the sandpaper letters that would spell it (but permit her to look at the letters at this beginning stage) and piece the word together.

Most children learn to write *before* they learn to read; with some, the reverse occurs. Give your daughter many opportunities to write her name, notes to the milkman, "thank you" notes for gifts, letters to grandparents, and the like. Make a "book" of the stories she dictates to you and then let her illustrate it. Encourage her to read the contents back to you. Before you realize it, she will be reading the items she originally dictated and then copied.

Encourage her to use a typewriter to copy a short note that you write as she dictates it. Becoming familiar with the letters of the typewriter will aid her to develop eye-discrimination and will serve to further familiarize her with the alphabetical letters. A *primary* typewriter (very large letters) is ideal for this purpose. The major problem of using a typewriter is that its keys are in capital forms, and your daughter should be taught to read the small letters first—rather than the capitals.

Continue the praise and appreciation as she succeeds; be supportive and patient until she begins to achieve. Many teachers hesitate to share these methods with parents, in the mistaken belief that they will not have sufficient patience and "know-how" to teach their children correctly and lovingly. We disagree. To the contrary, too many teachers are impatient and negative with nonachieving children, and too many parents (who really care about their children and their academic progress) are insecure about trying to teach their offspring. *You can do no harm to your daughter if you remember the following, cardinal rules:*

Always be patient and supportive; praise her when she tries, and laud her for her success. Never continue an activity or lesson when your daughter shows you that she is tired, bored, impatient, eager to do something else, or unable to continue (or begin!).

When one method does not produce learning, try another. *There is no single effective teaching method for everyone —or even for most learners!* Be certain to use multisensory methods (telling, showing, writing, pasting, printing, moving fingers in sand, water, paint and others).

When your daughter demonstrates only slow progress, recognize that children mature at different rates. She is an extension of yourself—so she must be potentially intelligent! Give her the amount of time and repetition that she needs in order to *enjoy* learning. Assuming that she is of normal physical and mental health, she is likely to read *before* she enters school if you use and re-use the varied methods suggested in this chapter.

SCHOOL-RELATED DECISIONS THAT YOU MAY NEED TO CONSIDER

"When researchers probe into the background of school-age children rated as gifted or mentally superior by I.Q. tests, they typically find a stimulating home life and often deliberate planning by parents to help their children learn to use their brains."[10] Contrary to still another stereotype that exists among some people, the youngster who emerges from such a planned environment is one who participates actively in many experiences, including athletics, intellectual pursuits, and hobbies.

Mentally superior students are those who experienced a home and school environment which stimulated them to learn and to enjoy learning,[11] and they are better adjusted emotionally than average children.[12] Their parents and other significant persons set examples of interest and attainment in education for them which they unconsciously imitated,[13] and these children have *fewer* emotional problems than most and are better able to cope with those they do have.[14] They also experienced early family training which produced a desire for personal achievement,[15] and, perhaps because of the circumstances under which they were raised, they are more emotionally stable and mature than classmates of the same age.[16]

Bright boys and girls participate in extracurricular activities, including sports, as much or more than their average-ability classmates. They have had wider-ranging experiences and have become more sophisticated because of them. They engage in more hobbies, know more games, have a better sense of humor and better reasoning power, and are better able to amuse themselves when friends are not available. They also have fewer illnesses.[17]

This information should provide the background for several decisions that you may have to make concerning your daughter's assignments in school. Some parents have been concerned that their bright or achieving youngsters, particularly if grouped in special high-ability classes, would feel superior, become conceited, and develop into an "intellectual elite." Research verifies that the reverse often occurs. Intelligent young people tend to underestimate their abilities and accomplishments, and, as a result, they boast *less* than other youngsters. They are more self-critical and usually rate the achievements and abilities of average classmates higher than they really are.[18]

If you raise your daughter as has been suggested in this book, she may well emerge as an extremely bright—if not gifted—girl. The day may come when you will be told that she "does not get along well with her peers." Be prepared for the jolt and be able to respond without feeling defensive. Are the children in her class *really* her "peers"? Are they on a similar intellectual level, and does she have enough in common with them to value their social relationships?

Teachers incorrectly assume that children of the same age group should be able to interact socially with each other. When examined, that thesis makes little sense. We do not select our friends because they are members of a similar age group; we choose our inner circle—even the associates we see occasionally—because of our common interests or our respect for them. Age does not determine compatibility; intellect and identical concerns do.

It is unreasonable to expect that mentally superior children will view youngsters of their own age who are intellectually inferior to be socially desirable. Your daughter *may* be extremely popular and *may* get along very well with her classmates, but during the elementary school years that is of little consequence. If she is happy, active, involved in a variety of interesting-to-her experiences, and a good student, do not be concerned. It is *preferred* that emphasis *not* be placed on popularity, sociability, and other, at the moment, comparatively nonproductive directions which can lead—at too early an age —toward concerns about her need to develop "feminine" characteristics (the misinterpreted ones such as passivity, permitting the favored boys to excel her, and *overconcern* with her appearance).

Decision 1: What will you do if told that she "does not get along well with her classmates?"

Decision 2: What will you do if told that she is bright enough to "skip" a class (or be given advanced studies) but that, since she appears to be "socially immature," you must consider whether being with older students (or having more work to concentrate on) will not exclude her from much needed peer-group interactions?

Decision 3: What will you do when told that she should be placed in a class of children with "mixed" (diversified) mental abilities, so that she can "learn to get along with all people" and will not become "an intellectual snob"?

Decision 4: What will you do when offered a choice of the kind of educational program in which she may be placed? If, as so many schools are wisely doing, hers provided a traditional classroom, an "open" classroom, and individualized classroom, or possibly other alternatives, which would be the best choice for your daughter?

Social Compatibility

Intelligent persons of all ages are aware of how to get along with people, because they have learned to (a) anticipate or understand what others are thinking or feeling, (b) express themselves on many levels when necessary, (c) withdraw calmly from situations that they view as being undesirable or uninteresting, and (d) solve problems created by others.

The more intelligent and the more self-actualizing your daughter is, the *less* she will appear to need or desire extensive social relationships with others. Both Maslow and Dyer emphasize that people who are "together" find many things to absorb their attentions—activities that stimulate and satisfy their needs for growth.

Permit your daughter to choose her daily activities; do *not* select them for her. You may provide her with choices, but she should make the decisions about those in which she chooses to participate. Do *not* overprogram her. A youngster who enrolls for dancing lessons, horseback riding, tennis instruction, and piano may be overextending herself and her productive use of time. At least one or two unscheduled afternoons each week should be available for her to try some extemporaneous and exploratory activities, and time should be available for homework, relaxing, and friends—if she so desires.

In response to Decision 1, we would suggest that some of the nonschool or after-school activities in which she engages should include children who are *older* than she, as might occur in learning how to ice skate, dance, or play tennis through *group* lessons. Piano and horseback riding are isolating activities; they are fine, unless she engages in them exclusively and, *in addition,* rarely socializes. Consciously encourage her involvement in sports or cultural experiences where she will meet and talk with youngsters older than herself and with adults. If she persists, permit her to plan her own time, so long as it includes productive or stimulating activities. Do not be concerned if she does not enjoy her classmates, or even if she is not very interested in other young people; be certain, however, that she *chose* to be self-involved and is content with her choice.

Advanced Placement (Acceleration)

Decision 2 should be apparent by now. If she is capable of advancing academically, encourage that move. She undoubtedly will enjoy the more challenging studies and the older children more than her present class.

Homogeneous Grouping versus Heterogeneous Grouping

If you have the opportunity to respond to Decision 3, choose the homogeneous group for your daughter. She will be challenged by intelligent children, she will feel at ease with youngsters of her own ability level and will find them interesting and compatible, and she will have little in common with less intelligent students. At the very least, some of her school's programs should include experiences with children who have equal ability or talents.

In classes of mixed-ability students, the youngsters segregate *themselves,* because they have little in common with either intellectually superior or inferior children. The brighter students often develop disdain (rather than tolerance or empathy) for the ones who cannot achieve, and the non- or slowly-achieving children recognize their own inferiority in contrast to the brighter ones and experience a lowered self-image and esteem which then permeate their entire school existence—and from which they may never recover.

Unfortunately, you probably will never have that choice. Homogeneity and "tracking" have been considered "undemocratic"—for they acknowledge that all human beings are *not* equal. By virtue of admitting all children into school at exactly the same time, assigning them to classes heterogeneously, and trying to teach an entire group through identical instructional methods (regardless of their readiness, learning styles, or abilities), the schools support the myth of human intellectual equality and the concept that the mixing of unequals will be beneficial to all. That, of course, is nonsense!

When students are grouped heterogeneously (mixed abilities), the learning rate of the class is reduced to that of the "average" child; the bright learn much less than they would if they were members of a gifted group, and the slower students cannot maintain the pace of the class and begin to lag behind. They eventually require "remedial work" (wherein they are taken out of their classes, regrouped, and taught with similarly nonachieving youngsters—all of which might have been unnecessary had they originally been grouped among children like themselves. In addition, during the period in which they realize that they cannot learn as much and as well as their classmates, these less able children suffer emotionally, and many become negative toward the entire institution of school and its purpose—education!

The Best Program for Your Daughter
Concerning Decision 4, do you know how to judge what kind of program is best for your daughter?
1. Structured or open?[19]
2. Basic or alternative?
3. Traditional or progressive?
4. Disciplined or permissive?
5. Fundamental or creative?
6. Subject-oriented or child-oriented?

Falling into the educational label trap is at least as dangerous as it is misleading. The generalized "conservative" versus "liberal" tag is a handy yardstick misused by both critics and supporters of education programs, whether they are new or old.

As teachers and administrators we become the rather easy targets of latter-day, self-proclaimed Pied Pipers who would have us, in turn, follow a new math program here and retreat to basic computation skills there; embrace contextual linguistics there and rediscover phonics here. We are moved back and forth like heads at an exciting tennis match, until either the proponent or the critic scores a telling point on the bewildered majority watching the changing game.

The way to win for your daughter (and each child!) involves one attitude change and two simple acts.

One Attitude: Draw a firm resolve to avoid the either-or, win-lose, your side-my side, correct-incorrect program controversy. The truth is that many of the current educational programs, if done well, will suit your daughter if they and she are properly matched. Each program represents a basic philosophy which assumes that most children learn in a pattern represented by that approach. Whether that philosophy and the teaching methods it advocates are good for individual children depends solely on the way(s) in which each youngster learns most easily. As you read in Chapter 4, how a youngster learns is called her "learning style," and it is important to correctly match that style with the appropriate program for her.

How will you know if she's had the right tailor? Once your attitude has broadened beyond the stereotype that certain programs are either "good" or "bad," you can identify those that are very appropriate (indeed, ideal!) and those that are just plain wrong for your child and others who learn as she does. Now you need to consider two acts.

Act 1: Read the next section and become knowledgeable about the programs that have received the labels. Measure the underlying philosophy of each against your own. Observe classes within your local school (and others if possible) and use the descriptions and scales in this section as your first map of exploration. Gradually, the terrain will become familiar, and you will begin to recognize the teaching trails and landmarks of different schools.

Act 2: Using the Learning Style Questionnaire in Chapter 4, occasionally retest your daughter to determine whether any changes have occurred in the ways in which she prefers to learn.

You then will be able to determine which of the educational programs that are available to you will be most appropriate for your daughter. In addition, you will be able to respond to demagogues, whether they are of the extreme right or left or in the wishy-washy middle of the educational spectrum. More important, you will be able to aid your daughter (and other youngsters in her school) by encouraging her teachers to match appropriate teaching strategies to various learning styles.

Unfortunately, the reverse occurs too often; children are forced to adjust their learning styles to whatever teaching approaches are used. This procedure may be damaging to their progress, because it makes learning more difficult than it should be, causes frustration, and decreases a youngster's confidence in herself. Conversely, when a student learns in ways that are natural to her, the outcomes usually are increased academic achievement, improved self-esteem, a liking for learning, improved basic skills, stimulated creativity, and gradually increasing learner-independence.

RAISING THE CURTAIN ON ACT 1: VIEWING CURRENT SCHOOL PROGRAMS

Here are the current in-vogue programs, their philosophies, and skills that students need to function successfully in each. Next to the required skills column is a description of the learning style a youngster needs to thrive academically under each approach. These explanations are not intended to promote one program over another. It is necessary to understand that each child learns in ways that are often extremely different from those of every other student and that generally each program proves advantageous to one learning style. Of greater importance is the reality that *no program* can respond sensitively to *every* learning style and that, should the wrong child be placed into the wrong program for *her*, her ability to progress academically will be severely hampered.

INSTRUCTIONAL PROGRAM: TRADITIONAL CLASSROOM[20]

Philosophy: The teacher is responsible for helping students to achieve (minimally) grade-level standards. Children are expected to "pay attention," "try," "work," "take their work seriously," and "be good"—all of which presupposes that they are each able to achieve through the method(s) selected by the teacher. Most of the instruction is through lecture and questioning occasionally supplemented by media. Lesson plans are written by the teacher for the principal as indications of what the class will be taught. Grades are determined by the student's achievement on group tests. All students learn sequential blocks of subject matter at the same time. A few students are permitted some "enrichment" if it does not interfere with the curriculum to be "covered." For all, self-selection of subject content and method of learning are rare.

Required Student Skills	*Learning Style Characteristics*
1. To pay attention for consecutive intervals of 20–50 minutes each.	Is motivated.

Required Student Skills	Learning Style Characteristics
2. To sit still for consecutive intervals of one to three hours.	Does not require mobility.
3. To refrain from needing a "drink," "a break," or using a lavatory, except during specified times (recess, lunch, etc.).	Does not require intake, except at correct times.
—or—	
To raise one's hand, interrupt the teacher, and publicly request permission to do any of the above during instructional time.	Is not embarrassed by being different from peers.
4. To concentrate on studies for several hours during the school day and while engaged in homework after school.	Is persistent.
5. To retain information by listening.	Is an auditory learner.
6. To learn at a table and chair or desk.	Requires a structured environment.
7. To learn at his desk wherever it has been placed.	Sound, light, and temperature are not factors.
8. To accept that what is taught is necessary, valuable, and interesting.	Is authority-oriented.
9. To conform to externally established standards and rules.	Is authority-oriented.
10. To accept being marked on a competitive basis regardless of inherited ability or environmental background.	Is authority-oriented.
11. To learn whenever a subject is being taught.	Time is not a factor.
12. To keep working at an item until it is mastered.	Is persistent.
13. To maintain a positive self-image and creativity while following directions, controlling normal body needs, learning in a way that prohibits use of personal learning style, studying what may be irrelevant and uninteresting, and avoiding conflict.	Is authority-oriented.

INSTRUCTIONAL PROGRAM: INDIVIDUALIZED CLASSROOM

Philosophy: The teacher is responsible for diagnosing, prescribing for, and guiding each student through the learning process. Recognizing the different elements of learning style, she permits students to work anywhere in the environment, in any sociological pattern that they choose. When a student evidences his ability to follow objectives that have been assigned to him, he is permitted to continue working as he prefers and is gradually permitted more and more options in objectives, resources, activities, and evaluation. When a student does not appear to be able to work independently, structure is added to his prescription, so that he works to varying degrees under the direct supervision of the teacher. Multimedia, multisensory resources are available to students, who may select from among them. Objectives are written on an individual basis and may be contributed to or developed by the student. When progress is not satisfactory, the teacher becomes increasingly directive. Grades are determined as a result of criterion-referenced testing related to each youngster's enumerated objectives.

Required Student Skills	Learning Style Characteristics
1. To identify those objectives, resources, activities, and assessment devices that need to be fulfilled. This will be done on their own by students who can function independently and with the teacher for students who need guidance.	Varied levels of responsibility.
2. To identify the resources through which the objectives may be achieved. These will be itemized by the student. When student progress is not apparent or appropriate, resources will be prescribed by the teacher.	Varied perceptual strengths.
3. To complete individual prescriptions. When this is not done, the instruction will become formalized and traditional. As the student shows achievement, options in the mode of instruction will become available. As options increase with evidenced achievement, achievement continues to increase.	Varied levels of motivation.

Required Student Skills	Learning Style Characteristics
4. To self-assess one's own progress. Students who are able to evaluate objectively their academic growth are permitted to continue doing so. Students who are unable to do so are evaluated by the teacher frequently.	Varied degrees of self- and authority-orientation.

INSTRUCTIONAL PROGRAM: OPEN CLASSROOM*

Philosophy: Children are permitted to select their own curriculum, resources, schedule, and pace of learning. Students may remain with a topic as long as it interests them and may study alone, with a friend or two, or in a small group. Since youngsters learn in very individual ways, the teacher is responsible for providing an environment rich in multimedia resources and for encouraging student involvement and the materials. Objectives, if used, are determined by the child and may vary from student to student and on a continuously changing basis. Grades are not given, but evaluations are made in terms of each child's demonstrated growth. A positive and "happy" attitude is considered very important for student progress.

Required Student Skills	Learning Style Characteristics
1. To learn without continuous direction and supervision.	Is motivated.
2. To avoid an essentially social, rather than academic experience.	Is responsible.
3. To discipline oneself to concentrate and to learn self-selected ideas, data, and values.	Is motivated and responsible.
4. To study in the midst of movement, discussion, and varied activities.	Sound, structure, and the mobility of others are not factors.
5. To interact positively with other children.	Is peer-oriented.
6. To retain information without drill reinforcement.	Is not in need of imposed structure.

*Because of the wide variety of multimedia and manipulative resources available to students involved in open classroom approaches, less motivated youngsters are often intrigued into active participation. In addition, the de-emphasis on grades permits an immature child to explore materials and experiences without penalty. These procedures afford such a student additional time in which to adjust to an academic environment. Children must be carefully watched, however, in the event continued exploration without substantial academic achievement over a two- to four-month period may become habit-forming.

INSTRUCTIONAL PROGRAM: ALTERNATIVE PROGRAMS*

Philosophy: Students are given curriculum choices, freedom, and objectives and are expected to gather and retain information independently. Students are usually permitted a voice in their program development. Since alternative programs differ widely, the degree to which options are provided concerning objectives, resources, activities, and evaluations is dependent on the individual program, not the student.

Required Student Skills	*Learning Style Characteristics*
1. To learn without continuous direction and supervision.	Is motivated.
2. To determine the scope, sequence, and depth of undertaken studies.	Is responsible.
3. To self-assess one's own progress and potential accurately.	Is self-oriented.
4. To discipline oneself to study and achieve.	Is motivated and responsible.
5. To retain information without drill reinforcement.	Is not in need of imposed structure.

It is important to remember that all of the four programs described are different from each other and provide discrete types of learning environments. They should not be confused with each other, although some teachers tend to use selected aspects of each inappropriately—inappropriate because each represents a separate philosophy based on differing concepts of how children learn. Since children learn in a variety of ways—dependent on the individual child—each program serves strong needs of *certain children; no single program is appropriate* for all children. The important thing to remember is that the placement of students should be based on the way they learn, and not on the supposed value of a given program.

FOLLOWING WITH ACT 2: MATCHING HER LEARNING STYLE WITH THE RIGHT SCHOOL PROGRAM

An extensive body of research knowledge exists on the ways people learn or are affected by various elements. Until recently, this research has been largely

*Because of diversification, it is assumed that such a program permits students to achieve in ways different from those of the traditional classroom. If an open-campus approach is used, students need not be present at all times and may be scheduled into programs of less than 5.5 hours of formal instruction. Student learning is partially self-directed and may occur out of the school building. Usually, this approach is used only with secondary students.

ignored by educators, partly because many of the studies were conducted in fields other than education, and partly because educators, too, have emphasized *programs,* rather than *individual* learning styles.

Compare your daughter's Learning Style Profile Form (provided in Chapter 4) with how students must behave (the skills that are required) if they are to achieve in each of the different instructional programs. This analysis will aid you in deciding which program is best for her. Whatever the educational program—labeled or unlabeled—both parents and teachers should be aware that only children with certain learning styles can succeed in each of them. All students, and certainly those with learning problems, should be analyzed to identify how they learn best. Then, based on the findings, the youngsters should be placed in the programs that best complement them—not the current bandwagon approach to education.

If you want your daughter to achieve well in school, be certain that she is placed in an educational environment that capitalizes on the way she learns best.

Illustrating the Relationship between Learning Style and an Instructional Program
Read the following case study and the analysis of Kathy's learning style as if she were your daughter. Then compare her learning style characteristics with those described for each of the instructional programs. See whether you agree with our placement of Kathy.

Case Study: Kathy Hightower. Kathy shook her head in a continuing expression of frustration. Her negative "body language" had become apparent at home, as well as in school. Her fifth-grade peers were just as upset with her wandering curiosity as she was with her teacher's repeated commands to sit still.

The teacher's voice began to rise as he fought to control his composure—and Kathy. "Return to your seat at once, or I'll have to send you to the principal." Kathy looked up from her friend's desk. She liked the principal; they often compared their opinions on the underlying symbolism in recent movies they had seen. For an instant, she toyed with the notion of saying something fresh, so that she could take the long walk down to the main office. Maybe the principal has seen "Jeremiah Johnson," mused Kathy. I'll bet he didn't notice Jeremiah preparing those tasteless Indian bread cakes toward the end of the movie, after his Indian bride had been killed.

She shook her head again. No, she really didn't want to get her teacher even more upset. Kathy went back to her seat.

Kathy strained to see the print. It was comparatively dark in her far corner, and she had difficulty reading the work assigned to the class. She stopped and shook her head again. She knew her answers were right; she had completed the vocabulary words and used them in sentences in one-fourth the time that was needed by most of the others. She smiled as she looked at her last math test: her sixth straight 100 percent!

She felt restless and tried to bring her work to the teacher, but he was talking to another youngster, and there were three more lined up, waiting.

Kathy felt the urge to eat again and sneaked a health food bar she had prepared out of her desk. She also attached a tiny earplug under her long brown hair and switched from an analysis of Beethoven's *Fifth Symphony* by Leonard Bernstein to "News of the Day" to catch the latest weather report. She felt a glow of achievement as the forecast from the hidden radio matched hers. She wondered if she should sneak home at lunchtime to check her rain gauge.

She was deeply into her homemade weather charts and maps (while munching and listening to *Aida*) when her name was called by the teacher in exasperation. He was ready to move the class onto the next topic and was irritated that Kathy apparently had "tuned him out" once again. She had not heard his crisp command, "Put all other materials away now and turn to page ninety-seven of your science book," and "Kathy, please stay with us this time!"

She shook her head. She already knew the material being presented on rocks. As a matter of fact, she had collected those rocks and compared them to samples in the high school science room last fall.

....

If we were to list all the data that relates directly to Kathy's learning style, we would note the following: She:

- Is able to listen while reading or completing other activities (listening to radio and working on weather forecasts).
- Seems to be uncomfortable in a low-light area (dark in her corner, has difficulty reading).
- Is highly motivated (pleased with good grades, has success in activities).
- Is persistent (stays with all tasks to completion).
- Is responsible (listens to requests despite frustrations; wants to be part of class).
- Is self-structured when interested.
- Likes to work with peers and adults (goes to their desks, likes to talk to principal).
- Appears to have multiple perceptual abilities (listens, sees, and is kinesthetic; for example, radio, films, weather station).
- Likes intake (urge to eat again).
- Appears to require mobility (went to friend's desk, felt restless, wanted to bring her work to teacher, thought about walking to principal and going home).
- Is authority-oriented (wants to please the teacher).

When considering what the case study does *not* tell us about Kathy's learning style, we would need to note that we do not know:

- The time of day in which she functions best.
- The degree of temperature she prefers.
- The balance required to produce the most effective use of her many perceptual strengths.
- The balance required to produce the most effective use of her ability to work alone and with her peers.
- The amount of structure, if any, that she might need if not interested in a particular topic or subject.
- Whether or not she learns best alone, with one or more peers, with adults, or in a designed combination.
- Whether she would be in need of mobility if she were "challenged" by appropriate studies.
- Whether she would learn better in a formal or informal design.
- Whether or not she could function independently on advanced studies in which she was not interested.
- Whether or not she has or can use the senses of touch or smell effectively.

Kathy's problems center about the fact that she is far brighter than her classmates and that her teacher does not design advanced studies for her. By requiring that all students participate in the identical curriculum, the teacher is ignoring Kathy's intellectual giftedness. Because she must listen to and repeat studies that she has already mastered, Kathy is bored, frustrated, and irritated. The other students in her class are not really "peers," for they are not able to function on her academic level. The teacher's disparagement (". . . please stay with us this time!") is causing the students to react to her negatively, too ("Her peers were just as upset with her. . . ."). Had Kathy been able to work with actual peers, she might have developed an excellent relationship with some of them.

Kathy's learning style characteristics that might respond to a traditional program include that she is motivated, persistent, authority-oriented, an auditory learner, and that time does not seem to be a factor for her. Those characteristics which would *not* respond to a traditional program include her apparent requirement for mobility and need for intake. Since traditional programs concentrate on grade-level studies and standards, and since Kathy can function far above normal grade levels, she would either need to be advanced to a higher (older) grade, or her program would need to be varied extensively.

Kathy's learning style characteristics would respond to an open classroom program with two exceptions: (1) we do not know if she is really peer-oriented, for she has not had opportunities to work directly with real peers and (2) we do not know whether she would need structure if required to learn mandatory subjects. Since an open classroom would permit her to self-select her own curriculum, this would be a good program for her.

An individualized instructional program would certainly respond to Kathy's learning style, for it permits wide flexibility for those students who require variations in the environment and the curriculum and, simultaneously, provides structure for those who are not self-directive. In this case, however, given the wide range of Kathy's abilities, her high degree of motivation, persistence, responsibility, and her high academic achievement, an open classroom would be our primary choice.

6.
What to Do during the Turning-Point Years; the Middle School or Junior High Interval: Ages Eleven to Fifteen

CHARACTERISTICS OF OUR ADOLESCENT DAUGHTERS

It happens to some as early as ten or eleven years of age; others are not affected until they are past sixteen. But somewhere between their emergence from the elementary school cocoon and their maturation into independent, able-to-fly-where-they-choose butterflies, our daughters pass through a metamorphosis called "adolescence."

At birth, during infancy and early childhood, and as she gradually progresses through her first years of formal schooling, a daughter is a joy. When she moves into this transitional stage, however, you often may find yourself thinking, "If I had known *then* what I know now about raising children, I might have never ———!"

If you are feeling frustrated or victimized, we offer the following consolation: The values that you labored to instill *prior* to these difficult years may be obscured, but only temporarily. Eventually, your advice and efforts to build a system of values will take root and strengthen the tree of your child's character and personality. What you need to be concerned with at this time (in addition to maintaining your equilibrium) are three management questions: (1) how to understand what she is experiencing; (2) how to help her to cope with life as she grows; and (3) how to communicate to her that she is worthy and well-loved, *in spite* of the fact that she is behaving like a stranger whom you do not recognize as the child you raised—and whom, at times, you do not like very much.

As noted earlier, girls tend to achieve better than boys in elementary school. This pattern continues into the junior high and high schools for most girls, but gradually the gap in their academic superiority over boys narrows, and, eventually, more boys than girls attend and are graduated from colleges and graduate schools.[1] In part, the change is due to the accelerating rate of male mental and physiological development between adolescence and adulthood.[2] Of great impact, however, is a basic attitude change among girls that *discourages* them from achieving.[3] Many girls stop trying to succeed because they believe that achievement is "unfeminine"; others become so involved in attempting to lure (without succumbing to) the opposite sex, that they abandon their studies in favor of cosmetics, constant combing, clandestine conversations and/or "cutting up" in classes. This is due to their perceptions of what attracts boys. Ask your daughter what boys *"really like"* in a girl, and you are certain to hear her use adjectives that focus on physical features—"pretty," "beautiful," "thin," "big eyes," "nice smile," "long hair," "good legs," or "big breasts."

What is happening to our daughters at this time in their lives is that they are being thrust into a microcosm of our very real world, for the social values of our adult population primarily emphasize a woman's physical attractiveness. On a scale of valued female characteristics, physical attributes are followed by personality traits. Next on the list would be her socioeconomic status, as determined by her *father's* occupation and possibly (but not likely) enhanced by a professionally involved mother. The very *last* item of consequence is a girl's intellectuality.

In our view, a comparison of society's ranking of a man's vital characteristics in contrast with those of a woman often is quite different. Of major importance is his potential earning ability, as determined by his career plans and his socioeconomic status. Next would be his education and grooming. The *last* item of consequence in evaluating a male in adult society is his looks!

The early teenage years represent for daughters a shaky crossing of the bridge between childhood and adulthood. They are fearful of going forward on their own, for they recognize their need for your support and protection. At the same time, they are irritated with themselves for needing that security, because they also want to become independent and self-directive. Daughters are both tempted and repelled by their emerging womanhood; they progress and retrogress on the path to maturity in a constantly oscillating pattern. Their inconsistencies and reversals can be maddening, and the ambiguity of not knowing what to expect next causes most parents concern, distress, and occasional pain. If your daughter's childhood experiences aided her in developing her self-worth and independence, she will come through this temporary period well and strong. Indeed, it is during this phase that she will determine and probably announce her future career decisions. For some (those who are less secure about their own ability or less independent of social mores), it will take longer to mature; this second group will not develop professional aspirations until later—perhaps toward the end of their high school studies when they will be required to consider seriously whether or not they will continue into college and how they wish to earn a living. If you have focused on the development of the skills and attitudes that this book has emphasized, it is very likely that your daughter will respond positively to the broad, generalized goals you hold for her. At any rate, you will want to understand the difficulties she is experiencing, so that you can respond to her needs knowledgeably and help her to become increasingly independent during this critical stage.

UNDERSTANDING YOUR DAUGHTER'S SOCIAL
DEVELOPMENT DURING ADOLESCENCE

Although your guidance and encouragement have been a major support for your daughter's school achievement and in the expansion of her interests and activities outside your home during the past few years, you will become increasingly aware of your diminishing influence on her behavior outside your home as she moves through adolescence. Between the ages of eleven and thirteen, your daughter will need many opportunities in which to make decisions, and you will need to develop confidence in her ability to remember the many valuable skills you have taught her.

One manifestation of adolescent behavior will be her occasional (if not frequent) negative responses or outright rebellion, but it is important for you to recognize that, at this difficult stage of her life (more than ever before), *your daughter will use you to help her to further develop and expand a commitment to values.* At the same time, the youngsters with whom she attends school will provide the basis for her behavior standards and for her many affectations and attitudes. This is the age when peers are exceedingly important to youngsters who (unfortunately) begin to conform to roles assigned by the group— sometimes rigidly. Boisterous behavior becomes typical, as the peer group influence intensifies and girls become extremely self-conscious about their bodies.

Two of the more difficult problems of this age (and there are many!) include experimentation with the use of alcohol, marijuana, tobacco, and other drugs and the development of interest in the opposite sex—although girls are more interested in boys than boys are in girls. The adolescent's growing sexuality becomes a critical concern. Information concerning what is done, what might be done, how to avoid involvements, what to do in case they cannot be avoided, and other titillating fantasies are shared with members of each "in-group." Crushes and hero worship are common for the same and the opposite sex, and team games become very popular.

One of the major differences between boys and girls in this phase is that girls exhibit more social amenities than boys, and their interests appear to be more divergent.

In this regard, experiences that may seem funny to adults can loom as tragic as an opera to our adolescents. One day our daughter Rana came home aglow, reporting that she had learned something important in her ninth-grade psychology class: "People establish relationships because they want something from each other. You can't have a relationship unless you get something in return." We tried to explain that a sharing relationship in which each person *gave* and received through the giving was the best type, but we realized that she really was not listening. New vistas of psychological insight had been opened for her, and she was impressed with her admittance into an adult world.

The next day Rana came home half-depressed and half-angry. "I told Dan," (her current boyfriend) "that everyone wants something from a relationship," she recounted. "He didn't know what I was talking about. He wouldn't tell me what *he* wanted. Finally, he asked me what I wanted, and I said 'companionship.' Then I insisted that he tell me what he wanted from me, and do you know what he said? He told me that what he really wants is for me to stop hanging around the bus stop. His friends are bugging him because I wait for him, and he wants me to stop!"

Youngsters moving into their teens require a great deal of patience and understanding from us. They do not have the experience or the analytical tools to piece together the significance of the tragicomic scene just described. Rana had begun to understand abstractions in a behavioral context, Dan was operating on a very literal channel, and they did not communicate. This caused pain and frustration for both of them. Talking it through with Rana and her brothers seemed to help. She ended the conversation by saying, "Serious relationships really require a commitment, don't they?"

The school your daughter attends is always important to her development, but at this stage it should be of major concern to you, primarily because of its student population. The peers with whom your daughter interacts between the ages of eleven and thirteen will contribute immeasurably to her view of herself, her future, and her determinations concerning her life values. If you have any doubts at all about the neighborhood in which you reside or the students who attend her school, do not hesitate: Move, if you can. If moving is not feasible, attempt to arrange friendships, class schedules, and programs that will complement your daughter's needs and growth stages.

The self-image that you have helped her to develop, her independence and decision-making skills, and her feelings of confidence may all lie dormant for a while during these years, when she may be feeling confused and frightened by her perceptions of a more complex and impersonal junior high school setting. She will begin to question school authorities and will occasionally oppose them, and although she will have many concerns about her classmates, her school will become the major environment for a variety of social experiences.

Panic will help neither you nor your daughter. During these very difficult years, remain her loving parent, in spite of her lack of willingness to communicate and her behaviors, which will, at times, cause you despair. If you lose loving contact with her, she will feel more isolated and alienated than she already does because of her physical and emotional stress, and she will be alone in a very difficult situation. She needs you as never before.

HOW TO COPE WITH THE INFLUENCES OF
FAMILY, FRIENDS, AND SCHOOL

The major way in which you may counteract the negative peer-group influences exerted on your daughter at this stage of her life is to behave *calmly* —as if you believe that she will be the fine, moral, charming person that she has been all along. It is necessary, however, to insist that the values in which *you* believe are important, should be preserved, and cannot be sidestepped. Let us consider how decisions are and should be made in some of the areas in which this advice applies.

Your daughter's maturation process should be encouraged and supported by permitting her to make decisions and to observe and feel their consequences. You will need to believe that, by this stage of her life, she will be aware of those behaviors that may lead to dire consequences for her. This does not suggest that you allow her to make decisions that might prove damaging to her safety, education, or reputation; it does suggest that you *cease* telling her what to do (and what *not* to do) *most* of the time. *Save the required directions for important issues,* such as whether or not she may attend school functions at night or be out after a given hour. Permit her to decide which clothes she wears, when she does her homework, and what she eats, to cite a few examples.

Parents often are concerned about the impressions their daughters make on teachers, neighbors, or other adults, and therefore emphasize what they consider to be appropriate clothing for special occasions, correct manners, and specific social graces. This is the time to *stop!* Your daughter *knows* the amenities, and, in fact, when you are not present, she will impress others with her gracious personal charm. She also knows what to wear—although her perceptions and yours may not always agree. Permit her to select her clothes, so long as they do not offend your sense of *propriety* (too "low-cut" or revealing, for example), for she is better aware than you are of what is acceptable in the school situation in which she survives each day. She cannot counteract the peer culture in every respect, and wearing the "in" clothes is a protective device to maintain her group membership and, thus, some security. Besides, her clothes are not really a major issue; you may have confidence that she will wear appropriate attire when she is a little older and more independent of her friends.

Her eating habits also may become a source of concern at this stage. Ignore her tendency to select only a limited sampling of foods available (unless it is only "junk food"), for these inclinations, too, will change. If she persists in bypassing breakfast, repeated admonitions of how vital it is to eat in the morning will become a source of irritation between you. Tell her once, and proceed to another topic. You must train yourself not to "nag" during this period.

Other issues that do not require confrontations might be the way she wears her hair, the fact that she frequently loses items like combs or pens, or that she is forgetful. These behaviors will irritate you, but because there are so many important issues on which you will *need* to focus, it is suggested that you overlook those that will not permanently affect her. (She really *will* change the hairstyle, the clothes, and the slang some day, and she may even remember not to lose her possessions!)

On these less important issues, you might say, "Do you like your hair down on your face that way?!" If she responds positively, and you contradict her choice, you are "knocking" her judgment—which you must build. There is nothing wrong with telling her (*once!*), "Your face looked so much longer when your hair was pulled back! I thought you looked beautiful that way," but if she keeps her current hairstyle (and she will), do not criticize her by word, manner, or implication.

What are the decision-making areas that *are* important in terms of requiring your active intervention? Again, the only issues on which you will be able to have an impact at this point are those concerned with *values,* and these are determined on the basis of (a) what is important to you and (b) what is important to your daughter's future. (Her *future* will not be affected by either the clothes she wears or how her hair is styled now; her tastes will change—as will the fashions—as she matures.)

Since you are aware that the group's mores will tend to prevail (at least on the surface!) during this period, be certain that you know what they are. It is easy, of course, to remain consciously ignorant of the various escapades of youngsters of this age, but that would be self-defeating. It is better to become so close to your daughter that she either confides in you (do not trust that what you are told is the entire story) or is not aware of your constant alertness to her telephone conversations, written work (letters are often revealing), or activities.

If you choose to say, "I trust my daughter and refuse to 'spy' on her," that is your prerogative. Be certain, however, that you are not assuming an "ostrich" posture because it is the path of least resistance. Your daughter, in this phase, should not be trusted—because during adolescence, she is not the "same child" you knew for the first ten years of her life; she is a product of her need to be part of a social group that is, at the moment, confused, frightened, striking out toward adulthood and simultaneously disrespectful of authority (either outwardly or undercover). It is too much to ask that she be strong, independent of her peers, and totally loyal to your upbringing at this point; that is why she needs opportunities to exercise independence in some areas and your warm, understanding, and insistently moral guidance in others.

You will need to make the decisions concerning the issues or values on which you feel strongly. For many families these include some or all of the following:

1. *Personal Cleanliness.* Habits like regular bathing, teeth brushing, or clothing and underwear changes that were initiated during infancy and early childhood will tend to remain, but at times may be neglected. An occasional, gentle reminder is all that is necessary. If these health-preserving procedures are overlooked, you will need to decide how important they seem to be. Your decision may be influenced by the degree to which your daughter resists and the other areas of difficulty that may require your guidance.

2. *Organization of Possessions and Neatness of Living Quarters.* Youngsters at this stage are so engrossed in their bodies, looks, clothes, and social relationships that their rooms, closets, drawers, and possessions appear to be of less interest and concern than, perhaps, they should. If you cannot tolerate disorder or dirt, calmly, charmingly, approach your daughter and say, "Honey, please try to keep your room (drawers, closet, things) in better order. It irritates me to see things so messy. if you need help in organizing (cleaning up, etc.), I will be glad to work with you, but things cannot remain this way."

She will need many reminders and a great deal of help. She will say things like, "It's my room, and how I keep it is my business!" If *you* do not like living in a home with disorder, tell her so—and insist that *her* room is in *your* house and that when she is old enough to have her own apartment or home, you will not tell her how to maintain it. And don't!

3. *Late Hours.* Time is relative, and what is "late" to some parents is acceptable to others. In this regard, do not be intimidated by what others permit. *Your* standards are the ones that should be abided by, and when you find yourself deliberating, "Am I 'old-fashioned?' " *stop!* Reassure yourself that *you* are the parent, and you are responsible for your daughter's safety. The cop-out, "Nothing can happen after 9:00 that cannot occur before!" is an absurdity. After the hour at which *most* of the youngsters are present, fewer people, less supervision, a feeling of recklessness, and a self-image of being "adult" (by virtue of being "out" at a later time) all contribute to the increased possibility (if not likelihood) that activities that might not be considered earlier could be introduced at a later hour.

4. *Evening School Activities.* Parents often assume that school-related events are well-supervised and safe. Nothing could be farther from the truth. To begin with, the degree of necessary supervision that *can* be exercised over fifty or more adolescents is minimal. Adults must remain with the larger group, and individuals, pairs, and small groups can always drift out of sight and into hallways, vacant rooms, closets, and the outdoors if they so choose. The lavatories in the school are often used as a place in which to smoke, try drugs, experiment with makeup, or sex, or to abuse the more innocent. Remember that many youngsters of this age begin to experiment with tobacco, alcohol, and drugs, and those who do, need to have others join them, in order to rationalize their own participation and to feel that they are part of a group. Your daughter may never be a *volunteer* for these activities, but she is almost certain to be exposed to them in school—particularly at class parties or dances, where the need to "put up a front" appears to be of importance.

When confronted with the perennial whine, "Everybody else's parents let them go to ———", you should respond with, "Nobody else's parents love them the way *we* love *you,* or, "That is not true. Many parents do *not* permit their children to go to ———, and those who do are not aware of what goes on at ———." If you take this approach, you will need to be strong, for her badgering will be relentless. She will taunt, tease, pout, express anger and resentment, and tell her friends that you are "mean" (or worse). Ignore it all and be resolute (if you can), for, eventually, she will express her admiration for you, because (a) you "knew" what was going on, (b) you were trying to protect her, and (c) you wouldn't "give in the way the other parents did!"

Another ploy used by girls of this age is, "You don't trust me!" Your response can be, "Of course we trust *you!* But you cannot be accountable for the other "kooky" kids, and we do not want to place you in a situation that you should not have to attempt to handle so early in your life!"

The only hesitation you may have in this area is that, "Unless she has an opportunity to learn how to socialize, how will she ever learn?" Our best advice is that she will learn to socialize very quickly and very well when she is older and that at this stage in her life you are permitting her to enter into situations that potentially are *dangerous* if you condone her attendance at night-time functions in most schools. Widespread experimentation culminating in negative experiences during these events has been *increasing,* rather than decreasing, both in the number of children involved and the seriousness of the activities.

5. *Social Events in Other Children's Homes.* Do not feel guilty about refusing to permit your daughter to attend after-school, evening events and then assuage your feelings by permitting across-the-board acceptance of invitations to other girls' homes. It is important that you *speak* to the inviting youngster's *parent* (not older sibling) and confirm that (a) she or he is aware that your daughter has been invited, (b) the hour at which she is expected to arrive

and leave, (c) a concerned *adult* will be present, and (d) boys will not be invited or permitted to "crash." Unless you have had similar experiences, you will not believe the number of times that parents have been assured that an adult would be at home for the entire time and then later learned that they were either in another part of the house and did not supervise or were called away and left an older teenager to oversee the situation.

After repeated reports of outwardly lovely parents who assured other mothers of their continuing presence *and* supervision at evening parties and in whose homes alcohol, pills, and sexual experimentation occurred, we are less than convinced that all parents are truly adult and responsible. If you do permit your daughter to attend selected gatherings, one or both of you should drive by the house and often "drop in" with a surprise of donuts or ice cream for everyone in attendance.

Remain alert to the clever scheming of this age group. If they are so inclined, they will bring beer or liquor to a youngster's house, leave it outside when admitted, and then go out and rescue it from its hiding place after things "get going." Once they have been admitted by adults, scrutinized, and have been at the party for a while, few question their need to get a "breath of fresh air" at about nine o'clock or nine-thirty. Sometimes they will drink outside and then return to the home. Sometimes they will slip a bottle into the house under a jacket or sweater. Girls of this age are *not* entitled to privacy; they are entitled to protection.

6. *Homework and Academic Studies.* It is at approximately this age and during the next three years that many girls develop a strong sensitivity to those mores that suggest that boys do not feel comfortable with girls who are their intellectual superiors. The girls, therefore, begin to de-emphasize their academic abilities. Many continue to excel, and most will retain their desire to achieve in spite of their developing conflicts, but be alert to how *your* daughter is doing. Do not encourage extensive television viewing, be highly selective about the programs she may watch, be certain that her grades are maintained, and continue to praise her extensively for well-done school work and good grades.

7. *Smoking, Alcohol, and Marijuana.* The data may include mixed conclusions, and the degree to which these items are detrimental to one's health may not be fully demonstrated, but no study or health or mental agency has ever suggested that smoking, alcohol, or marijuana are *healthful* for people, particularly when large quantities are consumed. An infrequent cigarette, drink, or "drag" may not be very harmful, but they *do* introduce an activity which makes children believe that they are "acting like adults" and which, therefore, extends their image of sophistication in their own minds and in those of their friends. These youngsters are *not* delinquent; they are immature and insecure, and the greater their immaturity and insecurity, the greater will be their need to "show" their peers how "cool" or "with it" they are.

There are very few girls who do not experiment with at least one, and probably all, of these forbidden items, and you would be realistic to assume that your daughter is *not* the exception. It is wise to tell her that all are harmful to her body, her skin, and her growth. A truly mature person cares about herself and doesn't abuse her body. It is foolish to threaten her with punishment or dire consequences if you discover that she has tried them. She will not be intimidated by warnings, the anti-authority sentiment of this age will cause her to attempt to defy you, and you will not follow through on extreme warnings anyway.

One of the better ways to cope with this very serious problem is to: (a) *avoid all of these items yourself;* (b) tell her how detrimental *you believe* them to be; (c) acknowledge that most girls her age do "try" them and that she probably will, but that it is foolish to take chances with her body and mind; (d) make her aware that individuals react differently to each of these, that her own reactions may be sickening or embarrassing, and that if she is going to try, to be certain that she is in her own home; (e) *refuse* to assist her to use any of these items. Further, do not condone their use among her peers; do not permit her friends to use them in *your* home, even if they have *their* parents' permission; and ask her to tell you about it (with impunity) if she does try.

You will need to insist that *you believe* that they are detrimental to her health, that you love her, and that you therefore cannot and will not permit her to use them. You will need to affirm that, since they are damaging, you do not want her in the company of young people who engage in their use, on the premise that it will be difficult for her to avoid joining in when confronted with widespread use by peers.

If you smoke and cannot stop the habit, you cannot expect your daughter to avoid smoking. If you do not have the willpower necessary for avoidance, why should the child, who is an extension of yourself, have more willpower than you? You are hypocritical and unrealistic if you set standards for your daughter that you cannot maintain for yourself.

If you and/or your spouse drink excessively (more than one an evening, as one standard), either desist from doing so in your daughter's presence or explain truthfully that one cocktail (or two, at times) for an adult is dispersed over a larger body area and is less harmful than for a not-fully-grown person. If you drink, so will she—eventually—and you would be wise, perhaps beginning in early adolescence, to introduce her to a quarter of a glass of wine (one ounce) at dinnertime, *occasionally*. She *will* drink if she sees you do so, and it is better to prepare her body for building a tolerance to liquor gradually than to hope that she will avoid alcohol and thus expose her to even greater danger when she drinks for the first time at a teenage canteen or party. Also, if she sees it in your home at dinner, the prospect of clandestine drinking may be less exciting or appealing to her.

If you engage in smoking marijuana or in using other drugs and cannot stop, you should anticipate your daughter's experimentation with them. Arguments concerning whether marijuana is more dangerous than either alcohol or cigarettes have no relationship to this aspect of the problem; they are all items that she does not need, would be better without, and *will use*—if you do.

As adults you undoubtedly understand that *all* adolescents do not do exactly the same things, in the same way, at the same time, or with the same effect. Most adolescents experiment with these unnecessary magnets—and they do so because they see adults use them and because demonstrating to their friends that *they* are adults is important to *their* value system. You have never heard of an adolescent surreptitiously drinking milk from a bottle or sucking on a pacifier, because adults do not do those things. Bear in mind, however, that although—for the most part—they *try* alcohol, cigarettes, and marijuana, most *do not continue* after a given period of time *if their own parents do not*. Some dislike the effects immediately and never (or rarely) repeat the attempt, others will continue for several months and then stop, and others may become involved in rather serious usage for one or more years and eventually discontinue the practice. Some, of course, do continue throughout their adulthood.

8. *Sex.* Because of our increasing knowledge of nutrition, health practices, and improved food intake, children are taller, larger, healthier, and mature sooner than ever before. One recent study of adolescent students verified that in the 1970s youngsters were equivalent in their *physical* maturation to people who were two to three years their seniors only two generations ago.

It is unrealistic to think that physically mature and awakening adolescents will not be sensitive to their emerging sexuality. When examined in the context of what adolescent society demands of its members in the way of conformity, it is only reasonable to admit that most girls between eleven and thirteen will be scrutinizing their bodies in an intensely curious manner and that they will be extremely self-conscious of every observable physical change that occurs.

Because most are not ready for real intimacy (either physical or emotional), they are titillated by the thoughts and discussions that help them to sublimate the sexual feelings that are beginning to emerge. They are preoccupied with acceptance by their social groups, however, and within the next three years almost all of our daughters begin to indulge in casual and intimate heterosexual activity and experimentation.

Each pair of parents must reach agreement and make peace with their own standards and regulations in this regard. You may decide that if your daughter eventually does engage in sex prior to marriage she should be alerted to contraceptive measures, rather than endure a premarital pregnancy —particularly at an early age. Providing your daughter with contraceptive information and measures will neither ensure nor prevent her sexual involvement, but they will permit her more of a choice in future pursuits than unwanted responsibilities that she is not ready to assume properly.

During this interval, despite the fact that peer influences will be very strong, your daughter will be developing and asserting her own value system. She will begin to understand ethical abstractions, such as the concept of justice, honesty, or integrity, and she will begin to become aware of and able to discuss selected social issues, such as friendships, group relationships, or true motivations. She will be living in a world (her own) with disparate values, for example, knowing that you disapprove of dishonesty, while, simultaneously, needing peer approval and knowing that some of her friends (wherever you reside) shoplift—which she understands is "stealing" and wrong. Although she will quietly and outwardly appear to accept her friends' actions, she will be considering them within the framework of her upbringing under your supervision and the beliefs that you hold. Through this process of examining, comparing, rationalizing, explaining, and extracting selected aspects, she will be developing the code of ethics by which she will live for the remainder of her young adult years.

Her self-concept development during these early adolescent years will be influenced strongly by her bodily changes. Her efforts toward achieving a personal kind of self-identity may sometimes include rebellion, and it is for this reason that you are urged to maintain a close, loving relationship with her, even if you find her rejecting you at times. The conflict she feels between needing your loving and wanting to be independent of it is normal and universal. This period of turmoil is reconciled in a later phase when you demonstrate your love for her and begin to recognize her ability to be independent and mature.

As your daughter moves into the fourteen-through-sixteen-year-old range, she will continue to be preoccupied with acceptance by her social group and will have a few close friends of both sexes. Previous to this period, she admired and was attracted to many different peers on a frequently rotating basis; at this point her friendships will last longer, and her primary group involvement will be with the same sex—with more heterosexual interaction. An increase in conflict between peer and adult roles will be evident, but the peer group influences will be greatly intensified—resulting in strongly expressed opinions and beliefs which may be contrary to those held by you and *your* peer group. Most girls continue to be more socially adept than boys, and, at about this time, their independent judgment emerges, *despite* their tendency toward conformity. When this happens, you will be seeing one of the first signs of your daughter's successful transition from childhood to adulthood.

One clue that our own daughter had begun to reach this stage was her response to one of the clichés at the beginning of this book. As we researched and developed them, we tested them on both youngsters and adults. To the myth stating that, "A career woman's marriage and children suffer," Rana snorted, "Are you kidding? I suffer when you *are* home. I must make my bed first thing in the morning, I have to do my homework before I go out, I can't talk on the phone too long, I have to remember to turn off the television and the lights if I leave my room, and so on. It's one big hassle. On the days that you work, it's great. You enjoy what you're doing, and we get some peace!"

We like to believe that her statement is partly exaggerated and partly humorous, but underlying the words is the suggestion that continuous maternal presence may be too directive and demanding.

UNDERSTANDING YOUR DAUGHTER'S
SELF-DEVELOPMENT DURING ADOLESCENCE[4]

As suggested previously, adolescence is an extremely unpleasant, difficult, and tension-provoking period for most young girls. They tend to be lacking in self-confidence and may be self-conscious, shy, and introspective—particularly with their parents. They worry a great deal about others' opinions—primarily those of their peers—and are sometimes moody and unpredictable; emotional outbursts are not unusual. Their need to conform to their peer group often results in an intolerance of other people's differences and opinions, and the physical changes that their bodies are undergoing often cause them great emotional stress—which they vent on their parents and siblings. It is important for your affection for your daughter to continue and be made evident to her during this period, although you should be prepared for either temporary outward rejection or ambivalence.

At times you will find that *your* feelings take precedence and that you are unwilling to grant her considerations that she does not "deserve" and does not appear to appreciate. When that happens, try to remember that the sometimes rude, often inconsiderate, frequently emotional "creature" that is your daughter, is a *child* caught up in a society that permits *children* to determine the culture of other children at the time in their lives when they most need adult supervision, guidance, and love. Remind yourself that you, an adult, are quarreling with a person vastly inferior to you in every way —someone to whom you gave life and who needs your undying affection and support. Force yourself to remember that it is more important to keep this confused young daughter secure in your love (which, during these days, is too often ephemeral) than to "win" the argument. Compromise, treat her as a very well-loved person, and stay as close to her as you can.

The tragedy of our times is that it is during this very erratic period in our daughters' lives—the in-between stage of the struggle from childhood toward adulthood—that they begin to learn their roles in heterosexual relation-ships and move toward achieving "femininity." Consider the four-way struggle our darlings endure.

1. Their bodies are changing and becoming bigger, more obvious, more sexual, and more uncomfortable, and they sense they are moving toward an adulthood which they simultaneously want and fear.

2. They are unsure of their ability to *be* adult and long for the safety and protectiveness of your arms and love—but are ashamed to admit it because they believe that they "ought to be growing up," and *we* repeatedly *urge* them to, "Grow up!"

3. The people who have loved them consistently throughout their lives, and who have served as their major source of security, are now intolerant of their attitudes, manner, speech, friends, and desires and are "always" chastizing and criticizing them—thus promoting, as a major source of encultu-ration, the peer group, which is equally (if not more so) anxious and confused.

4. Society communicates (via advertising, commercials, magazines, television, movies, the theater, and every major Madison Avenue outlet) that, first of all, it is important to be beautiful and futhermore, in order to be so, a girl must be slim (when she is blossoming in disproportion to her figure and features), attractive (when her parents refuse to permit her to wear makeup), less intelligent than boys (after she has been their mental superior throughout more than seven years of schooling), passive (when she has been required to assume leadership roles throughout the elementary years), and dependent (after having been trained at home to be independent—and just when her mind and body are reaching out for *increased* self-image and directiveness).

An entire revamping of the junior high and middle school structures is necessary to respond adequately to the needs of young girls today, but that describes what should be, and not what is.

As your daughter advances toward fifteen and sixteen, competitive peer relations will produce some distrust, although she will continue to confide more in her friends than in you. She will daydream a great deal and worry about her physical appearance and development. You may hear, "Do I look fat?" or, "Do I look too thin?" what seems to be a thousand times an hour. You should remember that this is her way of gaining the assurance of your acceptance and affection. Her emotional energies will continue to be expended toward physical change and developing heterosexual relationships, for this is the period during which many girls are described as being "boy crazy."

Becoming a woman raises serious questions and conflicts within many daughters: What does it really mean to be a woman? Will I be liked if I am not pretty? Isn't it important to be liked? How can I be popular and independent at the same time? How much of myself must I give up to be part of a group? Isn't being part of a group safer than being alone? Shouldn't I date? How do I handle a boy that I don't like too much? Why won't my parents trust me? They *say* they do, but they won't let me "be my own person." Why do they baby me? Why do they expect so much of me? I want to live my life my way! Can I live up to their expectations of me? I wonder what it's like to have sex. I'm not ready, but I'm curious . . . and interested.

Ironically, you will not be able to program her answers. She must go through the process of working out responses and then internalizing them by herself if she is to become independent. You can discuss experiences with her, to clarify their implications and to build her confidence. You can be a sympathetic sounding board. Above all, you can demonstrate your values, and even when they ostensibly conflict with hers, maintain what you believe, so that she has no doubts about where you stand on important issues.

Your daughter will rely more on your example and wisdom than you suspect. One day, a friend of our daughter's reported that in one of her classes Rana had revealed her feelings in a positive and insightful way. The teacher had asked each student to speak directly to another about her/his innermost feelings toward that person. Rana turned to her older brother, a senior in the same class, and said, "I really love you. I know I argue with you when you correct me, but I know you correct me because you care about me. In fact, everyone in our family cares. We have the greatest family—because every one *really* cares."

Rana is not a submissive young lady. She argues every point and resists every critical comment. She maintains her integrity at the cost of many turbulent hours and yet, somehow, she understands that if we did not care very deeply for her, we would not endure the turmoil. Your daughter, too, will understand that you love her and take the time and energy to guide her because she is very important to you.

Her interest in philosophical, ethical, and/or religious problems will develop at this time, and she will become aware of *and verbalize* contradictions that become evident to her in the moral code to which she has been exposed. Finally, for the first time, the group's beliefs will be extremely important in influencing her values—an area in which her home predominated formerly.

From this point on, her increasing maturity will be a blend of what you taught her during the first twelve or so years of her life and what she accepts from her peers. At the same time, she will demonstrate that she is developing socially responsible behavior, and you will note that she is also achieving new and more mature relations with age-mates of both sexes.

This is the "waiting period," for you can do little more than remain loving, supportive, and advisory when she seeks your assistance. You will need to be patient and rely on your faith in the effect of the many years during which you guided her growth.

UNDERSTANDING YOUR DAUGHTER'S THINKING AND
LANGUAGE DEVELOPMENT DURING ADOLESCENCE

Somewhere between eleven and fourteen, many girls are able to make the transition from concrete to abstract thinking, and they also begin to use abstract words in a discriminating and selective manner. Your daughter may be able to apply logic to solving problems and to think inductively. She will begin to consider alternatives, and if she also is creative, many of her ideas and "solutions" will delight and impress you. You may also note the emergence of independent, critical thinking at times, which is, unfortunately, subdued when she is with her friends—with whom she prefers to assume a more adaptive, supportive role, in deference to the group's status. She may also begin to make conceptual distinctions and, at times, will be concerned with the hypothetical, the future, and the remote, such as, "What do you think would happen if ———?" She will evidence an increased capacity for planning and will begin to consider long-range, rather than only immediate, purposes.

If she is very bright, she will be able to formulate and test hypotheses to consider many ways in which a problem can be solved, and she will deal with both logical and imaginary solutions. Bear in mind, however, that she is still in a transitory stage and will fluctuate between using abstract rules to solve problems and dissolving into tears (or becoming angry) at the slightest provocation—even when she should understand that she is being teased.

UNDERSTANDING YOUR DAUGHTER'S PHYSICAL
DEVELOPMENT DURING ADOLESCENCE

As our daughters approach the beginning of their junior high and middle school years, the onset of pubescence begins to occur. Hormonal changes cause the appearance of secondary sex characteristics, such as breast development, and menstruation begins between age ten and sixteen. It has been said that an early physical maturing is related to a more positive self-concept, but, at the same time, every parent will recognize the awkwardness their daughters experience in trying to cope with their rapidly changing bodies, when many of their friends' physical maturation has not, as yet, begun. Since boys tend to mature at a later time, girls are usually bigger, taller, more adult-like, and more socially aware than are their male classmates at this stage. By the time our youngsters reach their senior high school year, most have fully developed, have had physical contact of a sexual nature, and are continuing their struggle to learn socially approved outlets for sexual arousal.

Since the adolescent growth spurt is at its peak for boys later than it is for girls (there is usually a two-year difference), your daughter will begin to find "older" boys interesting at about the time she approaches her fourteenth or fifteenth year and will begin to "outgrow" the young fellows with whom she has attended school. It is at this time that her interest in or commitment to specific career goals will be most severely tested.

UNDERSTANDING YOUR DAUGHTER'S CAREER CHOICES

A substantial number of professionally successful women indicated that their career choices had been made extremely early in their lives—indeed, before twelve years of age by approximately 20 percent of the dentists, attorneys, and physicians in the New York University study. Furthermore, an additional 40 percent of the dentists, 30 percent of the lawyers, and 37 percent of the doctors had verbalized commitment to their intended professional fields *before they were fourteen*. Finally, 80 percent of the dentists, 51 percent of the attorneys, 66 percent of the physicians, 33 percent of the educational administrators, and 71 percent of the nursing administrators had made their career determinations *prior to college*.[5]

In this and other studies of developing career aspirations among women who became professional in a heretofore male province, early commitment to professional involvement and high parental expectations for their daughters, together with their continuing encouragement toward higher education and graduate school, were reported by all who had attained their career of choice.

If you would like to prepare your daughter, so that she is inclined toward and capable of becoming a professional woman, you should make your expectations known to her very early in her life. Suggestions for ways of doing this have been made throughout the text and include (a) continuing encouragement and praise, (b) the development of independence skills, (c) indications that you *expect* her to attend and complete college and to continue into graduate school, and (d) the development of strong social and humanitarian values of service and contribution for the benefit of others.

It is important that you understand that parents should *not* try to select the specific profession into which they hope their daughter will enter; that is the choice that must (and should) be made by their daughters. Suggestions may be offered if they are appropriate, but it must be understood that they are only alternatives. For example, a daughter who speaks well and enjoys verbal combat might be advised, "You'd make an effective attorney!" whereas one who enjoys caring for wounded pets could be told, "Since you love animals so much, you might be an excellent veterinarian!" Other than those suggestive comments, permit your daughter to choose her own profession.

In view of the data, begin early—when she is two, or three. Provide many interactions with professional women during her elementary school years and continuing into adolescence, particularly if no career commitments have been evidenced. Don't stop, because even though a large proportion of professional women actually made their career selections as young girls, choices for some continue to be made during the difficult adolescent years and into college.

However, parents should note that the younger their daughter is, the easier it is to influence her choice of a life style. Her junior high school and high school years are so fraught with physical, emotional, and socially engendered problems that she may not be able to concentrate very seriously on future career plans at that stage—although some do. In addition, as indicated previously, these years appear to be characterized by peer influences and a need for assertion. Therefore, it would seem that the period between eleven and sixteen—depending on the individual child—might be difficult for parents to be able to *launch* a successful program for developing career interests in their young daughters. They can, however, reinforce previously introduced concepts.

When your daughter reaches the sixteen-through-nineteen-year-old phase, she will have definite responsibility for making decisions concerned with her post-high school education. She will, again, be willing to accept your advice for important career, economic, and perhaps marital decisions. And, if she has maintained her academic interests, she certainly should be susceptible to continuing encouragement toward higher education and a profession.

This chapter has highlighted the experiences of many young girls as they struggle to establish their own uniqueness during their very difficult adolescent years. If you find that your daughter does not match the general description, if she does not experience the tensions or problems described herein, continue to encourage her academic excellence. Provide her with many opportunities in which to meet professional women, be specific about the level of expectations that you have for her, and praise her emotional stability—for you are a very fortunate parent, indeed!

TEACHING YOUR DAUGHTER TO COPE WITH AND CONTROL HER FUTURE THROUGH THE CONTINUING DEVELOPMENT OF THINKING SKILLS

Turning from social growth to the expansion of thinking skills, these are important exploratory years in which you can take positive advantage of your daughter's need to become increasingly independent and "her own person," for at this age she will exhibit boundless energy and enthusiasm—in between her moments of irritation and rebellion. She should be able to try out new ideas, to project herself into possible future roles, to fantasize alternative career routes, and to begin to measure her interests and abilities as they relate to the ways in which she can help people or improve society.

You will recall that the development of values, wherein women want to be of assistance to others and/or society, appears to be related directly to the development of their professional aspirations. Since the major way in which families seem able to influence their children during the early stage of adolescence is through the expansion of values, this is the time to capitalize on your daughter's natural interest in human relationships. In addition to creative daydreaming (tempered by a close hold on reality), your daughter should begin to learn how to analyze, apply, and use the knowledge she is gaining to solve problems and to make decisions. As she learns to control the environment and events through thinking skills, she will begin to plan, to cope with contingencies that arise, and to complete those plans, and thus to control her own future directions and goals.

Provide your daughter with many opportunities to climb through the various levels of thinking. Use the following samples to develop activities, experiences, and challenges to foster her ability to:

1. Recall and use knowledge.
2. Research and differentiate among facts.
3. Deduce and report.
4. Analyze and synthesize.
5. Conclude and elaborate on what she observed or found.
6. Set priorities and predict outcomes.
7. Solve problems or recommend solutions.
8. Plan and create new approaches.

As items of concern to her are brought to your attention, use them as a basis for expanding the thinking skills she has already developed. For example, if your daughter were to express concern about her figure or complexion, or if she were to describe to you how certain students are mistreating others, you could use the following (or similar) learning and thinking activities to enhance her growth and development as a successful, independent person:

1. Recall and use of knowledge.
- *Find* and *circle* all the nutritious foods in the Sunday paper.
- *Collect* such pictures and paste them together on charts to display balanced breakfast and lunches that could be eaten in school, and dinners.
- *Define* "natural" foods; list ten.
- *Identify* the additives listed on various food packages.
or
- *List* the things that the students who are *not* being bothered by the "bullies" might do to help the ones who are.
- *Itemize* what the students who *are* being bullied could do.

- *State* all the reasons that you can think of that might explain why certain students are bullying others.
- *Point out* the characteristics of the students who are doing the bullying. How are they doing on tests and report cards? What is their language like? What do you know about their parents? About their homes? About their brothers or sisters? About their friends? About their physical size?

Other verbs to use in this category include: connect, duplicate, recognize, repeat, sort, state, tell, underline, and so on.

2. Research and differentiate among facts.
- *Locate* information on balanced meals and their effect on your health, figure, complexion, or weight.
- *Classify* breakfast foods according to their vitamin, mineral, protein, carbohydrate, and calorie content.
- *Explain* the importance to you of eating a full and nutritious breakfast.

or
- *Suggest the reasons for* some students bullying other students.
- *Paraphrase* the things that the bullies actually say to the students that they are bothering.
- *Discriminate between* "kidding around" and "bullying."

Other verbs to use in this category include: compute, measure, say in your own words, or produce.

3. Deduce and report findings.
- *Investigate* the effects of cholesterol on the health and well-being of adults who are overweight.
- *Report* your findings to the family in the form of a television "special program."
- *Order* the foods with high cholesterol content from the most "criminal" to "moderate offender."

or
- *Gather data* on the kinds of students that the bullies seem to bother.
- *Illustrate* (graphically, verbally, or in writing) the things that bullies do.
- *Keep a record* of the people whom the bullies are bothering, the dates when each incident occurs, what is actually said and done, and who is present at the time.

Other verbs to use in this category include: give evidence for, find more about, omit, order, or present.

4. Analyze and synthesize data.
- *Compare* the cost of a nutritious breakfast with the cost of your typical morning snack.
- *Contrast* the amount of protein in highly advertised sugared cereal with the amount found in natural cereals.
- *Synthesize* the advertising techniques used to "sell" sugared cereals on television.

or

- *Interpret* what you already know about bullies to explain why they behave the way they do.
- *Justify* "telling on" the bullies to get help for the students they bother.
- *Organize* a campaign against the bullies in your class or grade.

Other verbs to use in this category include: find the central theme, identify the major ideas, rearrange, or generalize.

5. Conclude and elaborate on what you observed or found
- *Elaborate* on the value of eating three balanced meals and the disadvantages of "snacking."
- *Prove* beyond reasonable doubt that "one is what she eats."
- *Identify* the variables that would affect a person's weight gain or loss as she dieted or the ways in which a diet may affect a person's complexion.

or

- *Defend* a person's right and obligation to get help from authorities when people are being bullied.
- *Document* how people who "get away with" bullying others continue offending innocent persons.
- *Discover* at least three ways in which to help people who are being bullied and who are not able to help themselves.

Other verbs to use in this category include: critique, evaluate, expand, or extend.

6. Set priorities and predict outcomes
- *Rank* the foods you ate today in order of their importance to your general health, growth, energy levels, skin, eyes, bones, and blood.
- *Predict* the effects of a diet that: (a) reduces weight too quickly, (b) removes protein and minerals for an extended period of time, or (c) multiplies the level of protein intake.
- *Project* the results of eating three balanced meals for the rest of your teen years.

or

- *Develop some guidelines* for knowing when, and when not to alert authorities to incidents where people are being bullied.

- *Infer the results* of having alerted the school authorities to bullies and the students they have been bothering.
- *Lay the ground rules for* behavior in school and get a group of students to sign a petition in support of having the school authorities see that the rules are followed by all.

Other verbs to use in this category include: state the results or outcomes, establish criteria for, or develop a continuum.

7. Solve problems or recommend solutions

- *Design an experiment* to increase your energy on weekends.
- *Consider four alternative methods* of increasing our nutritional intake without increasing the family budget.
- *Formulate* a menu for one month's meals that will be both nutritious and appealing to the family's taste.

or

- *Recommend* some alternative courses of action that the school authorities might take to protect people against bullies.
- *Critically discuss* the problems related to bullies in school with friends of yours, your teacher, and the school authorities.
- Get the school authorities or the school Student Organization to *improve the procedures* whereby people who need help can get it quickly and without drawing attention to themselves.

Other verbs to use in this category include: hypothesize, prepare a model, improve the process or skills, and suggest improvements.

8. Plan projects and create new approaches

- *Brainstorm*[6] new types of food, recipes, and meals to try; *obtain concensus* on which to try first.
- *Hold a contest* to develop the most attractive, nutritious meals.
- *Award* a "Chef-of-the-Month" hat to the family member with the best idea for a delicious, nutritious dessert under two hundred calories.

or

- *Establish some time lines* for committees and/or individuals to
  a. *Develop and submit a new list of procedures* whereby people in school who need assistance can get it quickly and without drawing attention to themselves.
  b. Get the school authorities to *place on the "drawing board"* plans for eliminating or dealing with bullies and for reducing their impact.
  c. Write a "letter to the editor" of your local newspaper requesting parental assistance with handling the bullies in school and get at least fifty students to sign it. Mail the letter or, better still, take it to the newspaper office, accompanied by a large group of classmates.

Other verbs to use in this category include: design, implement, carry through, simulate[7], role-play[8], or set tasks.

With your daughter, move through these various levels of thinking in several areas, such as her choice of possible professional careers, her future, composition work, reading comprehension, family problems, raising daughters, federal and local government procedures, social problems, such as over-population, pollution, human relationships, poverty, the future of large cities, and other issues that require critical analyses. These suggested activities and experiences will aid her immeasurably in becoming a successful professional person.

7.
What to Do during the Difficult High School Years: Ages Fifteen through Eighteen

SELF ACTUALIZATION FOR GIRLS—TELLING IT THE WAY IT IS

The terrible middle school or junior high school years (ages eleven through fourteen) are followed by the even more difficult high school years. Girls rebel against their mothers and play up to their fathers (sometimes). They may act like mature angels with some friends and adults and like possessed creatures in their own homes. They have adult insights into their behavior at times but, like young children, may manifest uncontrolled emotions at others. They usually experience joyous "ups" and deep "lows." They resent authority figures but "lord it over" their younger siblings. Do not despair; most daughters emerge from these patterns as they grope toward a sense of their own identity and beginning self-fulfillment.

One of the more effective things you can do to begin to help her in this regard is to introduce topics such as "self-fulfillment" or "happiness" at the dinner table. (Better still, discuss this kind of thing *after* dinner instead of turning on the TV.) You will improve your relationships with her, because you will demonstrate caring and because the topic is likely to be of interest to her.

You might begin by mentioning the inner sense of direction or purpose that many adult men seem to have and the recent awakening of some women to the nature of their essentially domestic restrictive lives. For example, Betty Friedan called it "the problem that has no name." In the now classic *The*

Feminine Mystique, women are described as searching for love, for sexual satisfaction, for cohesiveness in their daily living patterns, and for a sense of personal identity. Our society tends to classify a woman as her children's mother, her husband's wife, her parent's daughter—but rarely as a unique, contributing individual. Friedan concludes that "We can no longer ignore that voice within women that says, 'I want something more than my husband and my children and my home.' "[1] The discussion might encourage your daughter to read Friedan, Maslow, Dyer, and other authors noted in the references of this book who have insights into self-realization.

Picasso was fond of telling about his mother's encouragement when he was young. She would tell him that he could be anything he wanted to be—a general, an architect, an engineer. "So, I became Picasso, the painter!" he explained. That single statement describes the ego strength and purpose that his mother's faith in his ability engendered in Picasso and should be noted by parents as one important way to develop self-confidence in children —particularly in daughters. They, too, can become what they choose to be. Certainly their belief in their own ability is essential to their development; their lack of it can only provide frustrating plateaus and set-backs.

Many definitions and terms have been used to describe "self-fulfillment." Professor Abraham H. Maslow studied people with high self-esteem and self-realization who exhibited no evidence of neurosis or more serious personality problems. He included public figures from the past and present, college students, and some older folks who were successful in various fields. Self-fulfillment, or "self-actualization," as he defined it, involves the full use and exploitation of one's personal talents, capacity, and potential. Such people seem to be continually involved in a variety of activities that challenge their intellectual and creative abilities. They are developing to *their* maximum capability. It appears to be the ongoing utilization and expansion of a person's intellectual, artistic, and/or physical talents in fulfillment of a mission (or "call," fate, destiny, or vocation) that seems to bring individuals a tremendous sense of satisfaction and accomplishment. In addition, the acceptance of each ". . . person's own intrinsic nature, as an unceasing trend toward unity, integration, or synergy within the person"[2] tends to lead toward a feeling of self-worth without guilt for participating in tasks we enjoy.

As might be expected, self-actualizing people are committed, have a sense of purpose in life, and rise above the petty details of everyday living. Maslow identified very few self-actualized women in his study (Eleanor Roosevelt and Jane Addams were the only two public figures), which suggests that either his research was limited or that the full use and realization of potential has been difficult, if not impossible, for many women in this society.

Maslow and others also concluded that self-actualizing partners take pride in each other's achievements and, as a consequence, find that both their individual and shared self-renewal and joy in living increases. Sexual activity, contrary to the myth concerning diminishing returns with the same partner, grows more fulfilling and gratifying, as each increases his and her sense of self. Then love can become a gift that is given and received in greater quality and measure.

High school girls often respond favorably to discussions of this type. Many are acutely aware of adult relationships and the personality strength of their parents and other adults. Once you have initiated a general discussion about self-actualization, you might cooperatively develop some personal charts based on your daughter's needs and goals as she views her life ahead. Maslow's hierarchy of needs[3] presents an ideal framework for examining one's present feelings and future goals.

People throughout history or within a single lifetime move through this hierarchy, from basic needs toward self-actualization:

Baby to Womanhood	Daughter's Self-actualization Path
5. Self-actualization	
4. Esteem (Ego-Status)	
3. Love (Belongingness)	
2. Safety (Maintenance)	
1. Basic (Physiological)	

Maslow's hierarchy of needs with blank spaces for you and your daughter to complete for her.

Example: One family responded to the hierarchy chart in the following manner. This girl is attitudinally well on her way to becoming a successful attorney.

Needs from baby to womanhood	Hierarchy	My self-actualization path
Growth, activity, achievement, happiness, leadership, contribution, creativity, self-understanding.	5	Political office or federal judge. Introduction of laws to aid women. Self and peer recognition; author of book on legal rights of women.
Organization memberships. recognition, titles, family roles and functions.	4	Trial attorney, judge, official of local professional organization, committee chairman, informal leader.
Sweetheart, lover, mate, loved ones.	3	Husband and children—later; professional career gatherings, conventions, committees.

Medical help, fire and police protection, insurance of various types.	2	Law career with sought-after skills, license to practice.
Food, shelter, clothing.	1	College, job, salary.

A second activity might involve a listing and discussion of the characteristics that she believes are representative of a self-actualizing person. You will be surprised to find that many daughters enjoy talking about the future, their aspirations, their views of happiness, and their own fulfillment. This may be an ideal time for her to begin to understand her own value as an individual and the essential need for each person to have an identity of her (his) own. You might read and discuss a short story by James Joyce, titled "Clay," about the friend of a family, whose unfulfilling existence is based solely on her doing things for the befriended family. She has no identity of her own and is molded and shaped by their needs. One night, while playing a game of divination she is assigned the word "Clay." Everyone in the room stops with instant awareness that the word symbolizes the heroine's existence; everyone, that is, except the poor, overly malleable woman about whom the story is written.

Now examine Maslow's compilation of thirteen characteristics of the self-actualizing person[4] with your daughter. Interpreting these qualities and associating them with actual examples from her experiences or her own observations of others will build your daughter's awareness of those traits she should develop in her own personality. Assure her that her own list may be as accurate for her at this stage of her life as Maslow's list is for accomplished adults.

Superior perception of reality.   This would include a knowledge of human weaknesses and strengths, a clear perception of events as they are, an understanding of people's motivations (both apparent and underlying), and an analysis of her own niche in the total environment.

Examples:

Daughter: Why did the teacher "put me down" in front of my friends?

Parent's questions: Why did his remarks upset you?

Do you feel insecure in the face of an honest challenge?

Exactly what did he say?

Does he have personality weaknesses?

Do you think that you upset him?

Daughter: What do you need to do to become a doctor?

Parent's questions: Would certain courses be necessary?

Would an independent study project at a local hospital give you a better idea than we could?

Would it be a good idea to speak to Dr. Epstein about that?

Increased acceptance of self, of others, of nature.   Your daughter should learn to accept herself, her friends, her family and those with whom she comes into contact realistically. The nature of life and death should also be considered and accepted.

Examples:

Daughter: Don't I look fat in this outfit?

Parent's questions: Do you *really* think you look fat? If you do, what are you planning to do about it?

Do you think it might be those clothes?

Are you feeling insecure?

Are you accenting your best features?

Are you seeking sympathy—or approval?

What don't you like about the way you look?

Daughter: Why can't they (her friends) ever do what *I* want?

Parent's questions: Do you want the same things that they want?

Are you different kinds of people?

Do you use the wrong approach with them?

Do you consider their individuality?

Are they less flexible than you?

Increased spontaneity. An active and eager personality spontaneously takes advantage of opportunities or situations that occur. Sometimes inactivity itself should spur action on a new project.

Examples:

Daughter: What can I do today?

Parent's questions: Why not go to ————?

Would ———— interest you?

Is there anything special you would like to try?

I understand that our local Congresswoman is speaking at the Town Club, and I wanted to attend. Would you like to join me?

Why not list all the possibilities of interest and then select the ones you like most?

Daughter: Where is my _____(any possession)_____ ?

Parent's questions: Can you substitute something else for it?

Have you looked where it should *not* be?

Do you need more storage space?

Do you want help in organizing your room?

Increase in problem centering (and solving). Too many people bemoan their fate and gain some sort of emotional solace in describing their problems, hurt feelings, and illnesses. They become "professional" complainers. To the contrary, however, life is a beautiful challenge! It is also a series of problems to be solved, a set of opportunities to be seized, and a sequence of goals to be realized through planning and doing.

Examples:

Daughter: Everybody's got a car! I want one too!

Parent's questions: Are you planning to save for one?

What jobs are available after school?

Could you save toward a car this summer?

What skills do you have that will help you to earn money toward a car?

Do you know anyone who would give you a job?

Have you been to the job center? Have you looked in the "Help Wanted" section of the paper?

Increased detachment and desire for privacy. "People who always need people" are not "the luckiest people in the world." We all need to be alone at times, to reflect on events and ourselves, to meditate, to become completely in contact with our own sense of being.

Examples:

Daughter: Why don't I want to go to that party?

Parent's questions: Is it the people, or do you want a "break" from conversation with your friends?

Do you try to plan time alone or do you always join people when they invite you to do so?

Have you ever tried being alone with a sunset? Or your thoughts?

Have you ever gone into a house of worship when no services are being conducted?

Daughter: Why does everyone make so much noise when I'm trying to do homework?

Parent's questions: Would more privacy help?

Can we rearrange your room, so that the sound does not carry so much?

Can we do something to create a study area in the basement? The attic? A closet?

Can you work at the library?

Increased autonomy and resistance to inculturation. Relatives and friends usually mean well, but they are, themselves, victims of cultural patterns. Their views of society and its mores often are stereotyped. They expect everyone, especially young people, to behave and react as they do. Their expectations may deprive youthful individuals of their autonomy and uniqueness.

Examples:

Daughter: Everybody's becoming engaged! Or getting married!

Parent's questions: Why are they tying themselves down so early?

Are they able to support themselves?

Are they ready to choose the person they want to live with for the rest of their lives?

Is marriage for everyone?

Are they giving up college?

Are they aware of the divorce statistics concerning youthful marriages?

Daughter: Mary's going to work and support John through college.

Parent's questions: Why? Is she less important than John?

Doesn't she want a college education?

Doesn't she want to be a professional?

Does she realize that she'll probably work at a menial job and for little pay? And that she'll be doomed to remain in the unskilled labor market?

Greater freshness of appreciation and richness of emotional reaction. Learning and growing help to build appreciation and deeper emotional satisfactions. The ability to stop, to observe, to use all of the senses in admiring and enjoying the world can be achieved through conscious effort and continuing awareness. The beauty of art or music can touch one's emotions deeply as an expression and extension of the artist's feelings.

Examples:

Daughter: How can I become more aware of life and the world of beauty?

Parent's questions: Why don't you start your own "whetstone club"—a group that meets to sharpen each other's awareness, appreciations, and experiences?

Has any specific event ever touched you deeply? Can you describe it—perhaps on tape or in poetry? Could it be replicated? How?

Can you compare the beauty of something that impressed you with another phenomenon?

Have you ever spoken to people involved in consciousness-raising? Or deeply religious experiences? Why not invite someone like that to address a group at the high school?

Higher frequency of peak experiences. Peak experiences approach perfection. They result in exhilaration and positive well-being that cannot be achieved in any other way. A great artist reaches this state when he views his work and recognizes that he has completed a masterpiece; an athlete, when he achieves a perfect combination of concentration, relaxation, and controlled tension that results in a seemingly effortless new world record; a writer, when the words seem to leap and flow from the typewriter as if they almost had a life of their own; lovers, when they soar to heights of physical pleasure that seem to carry them out of and above the physical world, as two who blend together into "one" perfect being in euphoric harmony.

Example:

Daughter: How can I have a peak experience? Aren't they reserved for very sensitive people?

Parent's questions: Don't all humans have emotions and the potential to achieve?

Have you ever reached beyond your grasp—and succeeded?

Do you know what it feels like to do something extremely well?

Have you ever felt exultation or a feeling of wonder at a beautiful natural sight? Or a particularly moving concert or recording? Or a painting?

Daughter: How can I learn more about peak experiences?

Parent's questions: Have you read anything by Abraham Maslow?

Have you read *Your Erroneous Zones* by Wayne Dyer?

Have you read biographies, autobiographies, or other accounts of the lives of Madame Curie, Eleanor Roosevelt, or Jane Addams?

Why not ask your English teacher or the librarian to recommend writings (including poetry) that describe the feelings of accomplishment and joy that peak experiences suggest?

Increased identification with the human species. Compassion for others, empathy with their problems, awareness of one's mortality, humanness and sensitivity to events that affect other people are part of your daughter's increased identification with the human species.
Examples:
Daughter: Why are we so involved with the problems of people in other parts of the world?
Parent's questions: Do they feel pain and hunger as we do?

Are their lives intertwined with ours in any way?

Would you want them to be concerned about us, if the situation were reversed?
Daughter: What is it like to be old? Or really poor?
Parent's questions: Can you form a group of volunteers and visit a senior citizen center? Or a Welfare Office?

Do the local hospitals need part-time volunteers?

Could you contribute some of your time to helping elderly people in our neighborhood?

Changed or improved interpersonal relations. Young girls who actively begin to pursue their own autonomy often fall prey to self-interests which exclude concern for others. This behavior usually results in confrontations, accusations, and recriminations that serve no constructive purpose. The ability to relate and interact positively with others is a manifestation of growth.
Examples:
Daughter: How can I understand someone better?
Parent's questions: Have you ever role-played that you were the other person?

Have you ever asked her (him) to describe what she (he) feels? And why? Do you listen intently?
Daughter: How can I learn to persuade or influence people without manipulating them?
Parent's questions: Do you know how to recognize a person's values or "frame of reference"?

Have you learned how to appraise background and experience?

Do you know how to ask "open-ended questions" and to listen objectively?

Have you considered what the "pay-off" or rewards would be to *them* if they agreed with you?

Daughter: How can I stop you from "ordering me around"?

Parent's questions: Have you ever asked for a family council?

Have you thought of any suggestions?

Can you suggest a compromise? Or alternative?

Would you like to be part of our decision-making process?

Greatly increased creativeness. Creativeness is at least partly learned. It can emerge from opportunities and experiences which allow your daughter to try something new. Options and alternative routes should be suggested to build confidence in creative arts.

Examples:

Daughter: I just can't think of an idea for a composition that's due tomorrow!

Parent's questions: [It will *not* help to ask why she waited for the last minute to begin!] Have you tried brainstorming some possible ideas? [Jotting down thoughts as they "pop" into your head and then analyzing them.]

Can you think of anything especially zany that would make it a humorous story? Sad? Frightening? Anger-provoking?

How about taking a fifteen minute "break" and getting it completely out of your mind? *Then* attack it with fresh thoughts!

How about pretending that you are someone else? Could you write the composition from *their* point of view? Based on *their* experiences?

Improved changes in the value system. Values can and should become broader, deeper, and more meaningful as your daughter grows. Contributing to others, learning, growing, caring, and helping to improve society are a few of the higher values.

Examples:

Daughter: How do you deal with people who are selfish or who live for themselves?

Parent's questions: Have you confronted them with specific examples of their own behavior?

Have you considered avoiding them and finding people who are more caring?

Have you tried to build their egos with supportive, caring behavior of your own?

To what extent is living for yourself selfish? Can it be a positive way of living?

Is it possible to "do your own thing" and be unselfish?

At a later date, follow these discussions with a review of some practical and real situations from the lives of people who appear to have some of the characteristics Maslow enumerated. Ask her to describe exactly what she would like her life to be like ten years into the future. What would she like to be doing, how would she like to be living, and what would she want to be (career-wise) if a genie told her she could be anything she wanted to be. Analyze with her the consequences and likely results of various choices. Examine the relationships (if any) between past events and her aspirations and build her knowledge of self and confidence to deal with the world as a strong and independent person.

Reduce your daughter's dependence on others by explaining that, with forethought and striving, she can become the kind of adult she would like to be. Assure her that her ultimate responsibility is really to herself—to her own happiness and self-actualization. As a maturing individual, she will be better able to cope, to love, and to accept love, recognizing that it is emotionally healthy to consider her own dreams and hopes first when deciding on important career and life plans. As she gains self-esteem and confidence, she will be less and less likely to be intimidated by society, peers, her future lover(s), or a demanding husband or child.

Consider this next list of ten basic suggestions that might aid your daughter in reaching a dynamic state of fulfillment. Discuss these together. Analyze examples of each suggestion in literature, in the media, and in your experiences. Help her to develop her personal self-actualization goals.

Love life and develop enthusiasm for living. Zorba the Greek lived and breathed life every minute. His feelings and emotions were so powerful that he danced to express himself whether he was reacting to tragic events *or* happy ones. Nor is age a barrier to living and loving. Colette, the French novelist, who also lived life to the fullest, wrote, on her eightieth birthday: "If only one were fifty-eight, because at that time one is still desired and full of hope for the future." But do not wait to become eighty or fifty-eight to learn about the joy of living:

> I would I were alive again
> to kiss the fingers of the rain.
> To drink into my eyes the shine
> of every slanting silver line,
> To catch the freshened, fragrant breeze
> From drenched and dripping apple trees.
> *Renascence (1917)*
> *Edna St. Vincent Millay*

Think positively about your continuing growth and accomplishments. As she moves through life, your daughter will hear people say, "If only I could live my life over," or, "If only I had a lucky break." Perhaps she'll hear, "those were the days." She probably knows that right now is where reality is, and what she does now affects the future. Remind her that doers seem to grow happier and younger by the year. Doers seem to *make* things happen. Doers enjoy their work and have positive outlooks concerning their tasks. Three young female lab assistants at a medical research division of a large drug firm were asked what they were doing. The first replied rather curtly, "Earning a living"; the second was more pleasant and replied, "Mixing these chemicals, according to instructions left for me this morning." The third smiled, then almost bubbled, as she replied, with eyes aglow, "I'm helping to find a cure for cancer!" Urge her to consider the three employees who are, perhaps, similarly qualified. Which one would your daughter employ? And why?

Learn to cope with new situations and problems. There seem to be "winners" and "losers" and "pillars" and "leaners" in life. Which is your daughter? Which will she become? Ask her to consider these two approaches to living and decide which pattern she would like to follow:

Life is an adventure in time. Each of us experiences valleys and hills, but learning both to climb and to coast is important. Every fork in the road brings the excitement of choice and the reward of new people and places, if we follow one of the paths. Every day (and night) brings new opportunities to live, if we stride forward with confidence and expectation.

Now contrast this positive approach with the "Life is a chamber of horrors" personality. These people might respond with: "Living is surviving, if you're lucky. If I climbed a hill, I would fall down the wrong side and break an ankle. I'm afraid to turn a corner—why meet trouble head-on? Every time I reach a fork in the road and make a decision, I choose the path with all the rocks, holes, and mud. And I wake up every morning with a headache, thinking about the problems to come. Sleeping is no bargain either . . . I have nightmares."

List some people you both know personally who fit into these categories; then do the same for persons in public office, the arts, and so on.

Constantly set new goals and remember that happiness is a process, not a product. Happiness is not just reaching an airport terminal; it's a way of traveling. Once you've achieved a destination or goal, establish another, and another. Even Shangri-la has entered our language as a quest, not a place. The Man of LaMancha speaks of his "glorious quest" or an "impossible dream." He is joyful in its pursuit. Coco Chanel, the famous French designer, once said that life was like a toboggan ride—fast and furious. The excitement and joy, however, is always ahead, so "never look back!" Explore this philosophy with her.

Achieve inner peace. The calmness of inner peace is not easy to define, but she will find it easy to achieve when she realizes that everyone has "ups and downs;" that problems should be dealt with immediately, and not be put off; that problems are easier to solve if discussed with loved ones or close friends; that change may be for the better and at least merits her consideration; and that problems are not as serious as they seem at the moment, when compared against the larger scheme of things and personal long-range goals.

Love your career and appreciate its rewards. Urge that she attempt to obtain work in an area of deep interest to her. Help her to consider the many rewards of a profession, not just the money. Focus on her self-worth, sense of identity, recognition, contribution to others, self-growth, and achievement.

Achieve pleasure in your avocations. Time should be used to live —to plan, to go, to do, to learn, to taste life, and to relax, too. One wise woman we know devotes spare time during each year to a new area of interest. If she knows nothing about photography, she learns all she can about it for one full year and enjoys that hobby ever after. Sketching and tennis are two more of her self-initiated and continuing pleasures and interests. Select objectives like these for you and your daughter, now!

Achieve prestige, recognition, and status in keeping with your changing goals. Prestige is the estimation others will have of your daughter. Recognition is the expression of that estimation to her and for her. Status is the place she will have in life: her career, her home, her family, her standing. Her changing aspirations will be closely related to the way she feels about herself and the active way in which she approaches living and doing. She should not accept the views of others when estimating these standards; their value should be determined by her. You might discuss these standards in relationship to her goals.

Contribute to the lives of others. Much has been written about our one life and the need to value what we do with it. Perhaps one of the most noble statements on the need *to do* for others, attributed to Etienne de Gullet (1773–1855), is, "I shall pass through this world but once. If, therefore, there be any kindness I can show, or any good thing I can do, let me do it now; let me not defer or neglect it, for I shall not pass this way again." It is not difficult to aid others, and the rewards of self-growth and satisfaction in such endeavors will contribute substantially to your daughter's self-actualization. Decide on a voluntary project or cause for both of you and do it!

Achieve and experience physical, emotional, and mature love for a spouse. Early marriages are not advocated, because the statistics on the failures of early marriages are sobering and frightening. Encourage your daughter to delay marriage until she completes her education, becomes involved in a career, and finds someone with similar interests and goals. The maturity that she will have gained, by virtue of her increased age and educational and career experiences, will aid her to select a partner to whom she will be well suited. Waiting is no guarantee of marital happiness, but the likelihood increases with age and maturity.

It is critical that you build awareness of self-actualization principles in your daughter early. Negative attitudes and forces in society are difficult to overcome, once they have had an impact. Slanted statements, misrepresentative procedures, and stereotypes are everywhere—even in the guidance offices of your daughter's high school—and it is important, therefore, that she feel secure about her intended life directions and her ability to accomplish her self-selected goals before she needs to obtain college or career advice from others.

THE LACK OF APPROPRIATE CAREER GUIDANCE IN HIGH SCHOOLS

Institutional constraints function like invisible strings that control puppets, and high school guidance department "services" are no exception. Guidance counselors, themselves, are the victims of stereotypical attitudes and too often impose restrictive forces on girls through the reinforcement of time-encrusted expectations of female roles and performance, Few students will dare to deviate from the expectations required of them by their counselors, for the majority see insistence on their individual preferences as producing "hassles" (unpleasant confrontations) that are ultimately counterproductive (they will not get praising letters of recommendation) or time-consuming.

Parents should be very concerned about the large number of girls who lose their motivation to study medicine, law, dentistry, engineering, or architecture during the high school years and should recognize that changes in vocational motivation can often be traced directly to the offices of school guidance counselors—who are sometimes outdated in their own expectations for women and are, in addition, lackluster and inadequate.[5] Those counselors who are able and inspiring are trapped by local expectations to get everyone into college; personal and career guidance and preparation are often neglected.

Guidance personnel should be able to detect signs of interest in the professions among girls and should encourage them—even when social pressure or difficulty with a particular subject causes a student to consider an easier path. Indeed, counselors should *develop* such interests in girls and open their horizons to careers that they never may have considered. Instead, in most high schools, counselors generally are misused as glorified clerical assistants who complete forms and schedules. They have a reputation among sophisticated students as being "behind the times," both in information and attitude, and for being inadequate as dynamic role models. It is not uncommon in high schools to have an ex–physical-education teacher or other subject area specialist become a counselor, and academically oriented students are quick to dismiss their advice because of their conspicuous lack of training in the student's prospective field, as well as their lack of empathy with student interests, aspirations, or uncertainty.

The report of the President's Commission on the Status of Women maintains:

> In quality as well as quantity, counseling is at present wholly inadequate. The recommended ratio of full-time guidance staff to secondary school students is 1 to 300; the actual ratio is 1 to 550, with great variation among regions and shortages greatest in low-income areas. Many counselors do not meet recommended standards of either the United States Employment Service or the professional associations in

the field. *Far too few have had supervised practice in counseling women.* Counseling based on obsolete assumptions is routine at best; at worst, it is dangerous.[6]

In large schools where vocational guidance and college placement are divided among two or more persons, college advisors assume the responsibility for all youngsters considering applications to institutions of higher education. In upwardly mobile, affluent, or suburban areas where the majority of a school's senior class is college-bound, the heavy work load, even for dedicated personnel, makes it difficult to devote much time to true *guidance* functions, and most of the human interactions are essentially peripheral or perfunctory. The college placement advice given to young and often confused applicants usually centers about completing the required courses in sufficient numbers to facilitate acceptance. Concerns relating to whether the considered field is "appropriate" for women or responsive to future career changes and multiple life branches are frequently met either with indifference or negativism.

Carol Lopate recounts the story of a young girl who wanted information about the field of medicine. She had never spoken to her counselor, but she knocked on the office door and, after being seated, asked: "I was wondering if you could give me some information about becoming a doctor. I'm very interested in medicine as a career." The woman looked at her narrowly, questioned her concerning the grade she was in, and retorted, "Come back in a year or two; I can't be bothered now." When the youngster persisted, saying, "But I'm really interested. I just want to know what I'll have to do . . . ," she was interrupted with, "Well, if you're dying, I mean, I can pull you out of a class some day and have a chat with you. Write down your name on that sheet of paper."[7] The girl *never* heard from the woman.

This story is not unusual; many high school counselors respond similarly to students who express strong career interests at an early age—not realizing that career decisions for many are made *prior* to high school and that such choices usually evidence strong personal commitment. Furthermore, many counselors lean too far backward to overcome the "pushy parent" syndrome—a reaction against an affluent, aspiring society that tends to advocate college attendance for many youngsters who might prefer alternative pursuits. In effect, guidance personnel try to hold a rational check on the "college panic" which presses students, parents, and teachers alike into increasingly earlier career strategies. Without recognizing individual differences or the effect of *not* strengthening a girl's motivation, they prefer to see a student's interests broad and uncommitted, at least until a first sampling of various subjects in the college liberal arts program.

This generalized and delayed approach to choices may be appropriate for some individual students, especially those who are not ready for college or able to complete an advanced education. Refusal to discuss career aspirations, however, may be a misplaced kindness, at best, or a disastrous discouragement, at worst. Here's one account, reported by an intelligent seventeen-year-old student, that is not as atypical as it ought to be.

When completing applications for admission into college, the student was asked whether she wanted to be a teacher. She replied negatively, confiding that she had "always" wanted to enter into law. Her counselor frowned. "You'll come into contact with criminals and corrupt politicians," she warned. "That's no life for a girl!" (There's the stereotype emerging again). The young lady assured the advisor that her interests were in the area of corporate law and that she would undoubtedly be meeting very refined, accomplished gentlemen. (The student was more sophisticated than the adult and recognized the counselor's biases and limitations; the response was a "put on" to elicit her acceptance, so that her application forms would be processed quickly!) "Even so," the woman countered, "it's a very difficult field for a girl! You'll have a hard time beating out the many men in the field, and you'll have to give it up when you start having children!" Amicably, the youngster confided that her father was the senior partner in a well-established legal firm and that he was priming her to assume a junior partnership. "Oh, in that case," the woman rejoined, "you seem to have made your decision between a career and a normal life."

The insidious nature of the entire episode (let alone the last remark) is ameliorated by our personal knowledge of the young lady's level of maturity and her ability both to cope with the incident and to accept it humorously. The implications of such counseling for less astute aspirants are far-reaching and lead us to support John Henry Martin's proposal that perhaps guidance and psychological "services" should be *removed* from the schools altogether and incorporated into an independent community institution, perhaps called a Community Family Guidance Center.[8] The lack of sensitivity and responsiveness on the part of guidance persons to the personal, career, and school advisory needs of students—particularly girls—is one of the major reasons that professional counselors have become an endangered species. Declining enrollments, rising tax rates, high inflation, and resulting economic pressures on school boards have made guidance a program in jeopardy of elimination as an essential school program. Unless the *quality* of service improves, we would suggest that *career* counseling be conducted by practicing professionals in the field (preferably of the same sex!) and that *admissions* counseling become the responsibility of an intelligent, concerned *secretary*.

Only women *in* the so-called "masculine" professions are capable of describing for girls what being in those fields meant (to them) in terms of study, participation in an essentially male-dominated field, employment, and the combination of practice and marriage and/or motherhood. Even though one person's experiences would not identically parallel another's, women in the professions would be less likely to disparage a girl's hopes for professional involvement than would persons whose personal experiences keep them securely protected in a "feminine," relatively "secure" job. Psychologically, there is an emotional dichotomy for counselors that prevent them from recommending a high risk, personal independence career for girls when they had selected a low-risk, bureaucratically oriented, dependent role for themselves. Encouraging boys toward professions is a daily, totally accepted task; providing the same encouragement for girls is alien and foreign to the beliefs and values of too many counselors.

One anecdote that reveals a type of extreme bias in favor of boys should be included here. While visiting a low-socioeconomic urban high school in 1976, we heard the counselor describe a procedure used with Black "problem" boys in attendance. This was an "alternative school," considered the "last chance and final opportunity" for attending youngsters to earn a certificate. These students had either "dropped" or had been thrown out of "regular" schools throughout the city and were accepted only on the provision that they maintained attendance and acceptable behavior.

Because these youngsters had a low tolerance for academic studies and because most of them had short attention spans and strong mobility needs, opportunities were provided for them to participate in "out of school" experiences. Included in the wide range of activities were visits to police stations, courts, hospitals, clinics, building sites, and so on, so that they could interview and "get to know" practitioners in many fields at first hand. These community experiences were offered as a means of maintaining them in "school" but, in effect, served to stimulate and *develop* their interests in a variety of fields. The counselor proudly recited the names of students who, after having visited, met, and spoken with *attorneys, peace officers, physicians,* and *medical technicians,* had decided that *they* would pursue those fields and *become* what their role models had been! In this case non-achieving, delinquent students had been inspired to become policemen and attorneys and were interested in aspects of medical service. They were being *encouraged* by their school counselors in an exemplary and largely successful program. Now contrast this good approach for difficult male students with the typical high school program, where bright, conforming, and able female students are not provided with career guidance and are even discouraged from entertaining thoughts of professional careers.

Career decisions are made at varying times in the lives of women, but many research studies demonstrate that students entering into the professional areas show early decision patterns. The American Association of Medical Colleges study on the background of medical students revealed a *median* age of sixteen for both sexes "first thinking seriously of becoming a doctor."[9] This research confirms that 50 percent of the doctors had made a career choice prior to the third year of high school.

The New York University study asked the women in that professional sample to check the point in their education at which they had decided to pursue their chosen careers: Thirty-seven percent of the physicians, 40 percent of the dentists, 30 percent of the attorneys, 16 percent of the educators, and 26 percent of the nursing administrators reported that their decision had been made *prior* to high school, while an *additional* 29 percent of the doctors, 40 percent of the dentists, 21 percent of the lawyers, 17 percent of the educators, and 45 percent of the nurses said they had made theirs before entering college.[10]

In another study concerning decision points for careers, this one dealing with six successive classes of medical students at the University of Pennsylvania, Natalie Rugoff found a correlation between the age of decision among those students and their certainty of having chosen the career that best suited them. Of those students who had decided before fourteen, a far smaller proportion had seriously considered other careers than medicine; and the earlier the decision, the more certain was the student that medicine was "the only career that could really satisfy. . . ."[11]

The negative impact of inadequate high school counseling is reduced when youngsters make their career choices early and receive stimulation, encouragement, and direction at home and in their classes. A high school with an atmosphere of intellectual excellence and positive competition often can succeed with minimal vocational counseling by its staff, especially if trips are made to professional and vocational centers and associations and outside professional speakers are invited to speak to interested students. It is probable that contact with the concrete ideas and personalities of a specific profession will contribute more to the final decision than any amount of traditional counseling, which only can provide second- or third-hand information.[12]

More than 99 percent of the students in a science-oriented New York City high school attend college, and the majority of those graduates study and enter into science or related fields. The stimulation provided by the academically able student body, the science-centered curriculum, the middle-class background of the majority of students with its emphasis on professional success, and the elite spirit which the students *feel*, all make vocational counseling somewhat academic. Once students embrace intellectual and personal growth, motivation becomes natural and easily maintained.[13]

In approaching potential solutions to inadequate or inappropriate counseling for those girls who do not make an early choice or do not have the benefit of a specialized or highly challenging high school, both the poor and affluent socioeconomic groups present areas for concern, regarding girls' motivation toward professional aspirations. A lack of stimulation and encouragement in the home and at school contributes to the scarcity of female (as well as male) medical students from lower-class and rural areas. Although financial limitations contribute, an excerpt from The President's Commission on the Status of Women focuses directly on the situation:

On the high school level, many guidance counselors themselves need to broaden their concepts of realistic opportunities for the young Negro women who want to go to college or who are weighing that possibility. This is particularly true in the newly integrated high schools, where guidance for Negro youth often is based on misconception of the individual's capacities and abilities and a lack of knowledge of the accomplishments of Negro women and of probable social change.

The attitude of expectancy toward obtaining an education is crucial. When families and children have limited hopes as to future vocational possibilities, counselors also may believe that a girl or a boy has no chance for a particular type of job.[14]

Margaret Anderson, one example of an outstanding guidance counselor, describes her experiences working with disadvantaged Negro youngsters to encourage them into service professions (medicine, social welfare, or counseling). She began by imposing her belief that they *could* succeed on the students, their parents, faculty, and the community and continued by providing (through her personal determination) compensatory education and prodding for students who might never otherwise have succeeded.[15]

We have no doubt that aware and determined parents who have many years in which to help motivate their daughters (if they begin early) will succeed as well as or better than typical guidance personnel who first meet disadvantaged youngsters after the age at which many career decisions, appropriate or not, already have been made. Nevertheless, realistic self-image and confidence in one's ability to learn, grow, and aspire to the professions is the task of both parents and counselors for females raised in poverty.

The reverse of the problem encountered among impoverished students is found in middle-income and affluent areas. Many of these girls have not considered the possibility of having needs beyond the life style of their immediate family. Never having experienced financial pressures that, within bounds, could not be handled, these youngsters unrealistically feel that either their parents, grandparents, or future husbands will always care for and protect them. Many cannot envision their own participation in the job market and, having observed their mothers' involvement in their homes, leisure, sports, and certain volunteer activities, they do not make the transference from the world they have known to the one they may have to occupy in the future.

No one acquaints these youngsters with the research that describes how technology has reduced homemaking to a routinized, dull occupation that is satisfying to only a small segment of the population. Counselors rarely advise them of the mental stimulation they will need for their own growth, to keep pace with their husbands' maturation, and to establish a role model for their children. And, certainly, no one has discussed with them soberly the constantly rising divorce statistics that suggest that they will undoubtedly spend twenty-five years or more of their lives earning an income, [16] whether single, married, or remarried.

The lack of effective counseling for both our poor *and* affluent daughters is serious; professional aspirations must be encouraged among our able girls, opportunities must be provided for their achievement, and encouragement must be given to their budding interests, so that they may live productively and well in a world that will be very different from the one in which they grew up.

Individual states are in the process of adopting specific procedures to implement Title IX of the Education Amendments of 1972, which prohibits sex discrimination in federally assisted education programs. This legislation prevents people in the United States from being excluded from particpation in, being denied the benefits of, or being subjected to discrimination in any education program or activity. The rules specifically require that materials used for appraising or counseling students may not differ on the basis of sex, and, furthermore, The National Institute of Education (NIE) stipulates that, within the context of career guidance, sex bias is defined as any factor that might influence a person to limit (or might cause others to limit) his or her considerations of a career, solely on the basis of gender. Until Title IX statutes are fully implemented, parents must accept the responsibility for exposing their daughters to sources and experiences that may provide inspiration and encouragement for them, because many teachers and counselors lack either information or sensitivity to widening professional and higher educational opportunities that result from changing attitudes and equal opportunity legislation. Moreover, parents *can* build aspirations, a sense of autonomy, and self-reliance in daughters, to counteract the too-little, too-late approach of too many of today's counseling offices.

WHAT PARENTS CAN DO FOR THEIR DAUGHTERS, TO SUPPLEMENT OR REPLACE TRADITIONAL HIGH SCHOOL COUNSELING

Interaction with Professional Role Models

It is important that your daughter meet as many professional women in as extensive a variety of fields as possible. Use a woman pediatrician, internist, dentist, dermatologist, or family physician from the time of your daughter's birth, so that the concept that women can and do serve well in medicine becomes natural. Your County Medical Association can recommend outstanding women physicans, at your request.

When you need an attorney call your local Legal Society and, similarly, request the names of women attorneys. This was one procedure used for the New York University study described in this book, and the author was amazed and impressed with the physically beautiful, intelligent, poised, articulate, and charming lawyers interviewed for the pilot phase of that research. Young girls who are exposed to professional women of the caliber described, are bound to be impressed with (and want to emulate) them. Start early—perhaps when your daughter is nine or ten.

Request that professional associations in your geographical area sponsor a "Meet Professional Women" evening once a month during the school year. Have women in every possible *professional* field address daughters and their *mothers and fathers* on "What It Means to Be a Woman" in:

1. Administration
2. Advertising
3. Aerodynamics
4. Architecture
5. Computer Technology
6. Dentistry
7. Engineering
8. Law
9. Marketing
10. Medicine
11. Politics
12. Research
13. Science
14. Space Travel

Encourage your daughter's friends to attend with her (and *their* parents, if possible).

Caution: Do not personally advocate one field over another; that must really be your youngster's choice. We are reminded of the young man who chastized his mother for telling him that he should become a doctor, claiming, "You should let me make up my own mind!" With an indignant flip of her head, his mother countered, "*Of course* you have to make up your own mind! You can be any kind of a doctor you want! A pediatrician, a surgeon, an internist, or opthalmologist! YOU decide!"

Analysis of Local Library Offerings

Girls can turn to career books and pamphlets which are available in most "young adults" sections of libraries, in the vocational guidance office at school, or, more recently, in simplified versions of adventure stories in federally sponsored "Career Education" programs offered in many school systems. Current literature on the professions as a career for girls is, for the most part, marked by a reserved, balanced tone—as opposed to the recruiting zeal of the books written for boys. When you examine what is available for girls, you will find that most of the books are careful to communicate an idea of the demands and sacrifices of the profession, as well as their rewards. You repeatedly will find mention of truncated family life, rigorous intellectual demands, and special personality requirements. (No mention is made, however, of the boys who perform marginally throughout high school and college and are refused admission into American medical schools, only to obtain their degrees in foreign universities and return to the United States to practice.)

An excellent example of a book written for adult women, but readable by secondary students, is *Enterprising Women*,[17] which describes how selected women competed and became financial giants in the economic world. *Medicine As A Career for Women*,[18] written for teenagers, is also good. Others are listed in Chapter 8 and are recommended by approximate age levels, although, in actuality, their suitability will be determined by the reader's ability and motivation.

Counseling literature generally reflects a conservative viewpoint without developing a realistic picture of what it is like to be a professional woman in the 1970s—a decade in which many young women are recognizing that, unlike pets, they refuse to be "domesticated" and are choosing, instead, the combination of marriage, motherhood, and high-income-producing careers, a pattern that is likely to escalate in the 1980s.

Finally, be certain that feminist literature is included in school libraries and that efforts are made to secure instructional materials, including textbooks, which portray women favorably in nontraditional roles.

Establishment of Career Clubs for Girls

Effective starting points for concerted efforts to attract more girls into the professions would be the establishment of high school career clubs that encourage meetings and discussions among practitioners and currently studying or interested college students. Participating college girls and professionals would ensure membership by high school girls. The clubs should be organized by the biology or science department for medicine, by the social studies and political science department for law and politics, by the math and art departments for engineering, architecture, and design, by the English department for journalism and dramatics, and so on. Local or regional professional societies should participate actively and bear some of the responsibility for attracting professional speakers, arranging for field trips, and for "A Day With A Woman ——— [any professional]"—permitting juniors and seniors the opportunity to assist or observe a professional person during a week-day in their lives.

Clubs like these include the Future Doctors' Clubs organized by Sandia Kiwanis groups in various communities, Future Physicians' Clubs, undertaken as early as 1960 by the American Medical Association as the recruiting arm of their organization, and the Ars Medica Club, established by the American Academy of General Practice as part of Project More. Activities provided through these groups to youngsters interested in medicine as a career include field trips, guest lecturers, practice in labs, training in the use of equipment, volunteer work as a doctor's or nurse's aide, and summer hospital jobs, whenever possible.[19]

Expansion of Counseling Information.

Provide counselors with updated information, so that all students may be encouraged to consider a variety of career opportunities, and not only those traditionally entered by persons of their sex. When you discover such items (books, pamphlets, brochures, articles, book reviews) send copies or originals to the guidance office, with a note to the director indicating that you ". . . thought this might be of interest to some of the girl students." Do not be afraid of incurring the counselors' disdain: If they are alert and aware, they will appreciate your efforts; if they are outdated, they need all the help you can give them! We are less concerned about *their* reactions than we are about our daughters' lack of motivating encouragement.

Consideration of Jobs and Placement Practices

Encourage your daughter to seek part-time employment as early as possible (thirteen or fourteen is not too early) for after school and summer or other vacation hours. Earning money is a fine way to develop an appreciation for it and the effort it takes, and, of course, having a job is one way of avoiding the fear of employment inadequacy. If possible, help her to become involved in assisting professional people in nontraditional areas. *Any* work is beneficial, but the closer her contacts with professionals, the more likely she is to be inspired by them and to test her potential interest in various fields.

If you are concerned about the difficulty of maintaining good grades while holding a job, you need not be. Again, research reveals that many professional women achieved excellent grades while, simultaneously, being employed.[20] Besides, a job is one more way in which she can be stimulated into thinking beyond the "feminine" needs for being overly concerned about her hair, make-up, clothes, and attracting boys or needing peer approval. Moreover, although there is evidence that having a car causes deterioration of academic grades, no such relationship has been demonstrated for part-time employment.

Investigate local and school job placement agencies and practices to assure students of employment opportunities without restriction because of sex and urge that students not be assigned to career or vocational classes or instruction by sex. And, certainly, do not permit assignment to classes segregated by sex, such as homemaking, industrial arts, or driver education. Such arbitrary divisions tend to further intensify the male-female categorization of jobs and roles by nonthinking tradition, rather than by interest or ability. Should you encounter resistance, try to obtain change by working with the PTA, local organizations, and the board of education.

Changes in High School Offerings

Meet with school officials (either alone or as part of a group, such as the high school Parent-Teachers' Association) and urge that the role of women become an integrated part of the high school curriculum. Request that programs be developed to alert the faculty to sexism and its wasteful, degrading, discriminatory, and illegal practices. Urge that sex-stereotyped material be eliminated from all school publications and that such passages be exposed and discussed wherever they appear in literature or other texts. Also, be certain that faculty assignments to classes and courses concerned with vocations and traditional roles are not made by sex—that is, a woman should *not* teach cooking, and a man should *not* teach driver education. True, this is reverse discrimination, but it can lead to the proper exchange of traditional roles and to the ultimate annihilation of sex stereotyping and its psychological (and economic) damage. At the very least, *both* men and women should teach these courses to integrated groups.

In addition, selected traditional offerings should be available to youngsters of both sexes. For example, "open shops" for girls and "open cooking" for boys (in addition to the regular coeducational classes) can provide both sexes with valuable options. Girls who are encouraged to use the woodwork shops during the free periods in their schedules may construct cabinets for their artwork, scenery for plays, and models for future architectural endeavors. Boys who are permitted to experiment with recipes, are likely to become self-sufficient as cooks and some then may aspire to become gourmet chefs. When opportunities are not provided, horizons are necessarily narrowed. Teachers should be available for instruction, assistance, and supervision of meaningful and rewarding experiences for those youngsters who wish to have more than the ordinary amount of training. Certainly, working in labs, libraries, shops, home economics areas, and art rooms would be more beneficial than sitting silently in the many "study halls" usually required of high school students; such requirements are administrative, rather than educational in nature, and tend to restrict, rather than to expand a student's skills.

Support the offering of a course in human growth and development which includes emotional and physical interpersonal relationships. Youngsters at the high school level know about "the birds and the bees," but their information concerning the ways in which people should live together to promote individual and cooperative, intellectual, emotional, and physical health is probably scant and faulty. Courses that explain how very much both parents are needed by their babies and young children during the formative years and how very much both parents need to feel loved, appreciated, respected, and accepted by each other are vital to the ultimate and continuing happiness and well-being of both daughters and sons—but these are part of the curriculum that is nonexistent in most schools. In this regard, high schools should offer courses on how to raise children, because of the critical importance of the first five years of life. People learn about their own needs through trial and error—sometimes when it is "too late" and often after the fact. Teaching about each other's human needs is vital, but, as with many other *important* issues, this area is not accepted as a "responsibility" of schools.

Aside from basic learnings such as reading, writing, and arithmetic, nothing should take precedence over teaching young citizens about the characteristics of healthy people in a healthy society and how to safeguard the vitality of both. Unfortunately, most teachers at the high school level have received training in subject-matter disciplines and have not been prepared to work with young people on critical areas such as mental health, self-image, and self-realization. Neither have boards of education nor administrators considered including these topics as part of the high school curriculum. It is time that we challenged restrictive high school educational philosophies and course offerings that perpetuate female-male stereotypes and deny preparation for successful human relationships.

Attitudes Toward Pregnancy

The National Commission on the Reform of Secondary Education confirms that most high schools continue to enforce discriminatory regulations against female students who become pregnant. Such youngsters either are required to leave school or to attend a center for pregnant girls that offers no chemistry, physics, or advanced mathematics. This is an illegal procedure. Court decisions consistently have held that girls who become pregnant must have the opportunity to continue in the regular high school if they wish to do so;[21] in no case should the student be counseled not to remain in school.

Ostracizing or "punishing" young girls who become pregnant in high school is *immoral*, as well as illegal. It is discriminatory, because the boys who impregnate them are rarely suspended or restricted in any way. They are allowed to pursue full academic programs. Further, suspension or expulsion is cruel and harsh, considering the social, emotional, and economic hardships that will burden the young girl who has made this one mistake. More important, curtailment of education and growth for these unwed mothers can deprive our society of future physicians, inventors, researchers, or architects who would have contributed to the well-being and quality of life of thousands of people —male and female. At the very least, these unfortunate, unskilled girls who cannot compete even for lower-level jobs, will not require public assistance if permitted to complete their education.

One last note for those parents who worry that the sight of a pregnant peer will encourage your daughter to follow suit. It is likely that the largeness and comparative unattractiveness of the later stages of pregnancy will do exactly the reverse.

Improvement in Girls' Athletics

The National Commission on the Reform of Secondary Education recommended that girls should "receive the same encouragement, opportunities, and aspirations as boys to become involved in the excitement of team and individual sports" and that the girls' programs should enjoy equal use of the physical facilities and funds that are available.[22] The Commission Report cites cases in which girls were not permitted use of a gymnasium during basketball season or where the girls' gym is selected for social events, whereas the boys' gym is preserved carefully for male sports.

The Commission has gone on record as supporting *coeducational* noncontact sports, believing that both sexes will benefit—especially in sports with adult carry-over, such as tennis, swimming, golf, archery, and so on. It also deplores the discriminatory pay differential between women and men coaches and urges that both female and male physical education classes be classified as major activities.[23] These concepts are no longer new and are gaining acceptance through federal law (Title IX), state regulations, and local attitudes and practices. They are long overdue. If girls are to consider themselves as important as boys, then society (certainly the schools) must demonstrate its belief in equality by providing them with teachers, facilities, and activities in the quantity and quality enjoyed by boys. An accepted adage in tennis is that, to improve, one should play with those who are slightly better. Since school is where youngsters should be learning to achieve to their maximum potential, there is no reason why boys and girls should not compete with each other in *noncontact* sports.

An excerpt from the official handbook of the National Federation of State High School Athletic Associations reads:

> There is a trend toward expansion of girls' interscholastic competitive opportunities in athletics in virtually all states. This is due to the belief that schools need to provide girls with challenging outlets for physical activities when their needs require more than intramural programs. For three decades, educators avoided sponsoring interscholastic programs for girls because of cultural restrictions and physiological half-truths. Many parents believed it was unladylike to participate in athletics and that girls who did became large, muscular, and nonfeminine in appearance. *This assumption has no validity.* From the viewpoint of equal opportunity, girls are just as entitled to competitive experiences as are boys. If athletics are beneficial, they must be good for girls as well as boys. Recently, the American Medical Association released the results of a study pointing out that women who maintain a high level of health and fitness can meet family and career responsibilities more effectively and can pursue avocational interests enjoyably.[24]

Related to the Association's statements, parents should know that Title IX of the Education Amendments of 1972 provides that schools must take affirmative measures to make available equal opportunities for both sexes to participate in athletic activities of their choice from among those offered. Further, if separate teams are established for boys and girls, there can be no discrimination on the basis of sex in providing equipment or supplies, although total expenditures for each team need not be identical. Moreover, where athletic opportunities for one sex have been limited, institutions must make affirmative efforts to inform members of that sex about the availability of equal opportunities and then furnish support and training that will allow them to participate.

Daughters need to be healthy, competitive in positive ways, and able to cope with "wins" and "losses" in everyday life. Toward this goal, full coeducational participation will enhance their abilities to plan, analyze opponents and situations, engage in team efforts, experience both victories and defeats, and learn from each situation, so as to improve in future events. These skills contribute to one's sense of self-control, power over the environment, and independence and permit the kind of personal growth and values that foster a sense of accomplishment that all youngsters should experience—particularly our daughters!

RECOMMENDED READINGS, EXPERIENCES, AND OPPORTUNITIES

An increasing number of inspiring books about women and their accomplishments have been published in recent years. We suggest that you read several yourself and then make the ones which you believe will be appealing to your daughter available to her. Do not present more than one at a time, but when you've found one that appears to be particularly good (and on your daughter's reading level), mention it to her, tell her a little about it, and then suggest that she browse through it. You really can't do more than that, because too much emphasis may cause her to react negatively to the entire concept of women's accomplishments. Use your judgment concerning how much focus to exert in this direction.

Encourage your daughter to register for high school courses that are usually attractive to males, such as industrial arts, agricultural science and mechanics, technical drafting, and executive management. Other courses, like carpentry, plumbing, electricity, electronics, radio and television service, automotive repair and mechanics, air conditioning, bricklaying, cabinetmaking, and furniture design also will be highly beneficial to her during her adult life. Unfortunately, girls tend to shy away from these areas. In addition, fields such as forestry, marketing, aerospace, computer programming, sheet metal work, machine shop maintenance, marine vocations, auto design, and animal husbandry offer extensive career opportunities to skilled persons, but, again, are vocations that have not attracted girls in the past. Finally, premed, predentistry, and courses in politics certainly should be advocated for intelligent girls who might be interested in pursuing these studies. If such courses are not available at the local high school, suggest that similar offerings be provided as introductory units (minicourses), either through the courtesy of local business-people or through vocational schools that may exist as part of a regional school conglomerate. These experiences will admit your daughter into a "society" that can expand her horizons. She will learn things that she undoubtedly will not have been exposed to previously. She will gain entrance into an essentially "male" enclave and be able to observe their methods of operation and response, so that she will no longer feel unable to compete in "a man's [economic] world." She will recognize that males are no more capable or secure than she. Finally, she will have been exposed to new ideas, skills, and processes that could lead toward interesting work and stimulating lives. A girl's horizon should be limited only by her abilities—not by a dearth of opportunity. Several of the fields suggested suffer from a severe lack of skilled employees, and a bright, capable, diligent young woman could exercise leadership and management skills that might change a particular "job" into a successful, innovative industry. Women, after all, have not been involved directly in some of these "male"-oriented areas; there is no limit to what a creative, skillful woman could do about translating an "old image" into a "new entity." In addition, many professions and businesses lend themselves to either part-time or "from-the-home" management.

Insist that options, such as independent study assignments out-of-school, be available to girls who demonstrate the qualities of independence and self-reliance appropriate to such a program and discussed at length in Chapter 4. Many high schools currently permit youngsters to spend part or all of an academic year working in industry, government, or one of the professions. Girls have been permitted to work as student apprentices to state legislators, medical researchers, authors, consumer organizations, attorneys, publishers, architects, engineers, and even builders in the construction trades and, as a consequence, earn credit toward degrees. Some have attended schools and universities overseas in programs aimed at specific studies, such as Canadian, Israeli, or Irish literature, Japanese transportation innovations, or Swedish social reforms. Others both have learned and contributed as teaching assistants in elementary schools in their own districts, as volunteers to senior citizen or hospital organizations, and as assistants on projects that provide positive growth experiences for economically and/or educationally disadvantaged youngsters.

Whatever the nature of her new learning experience, it should promote independence and growth opportunities that help her to realize that the world offers a wide range of possible career choices and that she has the ability to cope with many different alternatives and to successfully manipulate them to her advantage. Experience with new ideas and processes usually cause a growth in personal self-image and confidence and, eventually, provide a wider array of skills and talents from which to draw. Your daughter will be able to develop increased insight into her own abilities and interests and will, at times, feel the euphoria and movement-toward-perfection of a "peak experience." She undoubtedly will dislike some studies, be bored by others, and apathetic to some; her horizons, however, will expand, and she may find many areas that will be stimulating and energizing in their appeal. The broader her experience base, the wider her opportunities for developing interests and the better her chances for the direct involvement, achievement, and fine performance that leads to self-actualization.

Throughout this chapter we have stressed the need for providing your daughter with a variety of experiences that will broaden her opportunities for participation, achievement, and self-actualization in fields that historically have been considered man's domain. We have said nothing about the obvious advantage of the so-called masculine careers—that they provide their practitioners with increased financial security—a dividend that is most meaningful in our economic society. Money is important to most people, particularly in this era of constantly shrinking dollar-values, shortages of raw materials, and demanding tax requirements. Women, particularly those who become heads of their families through divorce, desertion, or widowhood, desperately need monetary security. The male-dominated professions produce the better incomes and, as a matter of legal and moral equality, they must be opened to all of our citizens.

One of the major traditional differences between the upbringing of boys and girls is that boys have been conditioned to earn money from early childhood on, whereas girls are taught they must marry a man with good earning potential who will take care of them. Young boys often talk about the salaries paid to professional athletes or physicians; young girls discuss boys, marriage, and children. This pattern must be broken. The huge number of women appealing for welfare and family court assistance verifies that women no longer should rely on males to support them; they must prepare to assume the financial responsibilities for themselves and for any offspring they may bear. Certainly, if they ever need to be income-producing, they should be able to command earnings that will provide them with the basic needs of life and the comforts enjoyed by males, who, up to now, have claimed the largest share of the world's income.

Furthermore, developments in the technologies of work, the household, contraception, and longevity have all contributed to freeing women from tasks which previously required their time and energies, thus allowing them many more years in which they are able to participate in the world of work. And, as described in detail by Patrick C. Lee and Robert Sussman Stewart in their recently published book on sex differences,[25] economic changes, changes in the "typical" American family, changing marriage customs, women's liberation, and the psychological consequences of the emerging sex-role changes have all contributed to the recognition that more and more women are and will continue to be income-producing for survival needs for longer periods of their lives than men actually lived only a century ago.

If our daughters are going to be required to work, they should be involved in the professional world, where they can contribute to the betterment of society while (1) determining their own hours, (2) being self-employed, (3) choosing the geographical location where they wish to reside and/or practice, (4) using their intelligence and skills, and (5) earning an excellent income.

8.
What to Do about Books and Television

SEXIST PROGRAMMING IN THE MEDIA

There is a rapidly growing awareness of sexist stereotyping in children's readers and textbooks and on children's and adult television programs. This knowledge, however, has not been accompanied by equally rapid changes in the material to which our daughters are subjected on a daily basis. For example, Women on Words and Images reported the following discouraging statistics based on 2,760 stories in 134 books from 14 major publishers[1]—books that are in current use in our public schools:

Boy-centered to girl-centered stories	5:2
Adult male main characters to adult female main characters	3:1
Male biographies to female biographies	6:1
Male animal stories to female animal stories	2:1
Male folk or fantasy stories to female folk or fantasy stories	4:1

A follow-up study by this group on readers published after 1972 did not reveal much improvement:

Boy-centered stories to girl-centered stories	7:2
Male illustrations to female illustrations	2:1
Male occupations to female occupations	3:1
Male biographies to female biographies	2:1

For the most part women are still seen in the "job" of unimaginative mother.[2] Sexist role-inequality in children's books is often subtle and difficult to counter.

One popular story that is praised for its message and quality is *The Little Engine That Could*. One letter to the editor of the New York Times[3] sums up the problem of this and the majority of the books our daughters read:

I am dismayed to see the acclaim currently being given to "The Little Engine That Could." Your writer, Richard R. Lingeman, praises it as a book which encourages children in the task of growing up (May 2). While on the surface it does have this message, it also carries another, much more subtle, and much less constructive message. In the story the "happy little train" which carries the dolls and toys over the mountain and the merry "Little Blue Engine" which assists her are both "she." But the shiny new passenger engine and the big strong freight engine which are too busy and important carrying people and machinery to help "the likes of you" are described as "he."

Are we going to give this same message for another fifty years—that the "big, strong" males do the important work in the world and can't be bothered with children's concerns and that only the "little, kind" females can be relied upon to help out children and become a part of their world? We understand the damage done by the racism implicit in stories like "Little Black Sambo," and it is time now to understand that books which project sexual inequality are just as damaging to our children.

Turning to television:

. . . Virtually every family in the United States, regardless of its economic status, has at least one television set; more Americans have T.V. than have indoor plumbing. The average set is turned on approximately six hours and eighteen minutes per day. By the time that average American children become sixteen, they have spent approximately 15,000 hours in front of a T.V. set—or about 4,000 more than they have spent in a classroom. Only sleeping engages more hours.[4]

Consider these data carefully. They suggest that your daughter is in the process of accumulating 15,000 hours of sex-biased drama, humor, news, cartoons, old films, talk shows, and commercials by the time she is sixteen! Her brain and emotions have been assaulted by color and black-and-white sexist stereotypes ever since she has been a tot. In addition to the perpetuation of myths concerning such "male" qualities as strength, dominance, bravery, and intelligence and "female" qualities like passivity, limited courage, and submissiveness, television is damaging because it is, itself, a passive and submissive activity. It tends to diminish the desire to read and the willingness to go and to do.

With change in the content of books, television programs, advertising, and films a slow process, indeed, it is critical that you and your daughter become skilled at analyzing and overcoming the male and female stereotypes that saturate our senses from the media that surround us. She is, in a sense, (a) drugged and pacified by television, (b) programmed by films and books, and (c) placed in inferior positions to males who are equally victimized by the repeated propaganda about the roles of men and women in this country.

GUIDELINES FOR SELECTING BOOKS

As an aid toward monitoring some of the materials to which school children are exposed, a set of guidelines for nonsexist education was developed that you can use to review the texts that your daughter reads at school, the books that you buy, or those that she selects at the library.

Guidelines For Non-Sexist Education[5]
Most textbooks used in schools today are sexist. While these texts are directly concerned with the instruction of skills and the imparting of knowledge in various subject areas, they are indirectly expressing the attitudes and values of society. It is important that everyone dealing with children become aware of restrictive, narrow, sexist attitudes portrayed in the majority of school curriculum materials.

Checklist for evaluative sexism in curriculum materials
The following guidelines may be used to examine individual books for sexism:

	Male	Female
1. Number of stories where main character is	___	___
2. Number of illustrations	___	___
3. Number of times children are shown:		
a. in active play	___	___
b. using initiative	___	___
c. independent	___	___
d. solving problems	___	___
e. earning money	___	___

	Male	Female
f. receiving recognition	———	———
g. being inventive	———	———
h. involved in sports	———	———
i. being passive	———	———
j. fearful	———	———
k. helpless	———	———
l. receiving help	———	———
m. in quiet play	———	———

4. Number of times adults are shown:

	Male	Female
a. in different occupations	———	———
b. playing with children	———	———
c. taking children on outings	———	———
d. teaching skills	———	———
e. showing tenderness	———	———
f. scolding children	———	———
g. biographically	———	———

Other considerations

When examining books or curriculum materials, these additional questions need to be considered:

1. Are boys allowed to show emotion?
2. Are boys and girls portrayed with a range of human responses—e.g., fear, anger, aggression, excitement and tenderness?
3. Are there derogatory comments directed at women and girls?
4. Are mothers shown in roles other than housework or child rearing?
5. Are mothers employed outside the home? . . . in a wide range of occupations or only stereotypical ones?
6. Are fathers shown in roles other than going to work or doing traditional chores?
7. Are all members of the family involved in household tasks?
8. Are boys and girls participating equally in physical and intellectual activities?
9. Are both boys and girls developing independent lives, independently meeting challenges and finding their own solutions?
10. Are there any stories about one-parent families?* . . . families without children? . . . are babysitters and day-care centers shown?
11. Are only girls rewarded for their looks or given "grooming" instructions?
12. Are there one or two bright examples of equal sex treatment in materials which are fundamentally dominated by male role models?

*It is estimated that more than 25 percent of the nation's children now live apart from one or both of their natural parents.

13. Are generic "he" and masculine pronouns used to represent all people, e.g., "mankind," "fireman" and "mailman"?
14. Is family responsibility assumed to be the domain of females while males assume a breadwinner position?
15. Are the changing roles of men and women discussed?

Classroom practices
Awareness of the existence of sexism in all curriculum materials is important. In addition, attitudes and practices of teachers in the classroom influence students' impressions of what is expected of them. The following are examples of classroom practices which are detrimental to the full development of every child.
1. Attendance taken by sex
2. Classroom tasks assigned by sex
3. Classroom activities different for each sex
4. Different extracurricular activities for each sex
5. Different expectations for each sex academically and socially
6. Differing expectations of acceptable (unacceptable) behavior for each sex
7. Differing treatment of acceptable (unacceptable) behavior for each sex

Classroom activities
The following specific activities are suggested to sharpen the student's perceptions of stereotypes:
1. Discuss the limiting aspects of stereotyping
2. Have students reverse roles
3. Have students point out stereotypes in their own books
4. Have students discuss stereotypes in television shows
5. Have students discuss "what they want to be" and assist them in identifying any sex role socialization as the basis for their aspirations
6. Set up displays of non-traditional jobs for males and females
7. Set up displays emphasizing the role women play in sports
8. Set up displays showing males in nurturing roles
9. Use non-sexist bibliographies for choosing books
10. Have a wide range of biographies of both men and women available in the classroom.

Either preview the books your daughter will read or read them together and analyze each story according to the guidelines. Discuss your findings with all members of the family; bring the results to your Parent-Teacher Association meetings or to teachers, administrators, and school board members in your school district. Ask your daughter how the stories and books could be improved and how girls and boys might be shown as equals.

Check on classroom practices with your daughter's teacher. Show her or him these guidelines. Ask the teacher's opinion about these practices.

OVERCOMING SEXIST STEREOTYPES AT HOME

The classroom activities that are suggested in the guidelines offer many ideas which can be adapted to home use. For example, your daughter and her brothers can pretend "to change roles." In addition, she could:

1. Analyze and discuss sexist stereotypes she finds in the books she reads.
2. Develop a list of biographies on outstanding women.
3. Complete projects on women in non-traditional roles or for her own developing aspirations.
4. Trace the trends and advantages to young girls of the women's liberation movement.
5. Find ten sexist "ads" in the Sunday newspapers and create a display to use in her social studies, physical education, or English classes. There are many which depict women serving men who "deserve" special attention, according to the ads.
6. Design a family contest to list and discuss sex stereotypes shown either during one evening's series of television programs or in an advertisement. For example, examine one sample sexist advertisement and compare each person's answers to the following questions:*
   a. Describe what is happening in this photograph.
   b. What are the man's mood, feelings, and expectations?
   c. What is the woman doing? Why do you think your explanation is correct?
   d. How do you know it is the man who is being served by the woman?
   e. Does the woman mind waiting on the man? Why do you think so?
   f. Is he good-looking? Does that make him deserving of being served?
   g. Who is the *center* of the advertisement? Why do you think the ad was designed that way?
   h. How does the "copy," or advertisement's words, try to get you to buy the product?
   i. Do you believe that anyone has been compromised?
   j. How could you redo this ad to provide equal treatment for the man and woman?
7. Create non-sexist advertisements depicting affectionate, giving, equal male and female relationships in traditional and non-

---

*Vary the questions and their difficulty, according to your daughter's age and stage of mental development, but do not underestimate her powers of observation or ability to abstract ideas.

> traditional roles and submit them to the companies who persist in
> showing stereotypes.
> 8. Redesign or create new children's stories and readers which treat
>   girls and boys equally and positively.
> 9. Take photographs or draw boys and girls behaving with intelli-
>   gence and ability in a variety of social situations.
> 10. List a series of positive and negative human emotions and keep a
>   log of how real men and women exhibit both. For example:

Positive Emotions

Tenderness: Mom and Dad helped each other when they slipped on the ice.
Confidence—Aggressiveness: Dad decided to apply for a better position.
    Sis registered for an advanced course in biology.

Negative Emotions

Anger—Immaturity: In one week we counted five men and two women acting
    angry and shouting about the ways others were driving.
Defensiveness: When Brother spilled the orange juice, he protested, "It wasn't
    my fault! The glass tipped!" (He should have held the glass as he
    poured.)

RECOMMENDED BOOKS AND EXAMPLES OF SEXIST LITERATURE

Much of the material in this section was abstracted from an excellent book on
children's literature by Professor Masha Kabakow Rudman.[6] Her text is divided into a series of critical issues, such as "Siblings," "War," "Divorce," the
"Female," "Using Children's Books in a Reading Program," "Sex," and so on.
There is a discussion of each issue, a section relating particular books to the
topic as exemplars of how that topic is treated in children's literature, suggestions for activities for young readers, and annotated reference lists of sources
and bibliographies. This excellent reference could be used at home and in the
schools to design more relevant curricula for girls (and boys).
    Though not covered specifically by Rudman in the annotations, be
wary of the popular fairy tales that we have inherited, such as those written by
the Brothers Grimm. Close examination will reveal how these help to perpetuate sex-role stereotypes. These nineteenth-century stories and fables portrayed independence, self-confidence, strength, aggressiveness, leadership,
ambition, a sense of adventure and objectivity as the valued characteristics of
males; women who exhibited these traits were disparaged. Conversely, the
females in these stories were treated positively only when they displayed
gentleness, tact, neatness, concern with appearance, shyness, or dependency.
Girls also were characterized as being vain and talkative. Males who had these
traits were, of course, considered to be weak or emotionally disturbed.

When selecting books for your daughter, be certain that the female characters represent the kinds of positive, dynamic persons that you would like her to emulate. Avoid those stories that portray women in exclusively traditional roles, such as housewife or nurse. Exclude books that tend to describe them with negative "feminine" personality traits, such as passivity, fearfulness, helplessness, or vanity.

Purposely seek themes that depict girls in active play, using initiative, being independent and creative, solving problems, earning money, receiving recognition, being inventive, involved in sports, coping successfully with difficult decisions, and being courageous.

Special attention should be directed toward identifying storylines that: (1) permit boys to show emotion; (2) portray boys and girls with a range of human responses, such as anger, aggression, excitement, courage, fear, or tenderness; (3) direct no derogatory comments or innuendoes at either sex or toward any religious, ethnic, racial, or cultural group; (4) feature mothers in roles other than housekeeping or child-rearing; (5) involve all family members in housekeeping tasks; (6) portray mothers employed outside the home in a wide range of occupations and fathers in roles other than "going to work" or doing traditional chores; (7) illustrate boys *and* girls participating equally in physical and intellectual activities; (8) describe both sexes developing independent lives, courageously meeting challenges, and finding their own solutions; (9) discuss the changing roles of men and women; (10) explain the "nuclear family," divorce, racism, poverty, one-parent families, families without children, babysitters, and/or day-care centers; (11) reward boys and girls for their looks, grooming, cleanliness or kindness; and (12) do not use generic "he" and masculine pronouns to represent all persons, like "mankind," "fireman," "mailman," "congressman," or "manhandle."

The following recommended books represent the kind of literature which best exemplifies current, realistic characterizations of independent, active, and thinking people to which your daughter should be exposed.

Recommended for Ages Three Through Eight

Adams, Florence. *Mushy Eggs*. Illus. Marilyn Hirsh. New York: Putnam's, 1973. (Ages 4–8.)

The women in this story are admirable and have several dimensions. The housekeeper-baby-sitter has her own friends and family, and the boys' mother copes well with her computer job and the boys. They all seem none the worse for wear.

Adamson, Joy. *Elsa*. New York: Pantheon Books, 1961. (Ages 6–up.)

True story of a strong, sensitive woman, her husband, and their lioness friend, Elsa. Easy to read with beautiful photographs of Elsa.

Allinson, Beverly. *Mitzi's Magic Garden*. Illus. George Buckett. Champaign, Ill.: Garrard, 1971. (Age 6.)

Mitzi busily plants a garden, gets wonderful results, and benevolently gives
away what grows.

    Andre, Evelyn M. *Things We Like to Do.* New York: Abingdon Press,
    1968. (Ages 5–8.)

A large picture book depicting children of both sexes in various activities that
are fun to do: play with friends, bake a cake, play with dolls.

    Bonsall, Crosby. *And I Mean It, Stanley.* New York: Harper & Row,
    1974. (Ages 5–8.)

The friendship of an active, imaginative little girl, who builds contraptions in a
junk yard, and a giant dog named Stanley.

    Budd, Lillian. *Calico Row.* Chicago: Albert Whitman, 1965. (Ages
    5–8.)

A friendship story of a boy and a girl working together to find the most
wonderful thing on Calico Row, where they live.

    Caines, Jeannette. *Abby.* Illus. Steven Kellogg. New York: Harper &
    Row, 1973. (Ages 3–8.)

Abby is Kevin's little adopted sister. He loves her; but sometimes, when he
gets annoyed, he upsets Abby by saying that he does not like girls. The mother
is seen reading and studying. Abby is active and clever.

    Clifton, Lucille. *Don't You Remember?* Illus. Evaline Ness. New
    York: Dutton, 1973. (Ages 3–7.)

Desire Mary Tate, black, four years old, and very lively, considers herself to
have the best memory in her family. She has three elder brothers, one of whom
has taken a year off from school to care for her. Her parents both work, and her
ambition is to grow up and work at the plant, "just like Daddy." Division of
labor because it must get done, not because of sex role.

    ———. *Good, Says Jerome.* New York: Dutton, 1973. (Ages 3–7.)

Jerome, frightened by many things, asks his sister for the answers. She usually
has good comforting answers for him and helps him deal with many aspects of
life. Jerome is not punished or derided for his feelings; he is permitted to
display them and to be reassured.

    Cohen, Miriam. *The New Teacher.* New York: Macmillan, 1972. Pb.
    also. (Ages 3–6.)

A group of boys and girls at a racially mixed city school get a new teacher and
decide that they like her. The activities of the children are not determined by
sex. The book is not a literary classic, but does provide a good model for
nonsexist activities.

    Credle, Ellis. *Down, Down the Mountain.* New York: Nelson, 1934.
    (Ages 5–8.)

Two West Virginia mountain children grow and sell turnips to buy themselves
shoes. In this story there is no distinction between men's and women's work,
unusual for a story which takes place so long ago.

    Goffstein, M. B. *Goldie the Dollmaker.* New York: Farrar, Straus &
    Giroux, 1969. (Ages 5–8.)

Goldie is an artist who lives in the forest making dolls. She is lonely for someone who understands her feelings about her work, but her confidence in these feelings is reaffirmed by the end of the book.

    Goodyear, Carmen. *The Sheep Book.* Chapel Hill, N.C.: Lollipop
       Power, 1972. (Ages 3–7.)
Describes the cycle of raising sheep for their wool, which then becomes yarn and eventually a garment. The illustrations by the author are appropriate to the text. The farmer is a woman. The message of the text is didactic without being oppressive.

    Handforth, Thomas. *Mei Li.* Garden City, N.Y.: Doubleday, 1938.
       (Ages 5–8.) (Caldecott Award.)
Mei Li, a Chinese girl, goes to a big circus, has many experiences, and gains some self-pride.

    Heyward, Dubose, and Zarssoni, Marjory. *The Country Bunny and*
       the Little Gold Shoes. Boston: Houghton Mifflin, 1939. Pb. also. (Ages
       5–8.)
A story about a rabbit who is a mother and a strong, proud Easter Bunny at the same time. While she is out delivering Easter eggs, her little bunnies, boys and girls alike, are taking care of the house. Note the early copyright date.

    Hill, Elizabeth Starr. *Evan's Corner.* Illus. Nancy Grossman. New
       York: Holt, Rinehart and Winston, 1967. (Ages 4–8.)
Evan's mother is busy with work and family. His elder sister and father also help with the care of the children. The family is poor but manages well.

    Katz, Bobbi. *Nothing But a Dog.* Illus. Esther Gilman. Old Westbury,
       N.Y.: Feminist Press, 1972. (Ages 4–8.)
Very active girl wants a dog. She is pictured wearing all kinds of clothing (even including dresses) and engaging in all kinds of activities. In the end she gets her dog, but the book essentially has no plot. It presents the image of the girl in a nonstereotypic manner.

    Kaufman, Joe. *Busy People.* New York: Golden Press, 1973. (Ages
       5–7.)
A book about community life and careers that includes women and men, Blacks and Whites, in nonstereotyped roles.

    Klein, Norma. *Girls Can Be Anything.* Illus. Roy Doty. New York:
       Dutton, 1973. (Ages 3–6.)
Marina's friend Adam tells her she has to be the nurse or the stewardess when they play. But Marina's parents tell her she can be anything, even the doctor, the pilot, or U.S. President. Marina tells this to Adam, and they change the way they play their games.

    Lasker, Joe. *Mothers Can Do Anything.* Chicago: Albert Whitman,
       1972. (Ages 3–8.)
This book demonstrates the variety of jobs that mothers can hold, including scientist, linesman, artist, and lion-tamer. The illustrations are fun, and the message is an important one.

Merriam, Eve. *Boys and Girls, Girls and Boys.* New York: Holt, Rinehart & Winston, 1972. Pb. also. (Ages 3–8.)
An unpretentious book showing children, boys and girls alike, exploring, being active and enjoying life.

————. *Mommies at Work.* New York: Knopf, 1961. Pb. Scholastic. (Ages 5–7.)
A book showing all the things that mothers can do outside the house — a very broad and varied range, all compatible with being a mother.

Miller, Arthur. *Jane's Blanket.* New York: Viking, 1972. (Ages 5–8.)
A little girl grows and her security blanket shrinks in size. She eventually relinquishes the blanket to some birds.

Mizumura, Kazue. *If I Were a Mother.* New York: Crowell, 1968. (Ages 4–7.)
A look at many different animal mothers for clues as to what a human mother would do.

Ness, Evaline. *Do You Have the Time, Lydia?* New York: Dutton, 1971. (Ages 5–8.)
Lydia and her brother live with their father, who is a florist. Lydia is a little dynamo. Her only problem is that she fails to complete most of what she begins. She is, however, sensitive to the feelings of others; and when she recognizes that her actions are irresponsible, she determines to change her ways—not to be less active, but to see her projects through to completion. The doctor and other characters in the book are Blacks; Lydia and her family are Whites.

————. *Sam Bangs and Moonshine.* New York: Holt, Rinehart and Winston, 1966. (Ages 3–7.)
Sam (Samantha) lives with her father near the ocean and has a very vivid imagination, which her father calls "moonshine." When a potential calamity is narrowly averted, Sam learns the difference between reality and "moonshine." Sam and her father have an excellent relationship. Respecting and accepting her special qualities, he does not impair her individual nature. He also helps her to become better adjusted to her mother's death.

Reavin, Sam. *Hurray for Captain Jane!* Illus. Emily Arnold McCully. New York: Parents' Magazine Press, 1971. (Ages 5–8.) (Children's Book Showcase.)
Jane, the protagonist, goes on a fantasy ocean voyage while she is taking a bath. The captain of the ship, she saves the ship from crashing into an iceberg. When she awakens from her fantasy, she plans to pilot a plane for her next adventure.

Reit, Seymour, and Goldman, Louis. *A Week in Hagar's World: Israel.* London: Macmillan, 1969. (Ages 5–8.)
A week in the life of a little Jewish girl who lives in a Kibbutz in Israel, illustrated beautifully by photographs. The nonsexist aspects of Kibbutz life are displayed.

Rockwell, Harlow. *My Doctor.* New York: Macmillan, 1973. (Ages 3–7.)

Description of a regular medical checkup, and the doctor is a woman. The description is matter-of-fact; the message is not intrusive.

> Scott, Ann Herbert. *Sam.* Illus. Symeon Shimin. New York: McGraw-Hill, 1967. (Ages 3–8.)

Sam wants to play, but his mother, father, sister and brother all send him away—they are too busy. When Sam begins to cry, they all realize the cause of his unhappiness. Mother finds a task for him; she helps him learn how to bake a raspberry tart. Beautiful illustrations. Loving, aware family. Child permitted to cry, not criticized. Nonsexist task for him.

> Sharmat, Marjorie Weinman. *Gladys Told Me to Meet Her Here.* Illus. Edward Frascino. New York: Harper & Row, 1970. (Ages 3–8.)

Irving is the narrator. He and Gladys are best friends. He arrives first for a meeting with Gladys and is concerned because she is late. Gladys is obviously an active, alert child. She and Irving have a friendship that is not based on sex roles. The story could have been narrated by a girl; the events could stay the same. Except for one negative reference to nurses, this is a nonsexist book.

> Shulevitz, Uri. *Rain Rain Rivers.* New York: Farrar, Straus & Giroux, 1969. (Ages 5–8.)

The author-illustrator poetically describes the positive effects of rain. The central character is an active and responsible girl. A boy could also have been this central character. The fact that it is a girl creates a positive basis for young readers' sex-role redefinition.

> Sukowiecki, Sandra Lucas. *Joshua's Day.* Illus. Patricia Reilly Vevitrall. Chapel Hill, N.C.: Lollipop Power, 1972. (Ages 3–6.)

Contemporary story of a single working mother and her son's experience in a city day-care center.

> Terris, Susan. *Amanda the Panda and the Redhead.* Illus. Emily McCully. Garden City, N.Y.: Doubleday, 1975. (Ages 3–8.)

The family functions in an equitable, unself-conscious manner. Father and mother both cook, clean, and nurture children. Clothing of mother, teacher, and children is comfortable.

> Thayer, Jane. *Quiet on Account of Dinosaur.* New York: Morrow, 1965. (Ages 5–8.)

A girl loves studying dinosaurs and grows up to be a scientist, museum director, and dinosaur-expert.

> Udry, Janice May. *Mary Jo's Grandmother.* Illus. Eleanor Mill. Chicago: Albert Whitman, 1970. (Ages 5–8.)

One snowy Christmas, Mary Jo visits her old but independent grandmother, who lives alone in the country. When her grandmother has an accident, Mary Jo gets help. Both Mary Jo and her grandmother are capable females.

> Waber, Bernard. *Ira Sleeps Over.* Boston: Houghton Mifflin, 1972. Pb. Scholastic. (Ages 4–8.) (Children's Books Showcase.)

Ira does not bring his teddy bear when he goes to sleep at his friend's house. He

finds out when he gets there that his friend has a teddy bear, too. Nicely
supportive of children and their feelings.

      ———, *Nobody's Perfect.* Boston: Houghton Mifflin, 1971. (Ages
      5–8.)
A series of small humorous incidents involving friendship between girls and
boys.

      White, E. B. *Charlotte's Web.* Illus. Garth Williams. New York:
      Harper & Row, 1952. Pb. Dell. (Ages 3–8.) (Newbery Honor Book.)
Charlotte, a clever and witty spider, saves the life of her "true friend" Wilbur,
the pig, in this story of a deep friendship. Fern, the human female protagonist,
changes from a girl interested in animals to a girl interested in boys—one of the
only flaws in this beautiful book.

      Williams, Jay. *Petronella.* Illus. Friso Menstra. New York: Parents'
      Magazine Press, 1973. (Ages 5–8.)
Petronella, the youngest of three children, sets off to seek her fortune and
rescue a prince. She finds a prince, but it turns out he is really just a parasite
dependent on the enchanter at whose house he is staying. Petronella ends up
marrying the wise, kind enchanter rather than the nitwit prince.

      Yolen, Jane. *The Emperor and the Kite.* Illus. Ed Young. Cleveland:
      World, 1967. (Ages 5–8.) (Caldecott Honor Book.)
Loyal Djeow Seow rescues her father, the Emperor, who has been captured by
evil men and locked in a high tower. Written in a poetic style, it is a story of girl's
love, courage, and ingenuity.

      ———. *The Girl Who Loved the Wind.* Illus. Ed Young. New York:
      Crowell, 1972. (Ages 5–8.) (Children's Book Showcase.)
Danina is kept from the outside world by her father, who wants to protect her
from all sad things. But despite the garden wall, Danina hears the wind's voice
and eventually accepts the wind's challenge to discover the world for herself.

      Zolatow, Charlotte. *William's Doll.* Illus. William Pene duBois. New
      York: Harper & Row, 1972. (Ages 3–8.)
William likes to do "male" things, such as sports and trains, but he also wants a
doll. His father, brother, and friends (male) are perturbed by this. No mother is
included in the story. Grandmother comes to his rescue by getting him a doll
and explaining that he can practice for the time when he becomes a father
himself. This book will serve as the basis for much discussion.

Recommended for Ages Three through Eight—with Reservations

      Baldwin, Anne Norris. *Sunflowers for Tina.* Illus. Ann Grifalconi.
      New York: Four Winds Press, 1970. Pb. Scholastic. (Ages 5–8.)
Tina, a black child living in the city, craves a garden. Her brother shows her
sunflowers growing in a vacant lot, and that makes her happy. She, in turn,
dances a sunflower dance for her grandmother, making the old woman happy.
The lot of the female in this book is not, in general, a pleasant one.

Black, Algernon D. *The Woman of the Wood.* Illus. Evaline Ness. New York: Holt, Rinehart, and Winston, 1973. (Ages 3–8.)

Three men on a journey carve a woman out of wood, make her clothes, and teach her to speak. They each want to own her, but a wise old man tells them that she belongs to herself and only she can choose whom and what she wants. Although the moral is useful, the presentation is flawed by the one-dimensional characteristics of the woman and the transformation of the old man into a handsome young one.

Blaine, Marge. *The Terrible Thing That Happened at Our House.* Illus. John C. Wallner. New York: Parents' Magazine Press, 1975. (Ages 4–8.)

When a young girl's mother resumes her career, the child feels as if her world has fallen apart. She is intolerant of the new arrangements that the family makes. Resenting her parents' new roles, she wants her old, comfortable life back again. After a confrontation, the family together decide on a course of action satisfactory to all. The solution is a good one, but the tone of the book is negative.

Bonsall, Crosby. *The Case of the Scaredy Cats.* New York: Harper & Row, 1971. (Ages 5–8.)

A group of boys make plans to get rid of the girls who have invaded their clubhouse, but the plan backfires. Unfortunately, this book encourages competition between the sexes.

Danish, Barbara. *The Dragon and the Doctor.* Old Westbury, N.Y.: Feminist Press, 1971. Pb. (Ages 3–8.)

A story with consciously changed sex roles (doctor is female, nurse is male) about a dragon with a sick tail, who is very grateful to the doctor for her help. Too labored and obvious to be effective.

Eichler, Margaret. *Martin's Father.* Chapel Hill, N.C.: Lollipop Power, 1971. Pb. (Ages 3–7.)

Martin and his father go through a typical day together. There is no mother, and the two males perform what is conventionally considered to be women's work. This would have been an even more effective book if a mother had been present, working alongside Martin and his father.

Hopkins, Lee Bennett. *Girls Can Too!* Illus. Emily McCully. New York: Franklin Watts, 1972. (Ages 5–8.)

A book of positive poems about what different girls can do, think, and feel. The only flaw in the book is the inclusion of poems encouraging competition between the sexes.

Horvath, Betty. *Be Nice to Josephine.* Illus. Pat Grant. New York: Franklin Watts, 1970. (Ages 5–8.)

Charlie unwillingly gives up his baseball game to take his cousin Josephine fishing, and finds that, despite himself, he has a good time. But he ruins his good behavior by succumbing to his friends' teasing.

Jewell, Nancy. *Try and Catch Me.* Illus. Leonard Weisgard. New York: Harper & Row, 1972. (Ages 4–8.)

An active girl is self-sufficient and energetic. As she goes about her play, a boy teases her and seems to disapprove of what she is doing. But in the end, he approaches her and invites her to join him in a swim. The competition somewhat mars the story, but both the boy and the girl are described in positive ways.

Levinson, Irene. *Peter Learns to Crochet.* Illus. Ketra Sutherland. Stanford, Calif.: New Seed Press, 1973. Pb. (Ages 5–8.)

Peter wants to learn to crochet but has trouble finding someone to teach him, until he asks his teacher, Mr. Alvarado. Somewhat artificial, but not unbelievable.

Levy, Elizabeth. *Nice Little Girls.* Illus. Mordicai Gerstein. New York: Delacorte Press, 1974. (Ages 5–8.)

Jackie, a girl who wants to be a boy, is teased by her classmates, scolded by her teacher, but listened to and reassured by her parents. Finally, another girl in class wants to become friends with Jackie, and she is no longer an outcast. Somewhat mixed messages are conveyed in this book.

Lystad, Mary. *Jennifer Takes Over P.S. 94.* Illus. Ray Cruz. New York: Putnam's, 1972. (Ages 3–8.)

Jennifer imagines how she would run the school, while sitting on the "punish bench" for kicking a girl who hit her first.

McCloskey, Robert. *One Morning in Maine.* New York: Viking, 1952. (Ages 5–8.)

Two sisters spend a lovely day with their father digging clams and going to the mainland by motorboat. Although life is not stereotyped for the little girls, it seems to be for the parents.

McGinley, Phyllis. *A Girl and Her Room.* Illus. Ati Forbey, New York: Franklin Watts, 1963. (Ages 5–8.)

Changes in a girl's room are followed as the girl grows from birth to early womanhood. Too sweet, too simple.

————. *Lucy McLockett.* Illus. Helen Stone. Philadelphia: Lippincott, 1958. (Ages 5–8.)

A fairly liberated story for its time. Although the expectation is that Lucy will be well-behaved and demure, she is permitted to climb trees, play active games with boys, and ride a bicycle. All of this is counterbalanced by her other activities, which are predominantly female-role-linked; but the book is not ruined by its flaws. Lucy emerges as a very lively girl. An updating of the illustrations would go a long way in alleviating the sexist message.

Phillips, Lynn. *Exactly Like Me.* Chapel Hill, N.C.: Lollipop Power, 1972. (Ages 3–8.)

A young girl will not permit herself to be boxed in by stereotypes. The writing in this little book leaves much to be desired, but the message is a useful one.

> **Rothman, Joel.** *I Can Be Anything You Can Be.* New York: Scroll Press, 1973. (Ages 5–9.)

This book is an open-ended argument between a girl and a boy revolving around the taunt "I can be anything you can be." It is unfortunate that the action revolves around a competition.

> **Segal, Lore.** *Tell Me a Mitzi.* Illus. Harriet Pincus. New York: Farrar, Straus & Giroux, 1970. (Ages 5–8.)

The three stories describe a contemporary Jewish family living in New York City. The males are subtly valued over the females in these stories, although that is not the intention of the author. Mitzi is a competent child, but Jacob is even more so for his age. Mitzi's mother almost never takes off her apron, and does nothing but housework. Mitzi's father participates in the house and also takes the children for outings. The relationship is a loving one except that the family expects the mother to ignore her own illness and to care for them. Luckily the grandmother is available to nurse them when they are all ill. Too many stereotypes mar the essentially positive message of the story.

> **Simon, Norma.** *I Know What I Like.* Illus. Dora Leder. Chicago: Albert Whitman, 1971. (Ages 3–7.)

Integrated pictures. Children like all kinds of different things; unfortunately, boys and girls are pictured in somewhat stereotypic situations.

> **Werth, Kurt, and Watts, Mabel.** *Molly and the Giant.* New York: Parents' Magazine Press, 1973. (Ages 5–8.)

Molly outwits a giant and is brave and clever enough to get herself and her sisters married to three princes in this modern tale. Perhaps some day there will be a different happy ending.

> **Zolotow, Charlotte.** *The Summer Night.* Illus. Ben Shecter. New York: Harper & Row, 1974. (Ages 4–8.)

When a little girl cannot sleep, her father tries all kinds of remedies for her sleeplessness and finally accompanies her on a walk. The father is tender and understanding. The reader assumes that the mother is absent because of death, divorce, or temporary reasons. It would have been far more effective as a nonsexist book if the mother had been at home and the father had still behaved in this way.

Recommended for Ages Six through Twelve

> **Baker, Elizabeth.** *Tammy Camps Out.* Illus. Beth and Joe Krush. Boston: Houghton Mifflin, 1958. Pb. also. (Ages 8–12.)

Tammy goes camping with her brother and her father and is teased for being silly and incompetent, until a landslide occurs and she must blaze a trail and seek help.

> Baker, Nina Brown. *Nellie Bly, Reporter.* Illus. W. Blickinstoff. New York: Henry Holt, 1956. Pb. Scholastic. (Ages 8–12.)

An interesting biography of a determined and intelligent woman. Contains telling commentary about early twentieth-century America.

> Blassingame, Wyatt. *Combat Nurses of World War II.* Illus. Gil Walker. New York: Random House (Landmark Books), 1967. (Ages 9–up.)

A historical recounting of the teamwork among those who were involved in the battles of World War II. Free of sentimentality and of the exploitation found in some depictions of war-related events.

> Brownmiller, Susan. *Shirley Chisholm.* Garden City, N.Y.: Doubleday, 1970. Pb. Archway. (Ages 9–11.)

A biography of Shirley Chisholm, the first black woman to become a U.S. Representative. the book provides an insight into the business of American politics.

> Buckmaster, Henrietta. *Women Who Shaped History.* New York: Macmillan, 1966. Pb. Collier Books. (Ages 10–up.)

An excellent compilation of short biographies of six women who were important contributors to our country's development. Well written, well balanced, and well selected.

> Burch, Robert. *Queenie Peavy.* Illus. Jerry Lazare. New York: Viking, 1966. (Ages 9–12.)

Queenie is a strong, intelligent, capable thirteen-year-old. Her self-motivation and determination help her to overcome her father's negative influence and the teasing that she endures because he is in the penitentiary. She does things that only boys are usually thought of as doing, is frequently in trouble, and almost gets into serious trouble. But in the end, the support of many adults and her own intelligence win out. The book is somewhat overly sweet, but Queenie's character provides a useful image for women in this kind of book.

> Burnett, Frances Hodgson. *The Secret Garden.* Philadelphia: Lippincott, 1911. Pb. Dell. (Ages 9–14.)

A bold, assertive girl comes to live in a new place, discovers a secret garden, a new friend, and how to care about others.

> Burt, Olive. *Black Women of Valor.* Illus. Paul Frame. New York: Messner, 1974. (Ages 9–11.) (Newbery Medal.)

Tells the stories of four black women who demonstrated their courage and ability: Juliette Derricotte, Maggie Mitchell Walker, Ida Wells Barnett, Septima Poinsette Clark. The book also contains a long list of other black women of valor. Valuable addition to information about black history. One would wish, however, that the author had not so facilely referred to each of the women by her first name.

Cleary, Beverly. *Ramona the Pest.* New York: Morrow, 1968. (Ages 9–11.)

Everyone calls curious, lively Ramona a "pest," but she has a different image of herself during her first few months of kindergarten. Overturns the image of the typical little girl.

Cleaver, Vera and Bill. *Ellen Grae.* Illus. Ellen Raskin. Philadelphia: Lippincott, 1967. (Ages 9–11.)

Ellen Grae is an unusual heroine. She is imaginative beyond belief, and is, in fact, not usually believed by the other characters in the book. A nonconformist in many ways, much to the dismay of her parents and other adults, she is, however, sensitive and appealing.

————. *Lady Ellen Grae.* Illus. Ellen Raskin. Philadelphia: Lippincott, 1968. (Ages 9–11.)

Another very well-written story by the Cleavers. Ellen Grae is the imaginative, sensitive, loving, bright heroine, who manages, despite her eccentricities, to endear herself to everyone. In this book, her parents decide that she should learn "ladylike" ways. The parody on stereotypic feminine characteristics is somewhat broad, but the demonstration that individual differences are far more acceptable than mindless conformity helps the reader to overlook the flaws.

Colman, Hila. *Diary of a Frantic Kid Sister.* New York: Crown, 1973. (Ages 8–11.)

Written in a narrative/diary form, this is the sensitive story of an eleven-year-old girl's relationships with her mother and her elder sister, all of whom are having difficulty coping with their roles.

Faber, Doris. *Lucretia Mott: Foe to Slavery.* Champaign, Ill.: Garrard, 1971. (Ages 8–12.)

The biography of a Quaker woman who spent her life fighting for voting and educational rights for women and Blacks.

Fitzhugh, Louise. *Harriet the Spy.* New York: Harper & Row, 1964. Pb. Dell. (Ages 9–12.)

An amusing, brash portrayal of a sometimes stubborn eleven-year-old girl who wants to be a spy and bluntly writes down all her observations of family and community life in her secret notebook. Harriet is clever, inventive, and not very sensitive to other people's feelings. The other children in the book are also not stereotyped.

Gardner, Richard A. *Dr. Gardner's Fairy Tales for Today's Children.* Illus. A. Lowenheim. Englewood Cliffs, N.J.: Prentice-Hall, 1974. (Ages 8–up.)

Four fairy tales loosely adapted from classical versions. The characters behave in rational, constructive fashion rather than adhering to traditional patterns. The stories are fun.

Gauch, Patricia Lee. *This Time, Tempe Wick?* Illus. Margot Tomes. New York: Coward, McCann & Geoghegan, 1974. (Ages 7–11.)

Temperance Wick, a bold unselfish girl, defies rebellious American soldiers in
order to protect her mother, horse, and house during the Revolutionary War.

> Goldreich, Gloria and Esther. *What Can She Be? An Architect.*
> Photographs by Robert Ipcar. New York: Lothrop, Lee & Shepard,
> 1974. (Ages 4–10.)

Part of the "What Can She Be?" series, this book maintains the quality of the
others. The information is well presented; the photographs are clear. This book
does not, incidentally, include as many women in professions as the others do,
but it is, nevertheless, a useful addition to any library.

> ———. *What Can She Be? A Lawyer.* Photographs by Robert Ipcar.
> New York: Lothrop, Lee & Shepard, 1973. (Ages 4–10.)

Part of the series devoted to describing women in professions formerly considered to be for men only. This book describes how Ellen Green manages to be
a lawyer, wife, and mother. Ms. Green has a varied clientele and is shown to be
an able attorney, as well as a competent, happy, well-adjusted woman. An
excellent, well-conceived book.

> ———. *What Can She Be? A Newscaster.* Photographs by Robert
> Ipcar. New York: Lothrop, Lee & Shepard, 1973. (Ages 5–10.)

A straightforward book about a woman who works as a TV and radio newscaster
and also has a good family life.

> Graves, Robert. *Two Wise Children.* Illus. Ralph Pinto. New York:
> Harlan Quist, 1966. (Ages 8–up.)

The friendship of Bill Brain and Avis Deed grows stronger after each experiences and then loses the magic power to be able to do or to know anything
beyond the ordinary. Their friendship is unusual because of the intrusion of the
supernatural.

> Heyn, Leah. *Challenge to Become a Doctor: The Story of Elizabeth
> Blackwell.* Old Westbury, N.Y.: Feminist Press, 1971. (Ages 9–13.)

The biography of the struggle of a determined woman to become a doctor
despite the discrimination evident in the all-male profession. Blackwell, in fact,
became the first woman physician.

> Henriod, Lorraine. *Marie Curie.* Illus. Fermin Rocher. New York:
> Putnam's, 1970. (Ages 7–10.)

A "beginning to read" biography dispelling the myth that radium was discovered accidentally. In simple but clear language it points out the care and study
that Marie Curie devoted to her profession.

> Hochman, Sandra. *The Magic Convention.* Illus. Ben Shecter. Gar-
> den City, N.Y.: Doubleday, 1971. (Ages 8–up.)

A girl goes to a professional magician's convention, sees an exciting performance by a woman magician, and decides more than ever that she wants to be a
magician.

> Hochschild, Arlie Russell. *Colleen the Question Girl.* Illus. Gail
> Ashby. Old Westbury, N.Y.: Feminist Press, 1974. Pb. (Ages 5–10.)

Colleen is an intelligent young girl who questions everyone about serious and confusing topics—race, discrimination, wealth, and status.

> **Hoehling, Mary.** *Girl Soldier and Spy: Sarah Emma Edmundson.* New York: Messner, 1959. (Ages 10–up.)

A well-written account of this unusual woman. The author always refers to her heroine as a woman, and it is as a woman that Sarah accomplishes her adventures. Her qualities are womanly, even when she is pretending to be a man. The author values women and presents the story so that readers may do so as well.

> **Howard, Moses L.** *The Ostrich Chase.* Illus. Barbara Seuling. New York: Holt, Rinehart and Winston, 1974. (Ages 10–14.)

Khuana, a young woman of the Bushman tribe, violates tradition by learning to hunt and to build fires. Because of these skills, she is able to save her grandmother's life and to conquer the desert. She nevertheless remains interested in womanly things as well. She is an admirable character.

> **Johnson, Elizabeth.** *Break a Magic Circle.* Boston: Little, Brown, 1971. (Ages 8–11.)

A boy breaks a magic circle of mushrooms and is enchanted. He is saved, though, and the magic circle fixed, with the help of a girl and her little brother.

> **Jordan, June.** *Fannie Lou Hamer.* Illus. Albert Williams. New York: Crowell, 1972. (Ages 6–10.)

A well-told biography of a brave black woman who fought for the rights of black people and who began a cooperative in Mississippi.

> **Keller, Gail Faithfull.** *Jane Addams.* Illus. Frank Aloise. New York: Crowell, 1971. (Ages 7–9.)

A clear description of the work and personality of Jane Addams. Simply, but in useful detail, her life is well narrated.

> **Kingman, Lee.** *Georgina and the Dragon.* Illus. Leonard Shortall. Boston: Houghton Mifflin, 1972. (Ages 7–10.)

Georgina Gooch is determined to live up to her suffragist great-grandmother's tradition. She crusades for equal rights and manages to raise the level of consciousness of her whole neighborhood. She is fun—her energy and intelligence are outstanding, An excellent book.

> **Klein, Norma.** *Mom, the Wolf Man and Me.* New York: Pantheon Books, 1972. Pb. Avon. (Ages 10–up.)

Brett, an illegitimate child, and her mother live together happily and discuss serious issues openly. When her mother makes friends with a man and eventually marries him, Brett is able to accept this change after an uneasy time.

> _____. *Naomi in the Middle.* Illus. Leigh Grant. New York: Dial Press, 1974. (Ages 7–10.)

Most of the characters in this book are female; all are individuals. They are pictured wearing comfortable clothes and doing activities of all sorts. The grandmother is an interesting character in her own right. She is not very fond of infants, preferring "more complicated" older children. The shop teacher is female. And so is Alice, Bobo's pet rat.

    ————. *A Train for Jane.* Illus. Miriam Schottland. Old Westbury, N.Y.: Feminist Press, 1974. (Ages 6–10.)

A verse-story telling how, despite all efforts of persuasion by her parents, Jane insists on a train for a Christmas present. It is fine for other girls to want "girls' " toys but she loves her train.

    Konigsburg, E. L. *From the Mixed-Up Files of Mrs. Basil E. Frank-weiler.* New York: Atheneum, 1967. Pb. also. (Ages 8–12.) (Newbery Medal.)

Claudia and Jamie run away from home and hide in the Metropolitan Museum of Art, where they get involved in a mystery centered around a work of art formerly owned by Mrs. Basil E. Frankweiler. Both Claudia and Mrs. Frankweiler are strong females with individual personalities.

    Krauss, Ruth. *I'll Be You and You Be Me.* Illus. Maurice Sendak. Lenox, Mass.: Bookstore Press, 1973. Pb. also. (Ages 8–up.) (*N.Y. Times* Best Illustrated Children's Books of the Year.)

Warm ideas, in poetry form, about friendship between boys and girls.

    Lawrence, Jacob. *Harriet and the Promised Land.* New York: Simon and Schuster, 1968. (Ages 6–10.) (*N.Y. Times* Best Illustrated Children's Books of the year.)

In verse and colorful pictures, this book describes the courageous black woman, Harriet Tubman, who escaped from slavery and helped many others to escape also. Her life was difficult and unconventional, as she persevered in her heroic actions despite grave danger.

    L'Engle, Madeleine. *A Wrinkle in Time.* New York: Farrar, Straus, 1962. Pb. Dell. (Ages 12–up.) (Newbery Medal.)

Meg is the heroine of this science-fiction adventure about two children who travel into space with three wise, magical creatures to find their scientist-father. Their mother, too, is brilliant and a scientist.

    ————. *The Young Unicorns.* New York: Farrar, Straus, 1968. (Ages 12–up.)

An elaborate mystery set in New York with a blind musician, Emily, and a scientific whiz, Sue, as heroines of the story.

    Levitin, Sonia. *Rita, the Weekend Rat.* Illus. Leonard Shortall. New York: Atheneum, 1971. (Ages 8–12.)

Cynthia is a second grader who hates being a girl. She has a rat named Rita, whom she cares for on the weekends. She begins to reconcile herself to being a girl, by the end of the book, but does not stop being active or taking care of Rita and her baby rats.

    Lofts, Norah. *The Maude Reed Tale.* Illus. Anne and Janet Grahame Johnstone. Nashville: Thomas Nelson, 1972. Pb. Dell. (Ages 10–up.)

The setting is the Middle Ages. Maude, about twelve years old, has a twin brother, who runs away from home to be a minstrel. Maude wants to be a wool merchant. The conflicts of personal and societal values, besides the cleverness of the heroine, make the book a vital one. The writing is of excellent quality.

>   Longsworth, Polly. *Emily Dickinson: Her Letter to the World.* New York: Crowell, 1965. (Ages 10–up.)

A nicely constructed biography of Emily Dickinson. Her recluse behavior is accepted as a logical result of her way of life, rather than being presented as a mystery.

>   _____. *I, Charlotte Forten, Black and Free.* New York: Crowell, 1970. (Ages 10–12.)

Charlotte Forten serves as the narrator of this fictionalized autobiography. Her life was an eventful, rich one. She meets and works against slavery with many famous people. the book describes other abolitionists, such as the Grimke sisters and William Lloyd Garrison, and tells the stories of such notable Blacks as Frederick Douglass, James Forten, and William Wells Brown, among others. The fight for women's rights is seen as a parallel and compatible one with abolition.

>   MacGregor, Ellen. *Miss Pickerell Goes to Mars.* Illus. Paul Galdone. New York: McGraw-Hill, 1951. Pb. Scholastic. (Ages 9–11.)

Miss Pickerell is an old woman who travels from one exciting adventure to another, all over the universe. She is much brighter than most of the males, and accomplishes more than most people. There is a long series of Miss Pickerell books, each with a new adventure.

>   Mann, Peggy. *Amelia Earhart, First Lady of Flight.* Illus. Kiyo Komoda. New York: Coward, McCann, 1970. (Ages 10–12.)

A biography of the first woman to become a well-known aviator. Earhart is one of the women most written about.

>   Mathis, Sharon Bell. *Sidewalk Story.* Illus. Leo Carty. New York: Viking, 1971. Pb. Avon. (Ages 9–11.) (Council on Interracial Books for Children Award.)

Lilly Etta Allen is the nine-year-old protagonist. By her refusal to accept an unfair situation, she manages to help her friend Tanya overcome eviction. Lilly Etta enlists the aid of the newspapers and also acts on her own to protect her friend's possessions.

>   Minard, Rosemary. (ed.) *Womenfolk and Fairy Tales.* Illus. Suzanna Klein. Boston: Houghton Mifflin, 1975. (Ages 7–10.)

Females are the major characters in all of the stories in this book. They are not all unstereotypic, but they do, in general, exhibit such qualities as intelligence, courage, and ingenuity. The introduction is a valuable addition to the tales themselves.

>   Myers, Walter. *The Dragon Takes a Wife.* Illus. Ann Grifalconi. New York: Xerox Education Publications, 1972. (Ages 7–9.)

Harry, the dragon, takes lessons from Mabel Mae, the good fairy, so that he can vanquish a knight. He does so, marries Mabel Mae, gets a good job at the post office, and never fights again.

> **Nathan, Dorothy, *Women of Courage*.** Illus. Carolyn Cather. New York: Random House, 1964. (Ages 10–up.)

Biographies of five brave women: Susan B. Anthony, women's rights crusader, Jane Addams, social reformer who worked for the poor, Mary McLeod Bethune, educator of black children, Amelia Earhart, daring aviator, and Margaret Mead, anthropologist searching for the "secrets of human nature."

> **Norton, Mary. *The Borrowers*.** New York: Harcourt Brace Jovanovich, 1953. Pb. also. (Ages 8–up.)

The first of a series of books about little people called Borrowers who live under the floors and in the walls of human's houses. In this book, Arietty, an adventurous female, is taken out by her father to learn how to borrow—something usually done only by males.

> **O'Dell, Scott. *Island of the Blue Dolphins*.** Boston: Houghton Mifflin, 1960. Pb. Dell. (Ages 10–up.) (Newbery Medal, ALA Notable.)

Karana, a young Native American girl, is alone on her home island after her tribe has left and her brother has been killed by wild dogs. She manages her own survival courageously for many years until, at last, she is rescued by missionaries.

> _____. *Sing Down the Moon*. Boston: Houghton Mifflin, 1970. Pb. Dell. (Ages 7–up.) (Newbery Honor Book.)

A courageous young Navajo woman experiences all sorts of dangers: she is kidnapped by Spaniards, endures the Long Walk to Fort Sumner, and manages to return, with her husband and child, to their original home. The story focuses on the character of the young woman rather than on the hardships of the Navajos.

> **Paustovsky, Konstantin. *The Magic Ringlet*.** Translated by Thomas Whitney. Reading, Mass.: Addison-Wesley, 1971. (Ages 6–10.)

A young Russian girl lives with her sick grandfather. She is given a magic ring that will bring her happiness and her grandfather health, but she loses it—and persistently tries to find it in a snowy forest.

> **Penny, Grace Jackson. *Moki*.** Boston: Houghton Mifflin, 1960. Pb. Avon. (Ages 8–12.)

Moki, a ten-year-old Cheyenne girl is dissatisfied doing "women's work," but she is put down every time that she tries to assert herself. This does not stop her, though. In the end she is awarded an honor rarely given to women.

> **Rich, Gibson. *Firegirl*.** Illus. Charlotte Purrington Farley. Old Westbury, N.Y.: Feminist Press, 1972. (Ages 8–12.)

A girl has ambition to become a fire fighter and learns all about what it takes to realize this goal.

> **Rodgers, Mary. *Freaky Friday*.** New York: Harper & Row, 1972. Pb. also. (Ages 10–up.)

A girl magically turns into her mother for a day and sees herself from a new perspective.

      Sachs, Marilyn. *Peter and Veronica.* Illus. Louis Glanzman. Garden City, N.Y.: Doubleday, 1969. Pb. Dell. (Ages 8–12.)

Peter and Veronica are good friends despite their differences of sex, religion, and social acceptability and despite pressures exerted by parents and peers. They finally realize that good friendship can sometimes be very painful. Veronica is strong, pugnacious, and awkward. She begins to change in physical appearance but does not want that to affect her relationship with people.

      Sawyer, Ruth. *Roller Skates.* Illus. V. Angelo. New York: Viking, 1936. Pb. Dell. (Ages 9–12.) (Newbery Medal.)

Lucinda is the lively, bouncy heroine of this story. The episodes take place in very upper-class old New York. Lucinda is unusual for her time but beautifully in tune with today.

      Simon, Seymour. *A Tree on Your Street.* Illus. Betty Fraser. New York: Holiday House, 1973. (Ages 6–9.)

A group of children, both boys and girls, studying the trees in their neighborhood, learn about the leaves, the bark, the variety of trees, and the animals that live in trees.

      Sorensen, Virginia. *Plain Girl.* Illus. C. Geer. New York: Harcourt, Brace, 1956. Pb. Scholastic. (Ages 9–11.) (Wel-Met Award.)

Esther is a member of an Amish family. The story revolves around the conflict between the teachings of her group and the rest of the world. Esther is a strong heroine because she struggles to think for herself and to make decisions about how she will behave.

      Supraner, Robyn. *Think About It, You Might Learn Something.* Illus. Sandy Kossin. Boston: Houghton Mifflin, 1973. (Ages 8–12.)

Written as a personal journal. Jennifer presents episodes of her life and her private thoughts about what it is like to be a preadolescent daughter, sister, relative, and friend.

      Taves, Isabella. *Not Bad for a Girl.* New York: M. Evans, 1972. (Ages 10–up.)

The true story of a little girl who prefers to play baseball than to play with dolls. Though the coaches object, her father takes her side.

      Travers, P. L. *Mary Poppins.* Illus. Mary Shepard. New York: Harcourt, Brace, and World, 1934. (Ages 9–11.)

The story of four children and their new nanny, Mary Poppins, who has magical powers and takes them on all sorts of fantastic adventures. The Banks household is sexist, and some of the episodes clearly display a "white man's burden" attitude. But Mary Poppins is decidedly not a stereotypic female.

      Wagner, Jane. *J.T.* Illus. G. Parks, Jr. New York: Van Nostrand Reinhold, 1969. Pb. Dell. (Ages 8–12.)

J. T. is a boy growing up in Harlem with his mother. Through his attachment for a scrawny cat, J.T. expresses his feelings and sensitivity for all the people in his life. He hates fighting and craves affection.

> **Warren, Ruth.** *A Pictorial History of Women in America.* New York: Crown, 1975. (Ages 10–up.)

A useful overview of the role of women in America's development. The book focuses on the women rather than the historical context. Many women are included. The text is interesting and well written.

> **Wilder, Laura Ingalls.** *Little House in the Big Woods and Little House on the Prairie.* Illus. Helen Sewell. New York: Harper & Row, 1932 and 1935. (Ages 6–11.)

The first two books in a series about a little girl growing up with her family and leading an interesting frontier life. The women, who actually lived, are accurately portrayed. Although victims of their time, they display courage and strength.

> **Yolen, Jane.** *The Girl Who Cried Flowers and Other Tales.* Illus. D. Palladini. New York: Crowell, 1974. (Ages 8–11.) (National Book Award Finalist.)

Three of these five tales have female protagonists. They are far from traditional: one contains a wise and frostily silent queen; one has a woman who takes upon herself the burden of designing the world's fate; one is destroyed by her desire to please.

> _____. *The Magic Three of Solatia.* Illus. Julia Noonan. New York: Crowell, 1974. (Ages 10–up.)

Sianna is a wise and strong and active heroine. The reader sees her grow from childhood into womanhood, retaining all of these qualities. These imaginative stories sustain a poetic and folkloric quality that is very satisfying.

> _____. *Pirates in Petticoats.* Illus. Leonard Vosburgh. New York: David McKay, 1963. (Ages 10–up.)

An engagingly written series of descriptions of female pirates. Interesting from a historical view. The book is in need of some updating but is, nevertheless, worth reading.

Recommended for Ages Six through Twelve—With Reservations

> **Babbitt, Natalie.** *Phoebe's Revolt.* New York: Farrar, Straus & Giroux, 1968. (Ages 6–9.)

Set in the Victorian era. A girl decides she does not want to wear ruffles and frills and likes her father's clothes instead. Finding that her father's clothes are not right, either, she finally finds a comfortable compromise. Somewhat of a cop-out but useful nevertheless.

> **Brink, Carol Ryrie.** *Caddie Woodlawn.* Illus. Trina Schart Hyman. New York: Macmillan, 1935. Pb. also. (Ages 9–12.) (Newbery Medal.)

A frontier story of the lively childhood adventures of Caddie and her brothers in the 1860s. Although Caddie's adventurous and active qualities are admired, the reader recognizes that she is expected to grow into a "conventional" woman.

Cleaver, Vera and Bill. *Delpha Green & Company.* Philadelphia: Lippincott, 1972. (Ages 10–up.)

Delpha accepts the responsibility for the world's welfare. A very self-reliant person, she manages to cope very well with seemingly insurmountable family problems, but the focus on astrology weakens the book. And the happy capitulation of almost the entire town is somewhat difficult to believe.

Coatsworth, Elizabeth. *The Princess and the Lion.* New York: Pantheon, 1963. (Ages 8–12.)

A folk tale in which the princess does the rescuing, assisted by a royal lion and a royal donkey. Yet, despite her courage and her cleverness, she must remain on the "servant" level of the king's women, while her brother becomes king.

Greene, Bette. *Philip Hall Likes Me: I Reckon Maybe.* Illus. Charles Lilly. New York: Dial Press, 1974. (Ages 9–12.) (Newbery Honor Book.)

Beth Lambert is black, eleven years old, and extraordinarily bright and competent. She is a lively, ambitious, successful young woman, who wants to be a veterinarian, and the reader knows that she will succeed. The major flaw in this book is that Beth and Philip, the boy to whom she is attracted, must always compete with each other. Competition is stressed between the boys and the girls. Though it works out "happily" in the end, the idea of one-upmanship mars the otherwise flavorful and excellent book.

Gripe, Maria. *The Night Daddy.* Illus. Harold Gripe. New York: Delacorte Press, 1971. Pb. Dell. (Ages 8–11.)

An unusual story about the relationship between a young girl and her adult male baby-sitter who stays nights while her mother works. The story takes place in Sweden; it is not yet realistic for the United States.

Jacobs, Helen Hull. *The Tennis Machine.* New York: Scribner's, 1972. (Ages 10–up.)

Story of a thirteen-year-old tennis champion who is trying to break away from her dominating father in order to think and to act on her own. She is only partially successful by the end of the book.

Konigsburg, E. L. *Jennifer, Hecate, Macbeth, William McKinley and Me, Elizabeth.* New York: Atheneum, 1967. Pb. also. (Ages 9–12.) (Newbery Honor Book.)

Elizabeth and Jennifer are friends. At first their friendship is based on the supposed practice of witchcraft, but both girls are outcasts, partly because they do not dress and behave as the other girls do. Jennifer is excluded also because she is black. The author values these two girls over the others, but adults would do well to guide readers to recognize the racist and sexist behavior of the other characters.

Larrick, Nancy, and Merriam, Eve (eds.). *Male and Female Under 18.* New York: Avon Books, 1973. (Ages 8–up.) Pb.

Comments and poems contributed by girls and boys, aged eight to eighteen, reflecting how they feel about their sex roles. The responses range from strong support of tradition to militant anger.

Lexau, Joan. *The Trouble with Terry.* Illus. Irene Murray. New York: Dial Press, 1962. Pb. Scholastic. (Ages 8–12.) (Wel-Met Award.)

Terry is a tomboy. Her mother, troubled about this, wants Terry to be more ladylike. Terry and her brother are friends, and she is accepted by her brother's friends. The book does not make great strides toward liberation, but it takes a few steps.

Lindgren, Astrid. *Pippi Longstocking.* Illus. Louis Glanzman. New York: Viking, 1950. Pb. also. (Ages 9–11.)

Pippi is a lively, independent heroine who lives, without parents, in a magical, adventurous world, which amazes her two friends next door. She stands out as painfully different and somewhat lonely.

Martin, Patricia Miles. *Dolley Madison.* Illus. Unada Gliewe. New York: Putnam's, 1967. (Ages 6–10.)

A "beginning-to-read" biography, the book somewhat oversimplifies the details of Dolley Madison's life. It also implies that her son, Payne, was loving and attentive, when history indicates that he caused her great problems.

Matsumo, Masako. *Chie and the Sports Day.* Illus. Kazue Mizumara. Cleveland: World, 1965. (Ages 8–11.)

Chie's older brother Ichiro and his friends disdain playing with girls. Chie's mother permits her to help prepare food for the Sports Day. The mother will cut short an important meeting to be able to attend. Fortuitously, at Sports Day, Ichiro needs a little girl to run the three-legged race. Chie and Ichiro come in first. No father is evident, but the mother seems to lead a balanced life, although it is clear that "boys are superior to girls."

Perl, Lila. *That Crazy April.* New York: Seabury Press, 1974. (Ages 9–12.)

Eleven-year-old Cress's mother is very much involved in the women's movement. Her father cheerfully participates in the maintenance of the house, and supports his wife's interests. Cress resents her mother's activities. In the end she realizes that she will develop her own interests and personality and will learn to survive on her own terms. The book is not a potential classic, but it raises interesting questions.

Rizzo, Ann. *The Strange Hocket Family.* Old Westbury, N.Y.: Feminist Press, 1974. (Ages 6–10.)

A self-conscious story in which male and female roles are absolutely reversed, and the "normal" stereotype is made to look peculiar.

Sorensen, Virginia. *Miracles on Maple Hill.* Illus. B. and J. Krush.

New York: Harcourt, Brace, 1956. Pb. also. (Ages 9–12.) (Newbery Medal.)

Marly and her family move to Maple Hill. Although Marly is an active, lively heroine, the characters have very sex-stereotyped expectations and behaviors. The story is a conventional but well-written one, demonstrating how the simple qualities and simple life are the best.

> **Vestly, Anne-Cath.** *Hello Aurora.* Illus. Leonard Kessler. Translated by Eileen Amos; adapted by Jane Fairfax. New York: Crowell, 1974. (Ages 7–10.)

A very didactic but charming story about a Norwegian family. Mother is a lawyer. Father, who is studying for his doctorate, stays home with Aurora, the young daughter, and Socrates, the baby. The father is not tremendously adept, but he and Aurora manage fairly well. The neighbors disapprove of the arrangement, and Aurora is uncomfortable; but the reader is totally drawn into the situation. Many values are stated in the book. The parents are too good; the world is too one-sidedly different from them—but the book is useful, nevertheless.

Recommended for Ages Twelve and Up

> **Carlson, Dale.** *Girls Are Equal Too, The Women's Movement for Teenagers.* New York: Atheneum, 1973. (Ages 11–up.)

This book raises strong issues and presents clear arguments reflecting the feminist position. Good sections on women's rights and job inequality and on the history of women's rights.

> **Cleaver, Vera and Bill.** *Me Too.* Philadelphia: Lippincott, 1973. (Ages 12–up.)

Lydia tries to teach her retarded twin, Lorna. Devoting an entire summer to her sister's education, she endures the hostility of neighbors and the desertion of a friend. She is clever, energetic, introspective, nasty at times, and a clear individual. She is free of sex-role stereotypes. She finally accepts the fact that her sister will remain retarded and that there is little that she can do for her.

> _____. *Where the Lilies Bloom.* Illus. Jim Spanfeller. Philadelphia: Lippincott, 1969. Pb. New American Library. (Ages 9–up.) (National Book Award Finalist.)

Set in Appalachia. A fourteen-year-old girl cares for her family after the sickness and death of their father, whom they bury and pretend is still alive. Her strength is impressive but is insufficient without the help of her siblings and outside circumstances.

> **Engebrecht, P. A.** *Under the Haystack.* New York: Thomas Nelson, 1973. (Ages 11–up.)

When deserted by her mother and stepfather, Sandy, a thirteen-year-old girl courageously manages to take care of her sisters and the farm where they live. She must work hard, defend herself, and cope with great responsibility.

George, Jean Craighead. *Julie of the Wolves.* Illus. John Schoenherr. New York: Harper & Row, 1972. (Ages 12–up.) (Newbery Medal and National Book Award.)

An Eskimo girl runs away from an unhappy situation. Living in the frozen wilderness, she courageously makes friends with the wolves and learns their ways of survival. She must face problems not only of individual survival but also of the changing ways of her people.

Greenfield, Howard. *Gertrude Stein, a Biography.* New York: Crown. 1973. (Ages 12–up.)

A frank and clearly written biography of the controversial woman. Her personal life is described and explained, as well as her public accomplishments.

Harris, Janet. *A Single Standard.* New York: McGraw-Hill, 1971. (Ages 10–up.)

Although this book contains a historical approach to the feminist movement, it stresses the sociological and psychological implications more than the history. The book relates to every aspect of women's lives.

Haskins, James. *Fighting Shirley Chisholm.* New York: Dial Press, 1975. (Ages 12–up.)

The dynamic black representative is described here in excellent detail. Haskins's book is very frank and inclusive.

Kerr, M. E. *Dinky Hocker Shoots Smack.* New York: Harper & Row, 1972. Pb. Dell. (Ages 12–up.)

A book dealing with many unique, individual adolescents not accepted by the adult community, and centering on Dinky, an overweight girl who is neglected by her community-oriented parents.

Klein, Norma. *It's Not What You Expect.* New York: Pantheon Books, 1973. Pb. Avon. (Ages 12–up.)

Oliver and Carla, fourteen-year-old twins, can find little to divert themselves from the pains of their parents' separation; so, for the summer, they decide to open a gourmet French restaurant. In general, males and females are not stereotyped.

Lader, Lawrence, and Meltzer, Milton. *Margaret Sanger, Pioneer of Birth Control.* New York: Crowell, 1969. Pb. Dell. (Ages 12–up.)

A biography of Margaret Sanger, a strong determined woman who fought to make birth control a right for all women, especially the poor. She was strong enough to maintain her own individuality.

Landau, Elaine. *Women, Women, Feminism in America.* New York: Messner, 1970. (Ages 12–up.)

Presenting a strong case for equality of the sexes, the author describes many instances of discrimination as the basis for her argument. She also tells of countries, such as Israel and Sweden, where great advances in the cause of equality have been made. A well-written, persuasive book.

Mathis, Sharon Bell. *Listen for the Fig Tree.* New York: Viking, 1974.
Pb. Avon. (Ages 12–up.)
Muffin Johnson, sixteen years old and blind, is extraordinarily competent. She
manages her mother and all of the details of housekeeping. She sews and shops
and has excellent relationships with people. Her mother is weak, and almost
destroyed over the death of the father. The male characters in this story are not
stereotyped, but Muffin is too super to be believed. The only chink in her armor
surfaces when someone attempts to rape her. She also relies too strongly on the
opinion of Ernie, whom she plans to marry. Her devotion and feelings about
her black heritage are a strong part of the book.

Meltzer, Milton. *Tongue of Flame. The Life of Lydia Maria Child.*
New York: Crowell, 1965. Pb. Dell. (Ages 12–up.)
A well-written account of the life and times of Lydia Maria Child, who fought for
such causes as abolition, women's rights, and rights of Native Americans. This
book is one of the excellent series of biographies entitled "Women of America."

Neilson, Winthrop and Francis. *Seven Women: Great Painters.*
Philadelphia: Chilton, 1969. (Ages 12–up.)
Serious critique of seven famous painters, from Angelica Kauffman to Georgia
O'Keefe.

Noble, Iris. *Emmeline and Her Daughters: The Pankhurst Suffra-*
gettes. New York: Messner, 1974. (Ages 12–up.)
Detailed story of the British Pankhurst family. The mother and three daughters
were ardent and active fighters for women's rights.

Ortiz, Victoria. *Sojourner Truth, A Self-Made Woman.* Philadelphia:
Lippincott, 1974. (Ages 12–up.)
In reading the story of this remarkable black woman, much history is learned.
The link between the feminist and abolitionist movement is described. So-
journer Truth, a pioneer for the cause of black civil rights, vigorously fought for
her people until her death.

Pfeffer, Susan Beth. *The Beauty Queen.* Garden City, N.Y.: Doubleday, 1974. (ages 12–up.)
A girl is coerced by her mother to enter the local beauty contest. She wins the
titles of Miss Great Oakes and Miss Harrison County. After much thought, she
realizes that being a beauty queen has no real meaning for her; she rejects her
titles and the values they represent.

Seed, Suzanne. *Saturday's Child—36 Women Talk About Their Jobs.*
Chicago: J. Philip O'Hara, 1973. Pb. Bantam. (Ages 11–up.)
Thirty-six women who have had successful careers in architecture, theatre, law,
carpentry, science, and so on, talk about their training, how they chose their
jobs, and how their jobs affect their families.

Thane, Elswyth. *Dolley Madison: Her Life and Times.* New York:
Macmillan, 1970. (Ages 12–up.)

An interesting description, not only of Dolley Madison, but also of the times she lived in and of several of the famous people she knew. Many details of life during the early development of America are described. Although not a complete description of the era, it should interest serious students sufficiently to lead them to further reading.

> **Wood, James Playsted.** *Emily Elizabeth Dickinson.* Nashville: Thomas Nelson, 1972. (Ages 11–up.)

A personalized biography of the poet, emphasizing the mystery of Emily's choosing to remain, for the last years of her life, inside her house. The description of Amherst during the nineteenth century adds flavor to the book.

Recommended for Ages Twelve and Up—With Reservations

> **Cleaver, Vera and Bill.** *The Whys and Wherefores of Littabelle Lee.* New York: Atheneum, 1973. (Ages 12–up.)

An independent, determined young woman overcomes the hardships of her rural mountain life. Her aunt does not conform to the feminine stereotype until she decides to discontinue her doctoring and settles down to be cared for by the man she loves. Each character, however, is an individual.

> **Dolin, Arnold.** *Great American Heroines.* Illus. Rafaello Busoni. New York: Lion Press, 1960. (Ages 12–up.)

The biographies of many American women, including Helen Keller, Pocahontas, Mary Lyon, Harriet Beecher Stowe, Susan Anthony, and Amelia Earhart. Sacrifice and hardship are stressed in these descriptions, somewhat overshadowing the women's own characteristics.

> **Hunt, Irene.** *Up a Road Slowly.* Chicago: Follett, 1966. Pb. Grosset and Dunlap. (Ages 12–up.) (Newbery Medal.)

Julie goes to live with a strict aunt when her mother dies. Julie learns to admire her aunt enough to want to stay with her instead of returning to live with her remarried father. Mixed messages about the role of women are communicated in this book.

> **Hunter, Kristin.** *The Soul Brothers and Sister Lou.* New York: Scribner's, 1968. Pb. Avon. (Ages 12–up.) (Council on Interracial Books for Children Award.)

Detailed portrayal of a group of black teen-agers, both boys and girls, growing up in Harlem. Lou is bright, active, and ambitious. There are other, less admirable characters, and the effect is, in general, not that of the liberated female.

> **Speare, Elizabeth George.** *The Witch of Blackbird Pond.* Boston: Houghton Mifflin, 1958. Pb. Dell. (Ages 12–up.) (Newbery Medal.)

Kit Tyler, orphaned as a young teen-ager, decides to leave her native island of Barbados to live with her maternal aunt, Puritan uncle, and two female cousins. Kit's upbringing has been aristocratic, and she has unquestioningly owned slaves. She has also been educated and encouraged to lead an active life. The role of the female in Colonial days, as well as the impact of politics and religion, is dramatically described in this book. The women in it are individuals, as are all the characters. Although the characterizations are not stereotypic, the males emerge as stronger and more highly valued. Nevertheless the book is excellent.

Recommended for all Ages
    Alcott, Louisa May. *Little Women.* Boston: Little, Brown, 1868. Pb.
    Macmillan. (All ages.)
Portraits of four sisters in a loving family, each with an individual personality and a different vision of her future life. A classic. Jo is one of the sources of the literary image of the active female.
    Herman, Harriet. *The Forest Princess.* Illus. Carde Petersen
    Duinell. Berkeley, Calif.: Over the Rainbow Press, 1974. Pb. (All
    ages.)
A modern-day fairy tale in which a princess wakes a sleeping prince with a kiss and then enchants him with her independence and self-assurance.
    Holman, Felice. *Victoria's Castle.* Illus. Lillian Hoban. New York:
    Norton, 1966. (All ages.)
Victoria is an only child with a wild imagination, with which she builds a castle and a fantasy world filled with unusual animals.
    Ness, Evaline (compiler and illustrator). *Amelia Mixed the Mustard*
    and Other Poems. New York: Scribner's, 1975. (All ages.)
A collection of poems dedicated to all females. Each one of the poems has a heroine at its center. The mood is light; the poems are well selected.
    Thomas, Marlo; Steinem, Gloria; and Pogrebin, Letty Cottin. *Free*
    to Be You and Me. New York: McGraw-Hill, 1974. Pb. also. (All ages.)
Collection of stories, poems, and songs dealing with people's potential to become whatever they want to become.

Recommended for All Ages—With Reservations
    Mosel, Arlene. *The Funny Little Woman.* New York: Dutton, 1972.
    (All ages.) (Caldecott Medal and Children's Book Showcase.)
This story is about a woman who is very content making dumplings and who laughs all the time—habits that get her into and out of trouble.

A BOOK FOR BOTH OF YOU

Enterprising Women by Caroline Bird (W. W. Norton, 1976) was created as a "Bicentennial Project" of the Business and Professional Women's Foundation and focuses on the outstanding female pioneers in various fields, from the revolution through to the present.
    This carefully documented and interestingly written book begins to

bring career women the kind of public exposure that they deserve. Incredibly, both women and men in our society think only of males when recalling or discussing giants of industry, economic leaders, innovators, inventors, or enterprising people who originally were handicapped by either their environment or circumstances and who eventually achieved fame, fortune, and status—perhaps with the one exception of Helen Keller.

What is needed to expand our daughters' horizons and to increase their aspirations is a clever use of the media approaches that bring politicians or performers before the public. Ms. Bird skillfully televises the previously hidden archives of great women and their achievements to the very receptive and empty (in this respect only) channels of our minds.

For example, only a handful of scholars in the entire country know that the Declaration of Independence—the version containing the authentic, original signatures of the signers—was printed by Mary Katherine Goddard (1738–1816), publisher of the *Maryland Journal*. Bird describes how this hard-working and skillful woman became one of the country's first postmistresses in an era when that responsibility was patriotically voluntary and, therefore, unsalaried. Mary Goddard served in that capacity without remuneration for years, delivering the mail as she distributed her newspapers, until the government decided to *pay* its postmasters and promptly dismissed her and appointed a male.

Bird also describes courageous Lucy Taylor (1833–1910) who, although born in a log cabin of poor parents, successfully fought a battle of conviction against institutions of higher education, the medical field and its practitioners, and the licensing procedures of her times. Ms. Taylor was one of those dedicated souls who had "always wanted to be a doctor." She was denied admission into medical school, because women, at that time, were excluded from the necessary preschool training that was required. She acquired enough education to become a teacher and then, over a period of many years, employed college professors and doctors to teach her through private lessons. Finally, she earned the support of a professor at the Eclectic College of Medicine who (also privately) continued her medical training but suggested that she consider practicing dentistry, which did not require a license in Ohio.

Eventually the dean of a dental college trained Lucy (obviously in private!) and encouraged her to seek an apprenticeship. She became the first woman dentist in the Midwest, established a practice that earned her a fine statewide reputation, and after she was recognized as being an outstanding and knowledgeable professional, was finally admitted into the Ohio College of Dental Surgery and became the first woman to receive the degree of Doctor of Dental Surgery in 1866. A romantic note: Lucy married a railroad car painter who subsequently became *her* apprentice and partner in a happy marital-professional relationship.

Read *Enterprising Women* with your daughter. The many interesting stories of women who became industrial, financial, and professional leaders in the United States are excellent for developing aspirations among young girls and for helping them to identify with the spirit, determination, and belief of the many American females who wanted more of life than a perennial second-, third-, fourth- or fifth-place position.

PUBLISHERS AND REFERENCES

An increasing number of sources of nonsexist materials are available for you and your daughter's examination. Selected organizations and publishers have produced books, pamphlets, and checklists to aid parents, teachers, counselors, and students to become sensitive to the insidious propaganda that perpetuates one sex's supposed superiority over the other.

Organizations:
- American Federation of Teachers. Women's Rights Committee. 1012 Fourteenth Street, N.W., Washington, D.C. 20005
- American Library Association. Task Force on the Status of Women. 4004 Whitman North, Seattle, Washington 98104
- Bethany Press. 2640 Pine Blvd., P.O. Box 179, St. Louis, Missouri 63116
- Change for Children. 2588 Mission St., Room 226, San Francisco, California 94110
- China Books and Periodicals. 95 Fifth Avenue, New York, New York 10003
- Connecticut Public Interest Research Group. P.O. Box 1571, Hartford, Connecticut 06101
- Council on Interracial Books for Children. 1841 Broadway, New York, New York 10023
- Educational Activities, Incorporated. Freeport, New York 11520
- Emma Willard Task Force on Education. Box 14229, University Station, Minneapolis, Minnesota 55408
- Feminist Book Mart. 162-11 Ninth Avenue, Whitestone, New York 11357
- Feminist Press. SUNY College at Old Westbury. P.O. Box 334, Old Westbury, New York 11568
- Feminists on Children's Media. P.O. Box 4315, Grand Central Station, New York, New York 10017
- Free to be Foundation. 370 Lexington Avenue, New York, New York 10017
- Joyful World Press. 468 Belvedere Street, San Francisco, California 94117

- KNOW Press. P.O. Box 86031, Pittsburgh, Pennsylvania 15221
- Lollipop Power, Inc., P.O. Box 1171, Chapel Hill, North Carolina 27514
- *Ms* magazine. 370 Lexington Avenue, New York, New York 10017
- National Education Association. Teachers' Rights. 1201 16th Street, N.W., Washington, D.C. 20036
- National Foundation for the Improvement of Education. Resource Center on Sex Roles in Education. Suite 918, 1156 15th St., N.W., Washington, D.C. 20005.
- National Institute of Education. Office of Education. 400 Maryland Ave., S.W., Washington, D.C. 20202
- National Organization for Women (local branches in each state). Central Office, 1957 E. 73rd St., Chicago, Illinois 60649
- National Organization for Women. Central New Jersey Chapter, R.D. 4, 25 Cleveland Lane, Princeton, New Jersey 08540
- National Women's Political Caucus, 1921 Pennsylvania Avenue, N.W., Washington, D.C. 20006
- New England Free Press. 60 Union Square, Somerville, Massachusetts 02143
- New Seed Publishing Company. P.O. Box 3016, Stanford, California 94305
- Resource Center on Sex Roles in Education. 1156 Fifteenth Street, Washington, D.C. 20009
- Sex Equality in Guidance Opportunities. APGA, 1607 New Hampshire Avenue, N.W., Washington D.C. 20009
- Women's Action Alliance. 370 Lexington Avenue, New York, New York 10017
- Women's Equity Action League. National Press Building, Washington, D.C. 20045
- Women's Heritage Series. Box 3236, Santa Monica, California 90403
- Women on Words and Images. P.O. Box 2163, Princeton, New Jersey 08540
- *Working Woman Magazine.* 110 East 59th Street, New York, New York 10022

Dictionaries:

- Houghton Mifflin. *American Heritage School Dictionary*, non-sexist definitions and illustrations with equal sex representation. American Heritage Publishing Company, Inc., 551 Fifth Avenue, New York, New York 10017
- Sutton, William A. *Sexual Fairness in Language.* Department of English, Ball State University, Muncie, Indiana 47306

TELEVISION: PROGRAMMING FOR FEMALE SUBMISSIVENESS

Women on Words and Images have published a number of valuable assessments of children's readers, career education materials, school texts, and television programs. *Channeling Children*[7] deserves special mention here, because its analysis of "prime-time" programs offers a way to appraise television programs with your daughter. The traits ascribed to males and females are revealed by what the characters say and their reactions to situations they find themselves in.

Analysis Chart:
For example, here is an analysis[8] of one episode of "All in the Family" shown from 8:00 to 8:30 on November 10, 1973. The three males portrayed are a factory worker, a student, and a priest. The females are a housewife, a wife who works to support her husband, and a nun.

Description of situation	Sex of Char.	Trait exhibited
Opening scene—Archie and Edith singing together at piano	M/F	Affection
Gloria is cooking dinner as a surprise for family; horsemeat to save money—nutritious, economical, just like other meat	F	Initiative Intelligence
Michael objects strenuously to eating horse (big laughs)	M	Squeamishness
Gloria tricks Michael into eating a piece of meat	F	Manipulating
Michael runs to sink, screaming that he has eaten horse	M	Hysterical
Gloria: "C'mon Michael, I saw that look . . . you really liked it."	F	Manipulating
Michael admits he did like it	M	Reasonable
Gloria reveals plan to serve horse to Archie and Edith, not tell them, Michael agrees	M/F	Manipulating
Edith thanks Gloria for cooking supper	F	Supportive
Michael sings "Camptown Races" (throughout show, continues to make innuendoes about meat—always gets big laughs)	M	Clever

Description of situation	Sex of Char.	Trait exhibited
Irene introduces her sister who is a nun—Edith replies to Michael's question about why Theresa is wearing street clothes, "Nowadays some nuns go around just like they was people."	F	Stupidity
Archie enters, rude to Theresa, demands dinner	M	Domineering Rude
Michael leaves to help Gloria in the kitchen (at Gloria's request)	M	Helpful
Irene leaves with humorous exit line	F	Humor
Archie demands that Edith remove medal given her by Sister Theresa	M	Prejudice Domineering
Archie tells why he doesn't like Catholics	M	Prejudice
Irene and Theresa give serious explanation of Catholic faith	F	Intelligent
Archie retorts with put-down of Pope and Catholics	M	Stupidity Prejudice
Doorbell rings, Edith greets Father Majerski, "You've grown a beard." Father Majerski: "Yes, I know." (big laugh) (Once again, Edith is made to look stupid.)	F	Stupidity
Father Majerski and Archie exchange insults	M	Derisive
Archie derides Gloria's effort to make supper: "It must be either the chink's or Colonel Saunders."	M	Derisive
Edith compliments Gloria on making supper	F	Kindness
Gloria whispers to Edith that meat is horse (so Archie can't hear)	F	Manipulating
Edith leaves table in horror	F	Squeamish
Gloria apologizes to mother for upsetting her	F	Affectionate
Edith says it's all right	F	Submissive need to conciliate
Edith describes day's events, gets jumped on by Archie who gets laughs for making fun of her	F	Victimized

Description of situation	Sex of Char.	Trait exhibited
Edith getting ready to leave gets made fun of by Archie who says she's running around like a loose weed	F	Victimized
Archie protests Edith's association with Catholics	M	Domineering Prejudiced
Archie visits Father Majerski, expresses fear that Edith will convert	M	Fear
Father Majerski tells Archie to talk to Edith himself	M	Intelligent
Father Majerski and Archie trade insults	M	Derisive
Archie tells Father Majerski to keep his hands off Edith or else	M	Threatening
Irene gets let in on the joke—horse for dinner —don't tell Archie	F	Manipulating
Archie calls Edith stupid for going to church	M	Derision
Irene retorts that that was dumb even for Archie	F	Assertiveness Defense of another
Archie gets really angry, waves finger in front of Edith's nose	M	Angry Domineering Authoritarian
Edith reassures Archie that she would never convert	F	Submissive
Irene defends Edith to Archie—important thing to love other people	F	Assertive Supportive
Michael affirms Irene's position—important to love other people	M	Supportive
Archie insults Michael	M	Derisive
Irene compliments Mike on Christian attitude	F	Supportive
Irene exits, saying she's glad the Protestants have Archie	F	Derisive
Archie tells Edith to leave the thinking to him, just do the useful things around here . . . get me a beer	M	Sexist

Description of situation	Sex of Char.	Trait exhibited
Edith complies	F	Submissive
Archie says he is hungry enough to eat a horse	M	Victimized

Many adults will argue that humor is "harmless," laughter is healthful, and that men, too, are derided and victimized by the "meat" in this TV segment. These defensive protests are unacceptable; they attempt to justify the stereotypical attitudes of males, exemplified by, "Leave the thinking to me. Just do the useful things around here. . . . Get me a beer!"

The snide exploitation of female (and male) stereotypes can damage your daughter's self-image. Insults, "put-downs," derisive innuendo, and dominance humor should be judged for what it is—low-level comedy used at women's expense. High-level humor involving irony, clever planning, achievement, problem-solving, and/or coping by both men and women should replace the former. You can begin by training your daughter to recognize stereotypes and inferior humor. Receptivity to intelligent forms of comedy elevates your daughter's mental sensitivity and thus increases her chances for self-actualization.

Women on Words and Images analyzes traits exhibited on twenty prime-time shows and adventure-type programs as a subgroup.

Use the "traits" checklist to assess some of your favorite television programs. If they yield negative data, write letters with suggestions for improvement to the producers and advertisers of sexist stories. More important, ask your daughter what she would (or should) have done (in contrast with what the female characters did) had *she* been in the situations described.

SUMMARY OF BEHAVIORS OBSERVED FOR MALE AND FEMALE FOR ALL TELEVISION PROGRAMS ANALYZED[9]

	Male		Female	
Behavior	Number of times observed	Percent of total behaviors	Number of times observed	Percent of total behaviors
1. Anger	165	13	77	10
2. Aggression	113	9	33	4
3. Cowardice	35	3	23	3
4. Incompetence	117	9	156	21
5. Dishonesty	63	5	54	7

	Male		Female	
Behavior	Number of times observed	Percent of total behaviors	Number of times observed	Percent of total behaviors
6. Harming Physically	22	2	2	0
7. Emotionality	71	6	48	6
8. Jealousy	15	1	10	1
9. Non-Supportiveness	15	1	11	1
10. Self-Sacrifice	4	0	7	0
11. Discrimination	87	7	52	7
12. Using sexuality	11	0	12	2
13. Vanity	21	2	13	2
14. Warmth of Feeling*	48	4	23	3
15. Bravery*	21	2	2	0
16. Competence*	298	23	131	17
17. Honesty*	23	2	10	1
18. Humor*	38	3	10	1
19. Supportiveness*	107	8	87	11
Total Number of Behaviors	1274		761	

*Positive Behaviors
Note: (Aggression was considered negative. Positive aspects of aggressive behavior such as leadership or assertion were placed under competence).

SUMMARY OF BEHAVIORS OBSERVED FOR MALE AND FEMALE FOR ADVENTURE-TYPE SHOWS[10]

	Male		Female	
Behavior	Number of times observed	Percent of total behaviors	Number of times observed	Percent of total behaviors
1. Anger	26	6	13	8
2. Aggression	46	11	8	4
3. Cowardice	7	2	14	8
4. Incompetence	14	3	53	31
5. Dishonesty	17	4	7	4
6. Harming Physically	10	2	2	1

	Male		Female	
Behavior	Number of times observed	Percent of total behaviors	Number of times observed	Percent of total behaviors
7. Emotionality	14	3	20	12
8. Jealousy	5	1	2	1
9. Non-Supportiveness	3	0	0	0
10. Self-Sacrifice	1	0	0	0
11. Discrimination	16	4	14	8
12. Using Sexuality	0	0	5	3
13. Vanity	5	1	3	2
14. Warmth of Feeling*	12	3	0	0
15. Bravery*	13	3	2	1
16. Competence*	197	46	23	13
17. Honesty*	8	2	0	0
18. Humor*	3	0	0	0
19. Supportiveness*	27	6	6	3
Total Number of Behaviors	424		172	

*Positive Behaviors

One last thought on the pervasiveness of male sexism in television: Gerbner found that 75 percent of the characters viewed by his researchers were middle-class, unmarried American males in the prime of their lives. "American women," he adds, "are generally portrayed as exuding sexual attraction, as marriage mates, or both; as lacking in social power and influence; and as much more likely to be the objects of victimization than men." As a communications specialist, Gerbner suggested a relationship between the extensive amount of violence exhibited on prime time television and the American males' social power structure, associating the two with the ". . . prerogative of a male free of responsibility."[11]

Another useful book to read with your daughter is *The Family Guide to Children's Television*.[12] This comprehensive guide assesses various types of children's programs and is a kind of "boob-tube how-to recipe" guide to what to watch, what to miss, what to change, and how to do it. Unfortunately, only one page is devoted exclusively to sexism, but, with a little translation for your daughter, the text offers valuable advice. For example, it includes the National Association for Better Broadcasting Guidelines for evaluating programs.[13]

Standard	Desirable–If	Undesirable–If
1. Does it appeal to the audience for whom intended?	It gives information and/or entertainment related to real life situations or interests.	Dull, boring, not related to experience or interests; exaggerated beyond believability.
2. Does it meet people's needs for entertainment and action?	Wholesome adventure, humor, fantasy, suspense.	Unnecessary morbid emphasis on cruelty and violence; loud, crude, or vulgar.
3. Does it add to one's understanding and appreciation of himself, others, the world?	Sincere; constructive; informative; balanced picture of life; encourages decent human relations; fair to races, nations, religions, labor and management.	One-sided propaganda; arouses prejudice; plays on emotions and lack of knowledge.
4. Does it encourage worthwhile ideals, values, and beliefs? (family life, etc.)	Upholds acceptable standards of behavior; promotes democratic and spiritual values, respect for law, decency, service.	Glamorizes crime, indecency, intolerance, greed, cruelty; encourages bad material success, personal taste, false standards of vanity, intemperance, immorality.
5. Does the program stimulate constructive activities?	Promotes interests, skills, hobbies; encourages desire to learn more, to do something constructive, to be creative, to solve problems, to work and to live with others.	Details of theft, robbery, smuggling and other crime; if probems are solved by brute force, or if situations are resolved by chance rather than by logical story development.
6. Does it have artistic qualities?	Skillful production as to music, script, acting, direction, art work, sets, sound effects, photography.	Poorly done job; confusing; hard to follow; action too fast, too slow; sound too loud, too low.

Standard	Desirable–If	Undesirable–If
7. Is the commercial acceptable?	Presented with courtesy and good taste, reasonably brief, in harmony with content and sound volume of program; delivered by announcer.	Too loud, too many, deceptive; poor taste in content and treatment.

An eighth "standard" should be added to the seven designed by the National Association for Better Broadcasting (NABB):

Standard	Desirable–If	Undesirable–If
8. Does it present an accurate and unbiased view of girls' and women's social roles and personal traits?	Girls and women are presented fairly, as human beings with strengths and weaknesses, with appropriate aspirations equal to those of men, with valued traits presented as desirable for both, and with warmth and love for each other and/or people.	Females are presented as scheming, inferior, deceptive, brainless, frivolous, powerless, undignified, in lesser roles, service-oriented, valued only for attraction and appearance, absent from the plot, or represented as decorative without significance.

Additional Standards Applied Specifically to Children's Programs:
1. Crime is *never suitable* as a major theme of a program for children.
2. There should be immediate resolution of suspense, and the program should avoid undue stress on fear.
3. A clear differentiation should be made between fantasy and fact.

Since 1953 the National Association for Better Broadcasting (NABB) has published evaluations of commercial television series broadcast by stations in the United States. NABB's purpose is to provide a guide to teachers and parents in the selection of programs for children who come within their care and influence. It is important to emphasize that these evaluations are designed as a guide—not an edict. The NABB encourages parents to use the analyses as a basis for determining those programs that each family views; it makes no pretense of infallibility in its conclusions. In fact, *Television for The Family* stipulates that programs change, the content in each sequence is varied, and that children react differently to identical content. It also stresses that it not only is important that children be exposed to selective television, but also that they be taught to understand *why* certain actions and behaviors depicted in programs may be unacceptable to their families. The introduction that accompanies the analyses states that children need guidance in evaluating the many varied attitudes and life styles that they see on popular television shows.[14]

This *Comprehensive Guide to Family Viewing* is reproduced here for your examination. Many of these programs continue year after year. View your daughter's favorite programs with her, read their critiques, and make her aware of their poor quality and stereotyping if they are among those analyzed as being negative, and of their fine quality and lack of sexism if they are rated as positive. In addition to helping your daughter develop an understanding of good program content, you will be aiding her to develop critical evaluation abilities that she may then adapt to other areas, such as literature, writings, and the theater.

The following assessments of television programs were excerpted from one of NABB's 1976 quarterly issues:

ABC AFTERSCHOOL SPECIALS—(monthly). Consistently high quality in a series that has set standards for afternoon programing for youngsters. Some of these shows are repeats from preceding seasons, but most of them are well worth such repetition.

ADDAMS FAMILY—Syndicated. Better than the run-of-the-mill animated shows. There are still traces of the original tone and flavor of the Addams cartoons.

ADVENTURES OF GILLIGAN—ABC, Saturdays. A silly, inept animated reconstruction of the original silly and inept live-action series. The network claims an injection of "positive social values." Wow!

AMERICAN BANDSTAND—ABC, Saturdays. Dick Clark and supporting rock performers in a show that keeps pace with the changing trends in youth-oriented music. A pleasant show presented with enthusiasm and good taste.

BIG BLUE MARBLE—Syndicated. A year ago NABB reported *Big Blue Marble* as the season's most outstanding entertainment series for children. Since that time it has continued to reap recognition and awards from various sources. More than that, it is building a solid following among youngsters throughout the world. It is lavish in production values and fascinating in its refreshing presentation of children of many nations. The series is produced and presented as a public service by International Telephone and Telegraph Corporation.

BUGS BUNNY/ROADRUNNER—CBS, Saturdays. Last year and in preceding seasons, NABB described *Bugs Bunny,* then on the ABC network, as a series with good production quality but with unacceptable content because the characters were slugged, clubbed, thrown off cliffs, and blown up without perceptible damage. Now the show is on CBS, combined with segments of *The Roadrunner.* In commenting on the switch from ABC to CBS, ABC's child program executive Squire Rushnell is quoted, "When Warner Brothers told us that in order to keep *Bugs Bunny* (one of ABC's highest rated kid shows) we'd have to take an additional half-hour of *Roadrunner,* we said no because *Roadrunner* epitomizes the old-style cartoons that play heavily on aggressiveness and action. The whole focus is centered on one creature trying to eliminate another creature." . . . Network people *do* sometimes look at their programs, don't they?

CALL IT MACARONI—Syndicated. Originated by the Westinghouse Group W stations, this is an imaginative, expertly produced series that deserves widespread distribution and the attention of audiences everywhere. Real-life adventure, live-action, with the adults involved showing a real interest in the subject matter and in the youngsters who view the show. The concept of the program is fascinating. Youngsters are taken from their own environment to participate with adults in activities in exciting and totally different surroundings.

CAPTAIN KANGAROO—CBS, Monday-Friday. This remains as commercial television's outstanding regular show for preschoolers. Appealing, low-key entertainment that has developed over the years, rather than remaining static in its format.

CHILDREN'S FILM FESTIVAL—CBS, Saturdays. Superior films with special appeal for children. A highlight of the week's schedule for youngsters.

DAVEY AND GOLIATH—Syndicated. An intriguing series with engaging puppet characters distributed by the United Lutheran Church. Expertly created by Clokey Productions.

THE DEVLINS—ABC, Sundays. The Devlins (two brothers and a sister) are animated principals in a motorbike stunt team in which one brother is the daredevil and the other the behind the scenes genius who works out the complicated stunts. Good family relationships.

EMERGENCY PLUS 4—NBC, Saturdays. This is a poorly conceived animated transition of the network's Saturday evening live-action *Emergency* that attracts millions of youngsters. Values of the original show are lost. Youngsters here are participants, and they are in constant peril. Not recommended.

FAR OUT SPACE NUTS—CBS, Saturdays. New this season. A silly live-action show comprised of mindless slapstick. The CBS director of children's programs says this is aimed at kids six to 12 and younger teens. It's a total waste.

FAT ALBERT AND THE COSBY KIDS—CBS, Saturdays. New episodes have been added this season, and it remains as a superior program with unusual values in characterization and story content. Action centers on the social and personal problems of black youngsters in an urban center. Bill Cosby's presence, with his obvious concern for children, gives the show added importance.

THE FLINTSTONES—Syndicated. Audience-wise, *The Flintstones* has been in second place among syndicated shows in the U.S. for the past season. (*Mickey Mouse Club* is first.) It is ingenious and funny, but it is also a classic example of bad sex stereotypes in most episodes.

GHOST BUSTERS—CBS, Saturdays. A very bad and stupidly contrived live-action show that is new this season. Production quality is terrible. We deplore the fact that talented performers such as Larry Storch and Forrest Tucker have let themselves be swept up in such garbage.

GO! U.S.A.—NBC, Saturdays. This is a live-action documentary style program covering a wide range of current issues and topics. Of special interest to older youngsters.

GOOBER AND THE GHOST CHASERS—ABC, Sundays. Reruns. Goober is an animated ghost who becomes invisible when he is excited. Frightening sequences make this unsuitable for children.

GROOVY GOOLIES—ABC, Saturdays. An animated Filmation monstrosity composed of plotless bits with vampires, wolf men, witches, bats, and other creatures in a haunted house background. The producers claim this is satire, but the satire is meaningless because it is based on people totally unknown to child viewers.

HARLEM GLOBETROTTERS—CBS, Saturdays. A live-action part fantasy with Globetrotter stars and guests in travesties on such tales as "Goldilocks and the Three Bears." Amusing and entertaining.

HONG KONG PHOOEY—ABC, Sundays. Fourth-rate animated Charlie Chan type series with silly, impossible stories. Background is crime and violence. Hero bungles his way to success over villains. Low quality artwork and production.

IN THE NEWS—CBS, Saturdays. Brief news features scattered through the CBS Saturday morning schedule. Produced by CBS News, these segments do not avoid presentation of controversial issues, but the excerpts are so short that they often do not permit adequate presentation. Production and treatment do not appear to be as sharp as they were a year ago.

JEANNIE—CBS, Saturdays. An animated version of the live-action Jeannie series, with juveniles now in principal roles. Childish and silly. A complete waste of time for any audience.

THE JETSONS—NBC, Saturdays. Space gadgetry is the attraction in this oft-rerun animated show. The gimmicks are fun. The stereotype roles are not.

JOSIE AND THE PUSSYCATS—NBC, Saturdays. Teenage characters in an animated really bad depiction of outer space adventure. Full of stereotypes and distorted situations.

KID POWER—ABC, Sundays. These are reruns, but there was quality in these episodes to begin with, and they can stand repetition. Characters are based on Morrie Turner's "Wee Pals."

KORG: 70,000 B.C.—Syndicated. A year ago this was a new one from

Hanna-Barbera for the ABC network. In an unguarded moment ABC's Squire Rushnell told a Broadcasting Magazine reporter that the series failed because it was too "educational" to hold interest. Whatever educational elements it contained certainly came from no qualified texts or responsible educators. It represents a totally unscientific and distorted picture of the era of the Neanderthal man, with dull and witless characters involved in situations contrived to emphasize constant peril and little else.

KUKLA, FRAN, AND OLLIE—Syndicated. In its weekly half-hour format, this is an attempt to revive the characters and situations that charmed millions of youngsters on a daily schedule more than 20 years ago. It is still in the same creative hands, but something seems to be missing. Maybe it needs daily exposure to build a following substantial enough to survive the ratings wars. It likely won't get the chance.

LAND OF THE LOST—NBC, Saturdays. Contrived sets and prehistoric monsters in situations that are confusing and sometimes frightening. Illogical plots.

LASSIE'S RESCUE RANGERS—ABC, Sundays. An outrageous animated distortion of the live-action Lassie series. Violence, crime, and stupidity. An insult to the perception and intelligence of any child over two.

LITTLE RASCALS—Syndicated. Old and dated, but these are still aired in many cities. They are sometimes fun and they have nostalgic interest, but the black youngsters are woefully stereotyped.

THE LOST SAUCER—ABC, Saturdays. Live-action. New this season. Of the many Sid and Marty Kroft shows this seemed to have the most potential, but instead of instilling creative entertainment qualities the producers have relied on gimmicks and stereotypes. It is a shame that the youngsters in the cast, who are charming, are lost in such undistinguished material.

MAKE A WISH—ABC, Sundays. An enchanting and visually refreshing program produced by the ABC public affairs department. In animation and live-action it covers history, geography, and literature.

MICKEY MOUSE CLUB—Syndicated. These half-hour programs, produced in black-and-white 20 years ago, still have enough class and entertainment values to draw ratings that outdistance the stripped-in crime shows aired in late afternoon hours. *Mickey Mouse Club* reruns, now broadcast on 70 or more stations, hold first place in the nation's syndicated shows for kids. It is unfortunate that Disney's producers did not integrate black and other minority youngsters into a show that is otherwise one of the brightest and most creative ever made for children.

MY FAVORITE MARTIANS—CBS, Sundays. Inane, silly, and witless animated versions of the live-action *My Favorite Martian* series. Reruns of recycled junk.

NATURE'S WINDOW—Syndicated. Although these beautiful

five-minute wildlife vignettes are usually integrated into children's programs with varying content and formats, the NABB committee is impelled to point out again that these are delightful, and well worth seeking out. More than 100 species of North American birds and animals are filmed in natural color. There are 130 segments. Recommended without reservation.

ODD BALL COUPLE—ABC, Saturdays. Squire Rushnell, head of children's programing for ABC, claims that this is "sophisticated enough to appeal more to 10-year-olds and older than to younger children." Actually, *Odd Ball Couple* has no sophistication whatever. It has lost the premise of the original show. It features distorted characters trying to outwit each other.

PARTRIDGE FAMILY: 2200 A.D.—CBS, Saturdays. An undistinguished animated show patterned after *The Jetsons.*

PEBBLES AND BAMM BAMM—CBS, Saturdays. Animated teen-agers from the Flintstone menage.

THE PINK PANTHER—NBC, Saturdays. Sometimes funny and cute, *Pink Panther* is among the more acceptable Saturday morning network fare. Parents should check other cartoons within the show to determine suitability for their children.

POPEYE—Syndicated. These frantic cartoons are classic models of the "hitting" violence that has plagued parents and teachers for years. Please see comments on *The Three Stooges.*

RETURN TO THE PLANET OF THE APES—NBC, Saturdays. This is typical of the "new" violence in children's shows that the networks claim is not violence at all. It is true that there are few evil characters, and few overt crimes. But there is much destruction by "natural" elements and constant menace to the human adults and youngsters stranded in the austere and unfriendly planet controlled by apes. Too frightening for younger children.

RUN, JOE RUN—NBC, Saturdays. Live-action with the central character a dog who is loved by children, but thought to be dangerous by adults. Previous army corps training has programed the reactions of the dog. Like Lassie, Joe is super smart.

SCHOOLHOUSE ROCK—ABC, Saturdays, Sundays. Brief but excellent animated films spotted on Saturday and Sunday mornings just before the hours or half-hours. Segments cover grammar, math, history, etc. Superior production qualities. Entertaining.

SCOOBY DO—CBS, Saturdays. A loud and unattractive frantic paced animated show that is full of menace and devoid of charm. Scary. Unsuitable for children.

SECRET LIVES OF WALDO KITTY—NBC, Saturdays. One of the season's worst new shows. Animation is low quality, but most appalling is the total destruction of the original Thurber story material. Grotesque and stupied nonsense.

THE SHARI SHOW—NBC and Syndicated. This is a welcome show that has charm for family audiences. The puppets are attractive and expertly handled. Credit Shari Lewis with a tasteful, cheerful program that is all too rare in TV.

SHAZAM!/ISIS HOUR—CBS, Saturdays. Combination animation and life action. The hour-long show is an expansion of the previous season's *Shazam!*, in which the show's young hero turns into Captain Marvel, a la Clark Kent/Superman. Adventures were steeped in robbery and dope traffic, and populated with hardened criminals. Now we have Isis, who was first conceived as a female criminologist, but transposed to a high school science teacher to downplay the crime emphasis. Both parts of the show rely on super powers of the principals to solve the problems encountered. In both shows the trick photography of the flying sequences is embarrassingly obvious.

SPECIAL TREAT—NBC, afternoon, monthly. This is an admirable new endeavor by NBC. It is comprised mostly of camera coverage of interesting events and places. For example, a recent episode visited six amusement parks in the U.S. An earlier episode photographed beautifully a spectacular sky glider descent from Mt. Fuji in Japan. Unfortunately, the narration for that program sounded like words from a dull textbook, thus missing the opportunity to enhance an exciting, imaginative experience.

SPEED BUGGY—ABC, Saturdays. Reruns of silly cartoons. Crime in story content. Unsuitable entertainment for children.

SPEED RACER—Syndicated. This animated monstrosity is an example of the worst that television has ever produced. The ultimate in crime, evil characters, cruelty, and destruction. No network would touch it. Some independent and affiliated broadcasters, however, flaunt their irresponsibility by stripping this in five days per week in afternoon hours when children are least supervised and most available.

STAR TREK—NBC, Saturdays. Good quality artwork and above average story treatment make this one of the more acceptable animated shows for children.

SUPER FRIENDS and Other "Super" Shows. These are the superheroes with their fantastic physical powers—Superman, Batman, Aquaman, and Wonderwoman. With invincible force they "fight injustice, right that which is wrong, and serve all mankind." When our institutions and constituted authorities are helpless we call on our Super Friends, and delegate to them all of our responsibilities to protect ourselves against a world full of weird menaces. We don't need anything else. Everything is settled for us by the violent use of super power. That's the message! . . . We deliver it to our children every time we permit them to watch one of these shows.

THE THREE STOOGES—Syndicated. Research on the behavior of children, and innumerable complaints from parents and teachers, have documented *The Three Stooges* as a prime incitement to unruly behavior by children everywhere. Indiscriminate unmotivated violence inflicted on victims who show no ill-effects from attacks that would kill or maim actual persons.

THESE ARE THE DAYS—ABC, Saturdays. An animated show about a family in the early years of the 20th century. The characters and situations are appealing. This is a Hanna-Barbera show with story qualities strong enough to maintain interest without crime or violence.

TOM AND JERRY/GREAT GRAPE APE SHOW—ABC, Saturdays. In the new segments, Tom and Jerry are now friends, instead of unremitting enemies. This part of the hour is still far from adequate as entertainment for children. The other half, *The Great Grape Ape* is a monstrosity of the first order. The huge grotesque ape grunts and croaks its way through sequences that are violent and almost totally mindless. There is no characterization. The production quality is terrible.

UNCLE CROC'S BLOCK—ABC, Saturdays. Combination animation and live-action, and it's difficult to determine which is the worst. Los Angeles Times critic Dick Adler called this "the biggest crock of the lot." ABC's children's programing chief Squire Rushnell called it "satire at the level of understanding of youngsters." The NABB committee calls it a monument of junk illustrating the network's irresponsibility in programing for children. An insult to the intelligence of any youngster.

UNDERDOG—Syndicated. One of the worst of the old crime-ridden series that have been discredited and are now unacceptable to any of the three networks. Nevertheless, this is still syndicated to independent and affiliated stations. Our latest report was that it is now beamed into 800,000 U.S. households. An illustration of the need for parents to be alert to what their children may be viewing.

U.S. OF ARCHIE—CBS, Sundays. Reruns of an animated series that purports to be an educational review of sequences from American history. Actually history in the hands of these uninspired producers becomes a background for deception and evil. It is a low quality program without merit.

VALLEY OF THE DINOSAURS—CBS, Sundays. Child viewers here will not be able to distinguish between fantasy and reality. Some of the scenes and situations are interesting, but peril is everywhere, and natural catastrophes add to the tension. Dialogue and story treatment are crude and illogical.

VISION ON—Syndicated. This is an outstanding series produced by the British Broadcasting Corporation. Although designed for hard-of-hearing youngsters, it will entertain kids and adults, deaf or not. It covers a wide range of subject matter with animation, live-action pantomime, and other techniques.

WESTWIND—NBC, Saturdays. *Westwind* is a clear and frustrating illustration of network television's sales-oriented approach to programs for children. This is NBC's most expensive Saturday morning package. It is a live-action series filmed on and under the sea in Hawaii. The scenic background is impressive, along with the ketch which provides the quarters for the appealing family. Unfortunately, with all of this, the scripts have been woefully weak in creative quality. NBC and the producers have superimposed contrived melodramatic situations to ruin what could have been the most refreshing and entertaining new program of the year.

YOGI'S GANG—ABC, Saturdays. This is a hodgepodge rerun of the many Yogi sequences, interspersed with cartoons of varying quality. Many of the segments are appealing and funny. Better than most animated TV.

Public Stations Air Superior Children's Fare   With exceptions as noted in the adjacent alphabetical listings of network and syndicated shows, the superior programs for children are generally aired in the United States by the noncommercial public broadcasting outlets. The NABB evaluations committee adds to this conclusion the comment that the motivations of commercial broadcasters are much different, and that these differences are reflected in the programs themselves.

Just renewed for another 65 episodes, and most welcome, is the bilingual (Spanish and English) Villa Allegre series that is fascinating whether or not the viewer understands both languages. The program is an artistic achievement in both production and creative content. Printed guide materials are available through the stations airing the series.

There are three other programs for children continuing chiefly on PBS stations. These are:

Mister Rogers' Neighborhood, the gentle and appealing program that was originated by Fred Rogers in April 1954 on public station WQED, Pittsburgh. This is an enduring program that utilizes fine creative talents in writing, performance, and production. Fred Rogers furnishes individual role models and a positive view of the world which both common-sense and scientific research have proved valuable. For these reasons, and because there is so little of this on public or commercial TV, this continues to be a most important program.

Sesame Street, still growing as it begins its sixth season with more than 12 million U.S. viewers between the ages of three and six. In addition to the 200 PBS stations airing Sesame Street, 50 commercial broadcasters are carrying it. It is produced by Children's Television Workshop.

Electric Company, another Children's Television Workshop program, now in its third season. This is an expertly produced experiment designed to help meet the problems of reading failure among elementary school children, but of interest to all youngsters. Created with the meticulous care that is typical of CTW enterprises.

ALL OF THE ABOVE programs are highly recommended by the NABB committee for the children and teens to whom they are directed.

Commercial Network Prime-Time Shows and Selected Syndicated Programs
ADAM 12—Syndicated. Although this program depicts the police as competent professionals, it does at times have an overload of criminal violence and

tense action. Now it is being broadcast up to ten times per week in some cities during late afternoon hours when viewing audience is composed primarily of young children. The NABB committee suggests that parents check the reactions of their own children. For older youngsters there is an emphasis on constructive values in law enforcement.

DON ADAMS SCREEN TEST—Syndicated (access time.) A gimmicky show with a noisy studio audience cued to cheer and applaud for the sound track. Candidates compete for chances to appear in TV film shows. Even if honest, it is a totally unprofessional way of seeking performing talent. Mediocre at best.

ALL IN THE FAMILY—CBS, Mondays. Very funny comedy, and still the most popular among TV's weekly shows. There has been much debate concerning the effects of *All in the Family* on American society. Whether or not the picture of Archie exposes bigotry, or whether there are millions of viewers who do not look at Archie as a bigot, but as a spokesman for things they themselves believe is, in our opinion, not the most important thing. Families will have to make their own decision whether or not to invite the Bunkers into their home. Archie is exposed. He is a real person, contradictions, bigotry, and all. This is what makes *All in the Family* worth watching, for families, whether or not they agree with Archie's views.

ALMOST ANYTHING GOES—ABC, Saturdays. Making its seasonal debut after the publication date for this guide, *Almost Anything Goes* will be viewed in the spring issue of the NABB quarterly.

AMERICA—Syndicated. This superior Alistair Cooke series is especially timely for this bicentennial year revival of interest in the true values of America's past and present. This is a magnificent program that is well worth a second or third viewing.

ANIMAL WORLD—Syndicated (access time). Bill Burrud's beautifully scenic presentation of wildlife in various locales. At times action and continuity appear to be contrived to heighten dramatic impact, but it is difficult to quarrel with this series as a whole. It is distinctly superior to most of the game shows that clutter the early evening "access time."

BARETTA—ABC, Wednesdays. A high-powered show that is tough, vengeful, and murderous. Robert Blake performs as an emotionally charged cop who operates as a "loner" rather than as a member of the team. Situations are sordid, with much emphasis on drug traffic and drug addiction. The violence is graphic and personal. In the Midwest, where the "family hour" *ends* at eight p.m., the kids see this just before bedtime. It is a frightening prospect for future syndication into late afternoon time periods.

BARNABY JONES—CBS, Fridays. This is a gimmicky crime show with Buddy Ebsen as a private eye. Routine network mediocrity.

BARNEY MILLER—ABC, Thursdays. A year ago the NABB committee criticized this program, based on the single premiere episode that contained sequences related to the bombing of public buildings. Subsequent episodes have convinced the committee that this may be the funniest program on the air, and that its characters comprise the most appealing and diverse group featured in any series, past or present. The situations presented here, and some of the guest characters who drift in and out of the precinct headquarters, will disturb some viewers (and possibly some of our readers), but this is a show where pathos and humor are mixed with great skill, and where cops are realistic without being cynical, compassionate without being maudlin, and outrageously funny without any gimmicky props. This could even restore some sanity to citizens' attitudes toward the police. Performances are superb.

BEACON HILL—CBS, Tuesdays. Although *Beacon Hill* is one of the season's earliest casualties, its passing should not escape some obituary comment here. The failure was most certainly not due to any inability of the TV audience to recognize and appreciate quality. *Beacon Hill* was lavish and expensive. It was obviously intended to outdo the British *Upstairs, Downstairs*. The disaster occurred primarily through the inability of the producers (and the CBS network brass) to understand what *Upstairs, Downstairs* is all about. They did not give us the true and appealing characters that make the imported series such a delight. They gave us an artificial glitter instead of real diamonds. the audience recognized the difference.

BIONIC WOMAN—ABC, Wednesdays. The counterpart of the Six Million Dollar Man, though not quite as expensive "because she is smaller." This is a form of Superman spin-off, although the Bionic Woman, like Achilles, has her points of vulnerability. Story treatment and characterization were well done in the first episode, but it is clear that plot direction will veer toward cliche presentation of espionage and physical violence. NABB suggests that parents should appraise this carefully.

THE BLUE KNIGHT—CBS, Wednesdays. An expertly produced police action program starring George Kennedy. Scripts and performances in the opening episodes have been on a high level. An entertaining show for melodrama fans, but this is definitely not for youngsters because of frightening situations and sordid, sadistic characters.

BONANZA—Syndicated. As westerns go, this is one of the best. Parents, however, should be aware that many episodes have excessive violence. Five episodes per week are a heavy dose of such material for younger children.

BRONK—CBS, Sundays. Jack Palance in a tough series with psychotic criminals engaged in violent crime.

CAROL BURNETT SHOW—CBS, Saturdays. This is probably the best of television's weekly variety shows. It is consistently entertaining and expertly produced with topflight performers. There has been a notable evolution from past seasons in which tasteless sequences plagued the program. Even though the show airs in the late evening, it is very popular with youngsters.

Due to the nature of the comedy skits, the NABB committee suggests that this show is not for unattended children.

CANDID CAMERA—Syndicated. Contrived and tasteless, despite occasional appealing and humourous sequences.

CANNON—CBS, Wednesdays. Sometimes interesting but essentially routine melodrama. Unsuitable for youngsters because of graphic violence and sordid story situations. Now aired at eight p.m. in the Midwest. This is another frightening prospect for syndication into afternoon hours when most children watch.

CHER—CBS, Sundays. Slim as she is, there is still a lot of Cher's skin on display each Sunday evening. It's all part of a series of intriguing costumes, and the effect is not vulgar. Unfortunately, it just hasn't been a very good show, aside from some of the music.

CHICO AND THE MAN—NBC, Fridays. There are still far too few Chicano characters on the air, and in that respect *Chico and the Man* has its plus side. Since its beginning a year ago the producers have responded to complaints by adding more characters and making this more of a "neighborhood" show. There is nothing really offensive about the program, but the stories and characters are superficial.

COLUMBO—NBC, Alternate Sundays. Intriguing melodrama, with emphasis on Peter Falk's character and deductive investigations. Good production and performance. For families with older youngsters. Not for children.

THE COP AND THE KID—NBC, Thursdays. An unlikely combination, with the cop as the unofficial father of a black youngster whose background has been the ghetto jungle. The series has possibilities. The principals are human and care for each other. They make mistakes, and try again.

COUSTEAU SPECIALS—ABC, (and syndicated reruns). Superb programs of rare beauty. Much of the charm comes from Jacques Cousteau himself and his obvious dedication to revealing hitherto hidden aspects of the sea around us.

DIRECTIONS—CBS, Sundays. A regular CBS Sunday feature that merits the attention of viewers who seek provocative discussions of social problems. Covers a wide variety of subjects.

DOC—CBS, Saturdays. An amusing well produced situation comedy. After a slapstick start, the show is taking time to develop characters and relationships. Has warmth and good human priorities.

THE DUMPLINGS—NBC. This new series will be reviewed in the spring issue of the NABB quarterly.

ELLERY QUEEN—NBC, Sundays. This show couldn't make it in the rough-and-tumble scramble for ratings at nine p.m. on Thursdays, but it will likely fare better in the softer Sunday evening period following the Disney hour. Jim Hutton as Ellery Queen may build a following among the fans of deductive mysteries. The pace and treatment are deliberately old-fashioned.

There is very little on-camera violence. The emphasis is on clues and deduc-
tion. Probably has little interest for youngsters.

      EMERGENCY—NBC, Saturdays. This program is one of the week's
leading attractions for youngsters of all ages. It is well produced, and it has
positive values in illustrating how paramedics rescue and treat victims of
accidents, fires, etc. The program may be too graphic and frightening for
unattended children. Interesting family viewing.

      THE F.B.I.—Syndicated. After years on the ABC network, this is
now syndicated and "stripped" Monday through Friday by many stations in
early evening hours. It is totally unsuitable as regular fare for youngsters. *The
F.B.I.* is not only an illustration of the misuse of official support (by the F.B.I.
itself), but also excessively violent and sordid in story content. This is a dismal
portrayal of the F.B.I. as our leading law enforcement body. More often than
not solutions are achieved by sheer luck and last-second rescues of terrorized
victims of criminals.

      THE FAMILY HOLVAK—NBC, Sundays (cancelled). The requiem
for this program must record the fact that the low ratings that caused its early
demise were not due to audience lack of appreciation of quality programing.
The networks and the producers were themselves responsible for the failure.
They began with a fine series concept, and they obtained one of the finest casts
ever to grace a TV series. Then they came up with a mishmash of melodramatic
and sometimes unpleasant story situations that made no use whatever of the
talents of one of America's most outstanding actresses—Julie Harris. There was
outstanding photography, but no trace whatever of any creative writing. A
waste.

      FAY—NBC, Thursdays (cancelled). Although this series was one of
the first casualties of the mumbo-jumbo ratings war, it merits comment here on
the possibility that ABC or CBS might pick up the program for future use. NBC
gave *Fay* no chance at all. The series had warmth and intelligence at an adult
level. . . . And it had Lee Grant as star. All it needed (or needs) was a proper
place on the schedule and time to develop an audience.

      GOOD TIMES—CBS, Tuesdays. An all-black series that is superior
because of the warmth of its characters and the realistic treatment of relevant
story themes. The entire cast is excellent. The writing is first-rate.

      GRADY—NBC, Thursdays. A new show concerned with an attractive
and appealing black family, with Whitman Mayo in the title role. With the
exception of *Good Times* it is more dimensional than other shows featuring
black families. *Grady* could become a fixture if the network gives it time to
develop, but NBC gave *Fay* no such chance in this same time period.

      GUNSMOKE—Syndicated. This long-lived CBS program has finally
completed its network run, and is now being syndicated to stations throughout
the world. Matt, Doc, Festus, and Kitty (and Kitty's "girls") will now be

available to children on a five-times-per-week basis. There are innumerable episodes. The NABB committee calls the attention of parents to the fact that many of these episodes, particularly those from the earlier years, have extreme violence and sordid story situations. Then, within episodes covering years, there is the background of the Long Branch saloon, where the prostitutes under Kitty's wing live in comfort and friendship while their more chaste sisters battle the elements and loneliness in scattered cabins 'way out on the prairie. As a view of history, *Gunsmoke* embodies exactly what is good escapism for adults and poor fare for children.

HALL OF FAME—NBC. Intermittent schedule. This season's schedule, with its emphasis on Americana, again adds stature and status to the quality of television entertainment in this country. *Hall of Fame* opened its 25th season with "Eric" on November 10. The bicentennial trilogy honors presidents Washington, Lincoln, and Truman, concluding with HST's "Meeting at Potsdam" on April 8. Hallmark Cards has been not only a supporter of the finest in TV drama, it has been also a model of good taste in the presentation of commercials.

HAPPY DAYS—ABC, Mondays. Light but appealing situation comedy based on the antics of high schoolers in the early 1950s. May help a little to bridge the generation gap between today's kids and their parents.

HARRY-O—ABC, Thursdays. David Janssen as a private eye in violence-ridden episodes devised to terrify and shock. Situations deal with dope, corruption and sadism, casual sex, beatings, and various forms of murder. A distorted view of the world. Not recommended for children under any circumstances.

HAWAII FIVE-O—CBS, Fridays. Graphic horror and brutality. Slick production by craftsmen who know all the tricks of milking thrills from sordid situations and psychopathic criminals. Strategically placed to be available to youngsters on their weekly Friday "freedom" evening.

HOLLYWOOD SQUARES—Syndicated (access time). This program has its clever and entertaining moments, but they are wedged so tightly between spot announcements and plugs for prizes that the essence of the program is its unrelieved commercialism. Someday the advertisers themselves will revolt against their own excesses.

IRONSIDE—Syndicated. This long-running melodrama has just left NBC and is now syndicated into early evening hours of a five-days-per-week schedule. An entertaining show for adults, but much too violent and crime-ridden for younger children.

THE JEFFERSONS—CBS, Saturdays. Archie Bunker's former black neighbors, the Jeffersons, are now established in plush New York East Side living quarters occupied by the racially integrated affluent. The program is based on the *nouveau riche* bigoted Jefferson who, like Archie, has a few subliminal appealing characteristics to soften his brashness and his sometimes unethical approach to day-to-day situations. But *The Jeffersons* is far less intimate in characterizations and in situations than *All in the Family*.

JOE AND SONS—CBS (cancelled). Another casualty of the rating war that deserved a better fate. The father (Richard Castellano) was involved in referable problems associated with bringing up two boys in a motherless home. The kind of program that television needs to sustain the significance of the medium itself.

JOE FORRESTER—NBC, Tuesdays. Lloyd Bridges in a tough and uneven series that depends largely on the depiction of violent crime. An addition to the mass of second-rate melodrama that floods the networks at the close of the Family Hour. Nowhere near the quality of the original *The Blue Knight* films from which it is supposedly modeled.

KATE McSHANE—CBS, Wednesdays (cancelled). Even though wiped out by TV's totally insensitive ratings race, this must have been a near-miss. There was substance and there was characterization. The program was cut off before it had time to develop roots.

KOJAK—CBS, Sundays. Despite its superior qualities in scripts, production, and performance, this is hard-core violence aired at a time when many millions of children and teens comprise a substantial segment of the target audience. This is aired at nine p.m. in the East and West, but at eight in the Midwest. Tough, hard-hitting melodrama. Subjects treated include violent rape, fights with knives, traffic in dope, etc. The dialogue and situations are sharply defined and realistic.

KUNG FU—Syndicated. Ostensibly, this preaches non-violence. Actually, it shows violence in minute detail and in slow-motion. It is far too strong and disturbing for unattended children.

LAST OF THE WILD—Syndicated. Lorne Green does a first-rate job as narrator for this interesting and entertaining wildlife series. Usually aired in early evening "access time" on network affiliated stations, this is a huge relief from the brash and greedy game shows that usually clutter these time periods. In spite of scenic quality, there are indications that reality is sometimes enhanced by contrived dramatization. However, the show is interesting and well worth watching.

LET'S MAKE A DEAL—Syndicated. This program, with its hypoed play on greed and frenzy, has no legitimate place on prime-time television . . . or anywhere else on the schedule, for that matter. It rips away dignity, and puts contestants through procedures that would be better suited to animal acts in a three-ring circus.

LITTLE HOUSE ON THE PRAIRIE—NBC, Wednesdays. Although there has been criticism of this program's failure to adhere to the stories and characterizations of the novels on which it is supposed to be based, the series still has enough qualities and appeal to give it a high rating on the very small list of network shows with real appeal for family viewing. The characters and the scenic backgrounds are attractive. In contrast to *The Family Holvak*, the emphasis here is on characters and situations, rather than melodrama.

MANNIX—Syndicated. *Mannix* is a rough and tough crime drama, with sex thrown in for the psuedo sophisticates. It has many psycho criminals involved in sordid situations. The show has left CBS and is now in the syndication marketplace. It is most likely to show up in late afternoon periods, "stripped in" five times per week. Parents beware.

MARCUS WELBY, M.D.—ABC, Tuesdays. Robert Young continues year after year as the image of the professional everyone would like to have as his doctor. Superior casting and first-grade production. Entertainment for adults, but a caution is due regarding this and other "doctor" shows. It is the nature of these programs that they depict rare and serious ailments as typical, thus building a distorted impression of the dangers of ordinary living. We have enough real woes, without adding the fear of others that are only remote possibilities.

M*A*S*H—CBS, Tuesdays. *M*A*S*H*, a solid hit show in preceding seasons, has been bounced around on the schedule this year, and it may have lost a few rating points in the process. It has not, however, lost its sharp wit and its often moving and compassionate treatment of situations created by the stupidities and brutalities of war. The NABB committee considers *M*A*S*H* to be a very funny program that adds distinction to the week's schedule, even though some of the subject matter and attitudes of the principals will offend some viewers. To view or not to view is a matter for individual family determination.

MAUDE—CBS, Mondays. Maude is a specialist in inciting controversy, and she has been the center of many provocative episodes. This is a place where the decision to view or not to view is properly delegated to internal family decree. Maude herself tackles any subject, and she takes a stand that often disagrees with the views of large segments of society.

McCLOUD—NBC, Sundays (intermittent). Dennis Weaver as a cowboy cop in New York City. Sometimes entertaining but usually melodrama. The NABB committee believes that this is unsuitable for unattended children.

MEDICAL CENTER—CBS, Mondays. Medicine at a pace of hypoed melodrama. We hesitate to use the term "phoney," because that implies premeditated deception. Let's just say that any resemblance to legitimate medical practice is accidental.

MEDICAL STORY—NBC, Thursdays (cancelled). It is ironic that NBC has cancelled this series, and added Danny Thomas' *The Practice* to the network schedule at midseason. *Medical Story* has been a strongly dramatized treatment of hospital situation and behind-the-scenes administrative conflicts.

It may have been a little heavy on the crusading side, but it was expertly produced by the same people who are responsible for the superior qualities of *Police Story*.

MOD SQUAD—Syndicated. Distributed widely as a five-times-per-week program aired in early evening hours readily accessible to children, *Mod Squad* is misleading because of its effort to appear timely and believable. While it has some merit through occasional involvement in social problems, it is more often than not far too engrossed in violence and sordid story material to be acceptable as fare for children.

MARY TYLER MOORE SHOW—CBS, Saturdays. One of the happy aspects about this show is the fact that in addition to its bright sophistication, its characters are adults, who can be comfortably associated with viewing teens and children. The series, as always, is beautifully produced with an outstanding cast.

MOVIN' ON—NBC, Tuesdays. Before the season began, the producers declared that they were changing *Movin' On* to make it more suitable for its new time period within the Family Hour. Announced changes included more "action" at the beginning of the show to attract youngsters, and a modification of adult story content. The result we see is less characterization, and more crime-oriented story content. This is not, in our opinion, good family entertainment, nor a constructive response to the "family hour concept."

BOB NEWHART SHOW—CBS, Saturdays. Fair and funny depiction of husband and wife relationships—concern for family and friends. Scripts are carefully written and well constructed. As in the Mary Tyler Moore program, these are people you would invite into your living room—or to visit your children.

NIGHT GALLERY—Syndicated. This is included here because *Night Gallery* has been promoted and sold as an "ideal" series for early evenings, Monday through Friday. In such time periods it attracts thousands of teens and children. Tales of horror and the supernatural produced to thrill adult audiences in late hours on a one-time-per-week schedule. At the pre-bedtime hour it is a terrifying, nightmare-inducing show that ought not to be accessible to children.

ON THE ROCKS—ABC, Mondays. This is a humorous show with bright dialogue and an expert cast. It also has one of TV's brightest comedy stars in Jose Perez. But *On the Rocks* has reminiscences of *Hogan's Heroes*, which disturbed and even distressed many persons by its cavalier treatment of prisoner-of-war camps in Germany. This is not to suggest that American prisons are comparable to the German camps, but doesn't this show, with its relatively bright inmates and relatively gullible guards, provide today's youngsters with an impression of prison that is too comfortable and too free in the living conditions of the inmates? The setting here is like that of a boarding school. It is nothing like a prison.

TONY ORLANDO AND DAWN—CBS, Wednesdays. Consistently pleasant variety hour featuring appealing personalities and musical talents of its three principle performers. Humor and warmth. The show generates a real sense of audience participation, both in the studio and at home.

DONNIE AND MARIE OSMOND—ABC, Fridays. This new music-variety program made its debut January 23, too late for the copy deadline for this guide. However, the Osmonds as personalities and as performers are favorably known to the NABB committee. This will be a bright and entertaining show if the producers use these talents to advantage.

OTHER PEOPLE, OTHER PLACES—Syndicated. Usually aired in early evening "access hours," this travel series is entertaining and interesting. A good family program.

PHYLLIS—CBS, Mondays. The one solid hit among the new comedy shows of the 1975-'76 season. Success is the result of superior scripts and the outstanding talents of Cloris Leachman as Phyllis. Pathos and humor, all in the same moment, as in the masterful episode when Phyllis and her daughter sat up all night in an unsuccessful attempt to learn to "communicate."

PETROCELLI—NBC, Wednesdays. Undistinguished melodrama with a good measure of violence and Godfather-type characters. Treatment is more deductive than in some other cop show. Okay entertainment for adults.

POLICE STORY—NBC, Tuesdays. Not for children, but this is far superior to most police action programs. It is produced by responsible people concerned with creating a realistic series in which the characters are "human" and the violence is integral to the story situations. If older youngsters are going to watch this, we suggest that parents watch with them.

POLICE SURGEON—Syndicated. Wherever this shows up, the NABB suggests that the audience skip it. Mediocre and contrived, as well as sordid and excessively violent.

POLICE WOMAN—NBC, Tuesdays. From its inception *Police Woman* has been a crude and distasteful crime show that has used all kinds of devices and sleazy backgrounds to incite the prurient interests of viewers. This is a kill-for-thrill show dealing with twisted psycho characters involved in the most sordid situations. Now, in the Midwest, one-third of the nation's teens and children have the opportunity of seeing this at eight p.m. In the West and East, the kids have to wait 'til nine. The three-network rate-race for ratings supersedes all other responsibilities.

POPI—CBS, Tuesdays. Amusing, with cute kids, but there was no indication from the opening episode that this will be anything more than contrived routine comedy. A Puerto Rican widower raises two sons. Not as appealing as the cancelled *Joe and Sons,* in which the boys were older and the situations more realistic.

THE PRICE IS RIGHT—Syndicated. Lavish prizes. Excessively commercial. Not as bad, however, as other game shows that exploit the avarice of contestants and viewers.

RHODA—CBS, Mondays. An appealing and entertaining show. No woman's lib here, but the characters are warm and funny.

THE ROCKFORD FILES—NBC, Fridays. An episode will begin with humor and a tongue-in-cheek treatment of the characters and the crime situations in which they are involved, then whamo!, the tone changes and everything is brutal and deadly serious. There is much hard-core violence, and much sordid corruption involving law enforcement officials and leading citizens. The way to survive, Rockford implies, is to trust almost anyone except the police. This is adult escapism . . . not for youngsters.

THE ROOKIES—ABC, Tuesdays. This long-running cop series is now offered in the syndication market, and has been promoted as an "ideal" show for family viewing. Yet ABC moved it to 9 p.m. in the East and West this season to comply with the "family hour" edict of the three networks and the National Association of Broadcasters! Irony and cynicism. The extreme violence and sordid story content of many episodes may be acceptable for some adult viewers, but they certainly do not belong in late afternoon or "family hour" time periods where youngsters will be the predominant audience. The youth and sincerity of the characters offer attractive models for young viewers, thus compounding the potential unhealthful influence.

ROOM 222—Syndicated. This is a first-rate series with a thoughtful, gentle, and entertaining approach to student-teacher issues. Excellent cast. A natural and appealing treatment of racial integration.

SANFORD AND SON—NBC, Fridays. It is good to have people from less affluent economic situations in prominent roles in successful regular series. It is also good to have black characters as stars in any regular TV program. But the NABB committee still has some reservations about *Sanford and Son.* Even though the principals are likeable and appealing, they are also broad and not too far removed from stereotyped presentation.

SIX MILLION DOLLAR MAN—ABC, Sundays. This is a big show with teen and child viewers. It also illustrates a world full of evil and constant menace. In part it is recycled Superman. Fantasy and reality are mixed so that youngsters won't be able to distinguish between the two. Not recommended for kids.

SIXTY MINUTES—CBS, Sundays. After a too-long hiatus, *Sixty Minutes* returned on December 7 into the best time period it has ever enjoyed. This is a public affairs program that is both sharp-edged and timely. Morley Safer and Mike Wallace are experts at their trade, and they appear to have a generous budget to prepare their exposes and investigations. This is a valuable, provocative program, whether or not we agree with the viewpoints expressed. It is worth sitting the family down to watch.

SPACE: 1999—Syndicated. This is an hour-long British import that has unusual qualities in space gadgetry and other visual effects. It has even won citations from scientific bodies, but the NABB committee strongly suspects that the scientists responsible for the citations looked at the gadgetry without in any way considering the scientific accuracy of the dramatic content of various episodes, which present utter destruction and absolutely terrifying aspects of outer space. Even a TV-hardened kid would be frightened out of his wits by scenes such as the close-up of a victim writhing as he is burnt to a crisp by a ray gun or the horrible transformation of a beautiful living woman into a decayed body. Production expertise devoted to showing exotic terror in outer space may be a science fiction tradition, but it is not good for young viewers.

STARSKY AND HUTCH—ABC, Tuesdays. A fun game composed of murder and violent organized crime. Knives, guns, sadism, beatings by hired hoods, and the crime boss living elegantly in plush luxury. For example: the December 10 episode included a victim stabbed to death in a phone booth, with the killer smiling as he watches the body collapse. A little later he stabbed a girl while making love to her, although the actual murder was off camera. Stylish production and the attractive relationship and characterizations of the principals have made this a popular show. We suggest that parents draw the line here, or watch it themselves.

STREETS OF SAN FRANCISCO—ABC, Thursdays. Tough and brutal, with graphic presentation of murder and other crime. All the bizarre gimmicks that come from the manufacturers of second-rate melodrama. Girls commit murder and are murdered themselves. Promiscuous sex is commonplace. Plots are thin, without logic or rational motivation.

S.W.A.T.—ABC, Saturdays. They've been toning this down ever since the critics blasted its first episodes, but the storm trooper approach to law enforcement still provides the beat—in music, story, and tempo—for this callous exploitation of viewers' appetites for graphic violence and sordid situations featuring psychopathic murderers. Episodes show the weakness of traditional police and the necessity for society to delegate its protection to wartime commando-type squads. The theme is Superman in real life. Violence is the *only* solution for most of society's ills.

SWISS FAMILY ROBINSON—ABC, Sundays. An attractive family with good priorities and concern for one another. Acceptable as family entertainment, although the producers have neglected the basic appeals of the original story to emphasize melodramatic incongruous elements that are far afield from the classic book. Some sequences too frightening for unattended children.

SWITCH—CBS, Tuesdays. In the pilot episode (August 28) the plot centered on a group of adults playing like kids in a cops and robbers game.

Robert Wagner has a role similiar to his characterization in "It Takes A Thief," which was much superior to this in plot and dialogue. Eddie Albert appeared to be badly miscast in a dull and almost plotless program. There wasn't much violence. Subsequent *Switch* episodes show everybody conning everybody, with Albert and Wagner using any means to outwit con men who have violently criminal tendencies and motives. There is a heavy emphasis on casual but expensive sex. Obviously a series that is unsuitable for youngsters, but scheduled at eight p.m. in the Midwest (nine p.m. in the East and West.)

THAT'S MY MAMA!—ABC (cancelled). Even though this was sometimes funny, its loss is no tragedy to the public as a whole. It relied entirely too much on superficial gag comedy that was played for cheap laughs at the expense of good taste.

THRILLSEEKERS—Syndicated (access time). Glamorized "heroes" risking their necks in spectacular stunts. The program does not show consequences of destructive accidents resulting from reckless risks. Would this induce your youngster to emulate foolhardy actions?

TREASURE HUNT—Syndicated. A game show with lavish prizes and excessive commercials.

UNTOUCHABLES—Syndicated. This brutal and irresponsible series is still in widespread circulation, so we need to include it here to caution parents about its availability to children. Critic John Crosby described this as the "worst program ever made for TV." His evaluation still stands, although today's critics never look at it and never write about its menace. But the kids can still find it, and we still have broadcasters who are callous enough to place it within their reach.

BOBBY VINTON SHOW—Syndicated. An "access time" program that tries to have something for everybody, but winds up as an unsteady hodgepodge that wavers between bright musical entertainment and sometimes distasteful skits that border on the vulgar. Celebrities in guest appearances. The commercials larded into the pre-network prime time period are interminable.

THE WALTONS—CBS, Thursdays. Earl Hamner's *The Waltons* is now an established success that is enormously influential in demonstrating what can be done when excellent writing, production, and performance are applied to the portrayal of a family that has principles, and warm feelings for each other. The appeal of *The Waltons* is its dramatization of the success of a family, collectively and individually, without dependence on economic affluence. *The Waltons* has been maligned for its "wholesomeness" and it has been imitated because of its huge and unexpected success. But the imitators—*Apple's Way, The Family Holvak,* etc.—have missed the basic concept that intelligent socially-minded people placed in realistic situations can be more dramatic and appealing than other so-called decent people forced into artificial backgrounds and sometimes contrived melodramatic situations.

WELCOME BACK, KOTTER—ABC, Thursdays. Kotter is an unorthodox teacher, and that is fine—and some episodes are really funny. But the overall treatment is shallow, and the laugh-track is artificial and obtrusive. Situations that could be poignant and appealing are aired in a flat dimension that fails to recognize that TV comedy could be more than a routine comic strip.

LAWRENCE WELK SHOW—Syndicated. The longest-running and most successful musical program on TV.

WILD KINGDOM—NBC, Sundays. This show is listed here rather than under "Children's Programs" because of its wide appeal to adults as well as to youngsters.

WILD WORLD OF ANIMALS—Syndicated. A superior series beautifully photographed with apparently authentic portrayal of wildlife. Narration stresses information without contrived sensationalism.

WONDERFUL WORLD OF DISNEY—NBC, Sundays. Year after year this series maintains standards in production and in story material. At times the Disney producers distort literary classics, but on the whole this show is probably the best regular weekly national network prime-time programs for youngsters and family viewing.

THE WORLD AT WAR—Syndicated. An excellent documentary of World War II in hour-long episodes. This is full of historic footage acquired from opposing forces in history's greatest war. For the perceptive, war is set forth with all of its horrors. This series is not intended as *entertainment*. It is for mature audiences seeking a realistic view and understanding of immeasurable tragedy.

WORLD OF SURVIVAL—Syndicated. A wildlife series that features portrayal of species threatened with extinction through man's neglect. Produced with aid from the World Wildlife Fund.

Commercial Brainwashing

A great deal of money is poured into television commercials. Huge production crews, top-flight actors and directors, and outstanding designers are used on the same kinds of settings employed on the best programs. Some tend to be obnoxious and repetitive on the theory (supported by research) that we remember the irritating commercials, rather than the pleasant ones. Whether soothing or nerve-wracking, these "shorts" tend to portray each sex in roles and activities that are fairly traditional. Women are generally depicted engaged in household tasks where their all-encompassing preoccupation is with getting things sanitary, clean, sweet-smelling, or in such excellent shape that they will be the envy of their neighbors (as if one's floors, wash, bathrooms, or drains were any of their business!). If they are not observed involved in domestic tasks, women are cast as sex objects and wearing, as is, the most beautiful and exotic make-up, hairdos, and clothes; they float through ocean sprays, mountain winds, and other natural phenomena while maintaining their glamourous smiles and composure. Few females are shown as intelligently or competently involved in higher-order tasks. [15]

It is critical that your daughter gain the ability to evaluate objectively the commercials that appear daily on her screen, for she will *have viewed approximately 350,000 of these brainwashing gems before she is eighteen!*

Consider the sexism that reaches young girls' ears under the guise of selling a product. In 93 percent of the cases in which a narrator's voice was used over a picture, that voice was male and said things like: "She's not innocent, not ordinary any more" (Revlon Color Silk). Is "innocent" equivalent to "ordinary"? And, if it is, since no adolescent girl wants to be thought of as "ordinary," should she, therefore, surrender her innocence in order to become unique?

In another commercial a father and son are racing on motorcycles, eating Wheaties. [16] The words spoken are, "He knows he's a man!" Apparently, men are foolish creatures who do not recognize the danger of (a) racing, (b) racing on motorcycles, or (c) diverting their attention from the driving by eating. Obviously, the appeal is to the macho nature of the male—reckless, carefree, chance-taking, and hungry. The image is stereotypical however, for many males are sufficiently intelligent either to avoid motorcycles or to drive them safely—without racing, whereas there must be some women who are sufficiently unthinking to emulate the actors in the commercial script. Further, there are women who drive and enjoy motorcycles, cars, planes, and motorboats.

Listen for the voices of the women who speak in commercials: "He touched me, and suddenly nothing is the same!" (Chantilly). Or, perhaps, you recall the scene in which a woman at a square dance is involved—not in dancing, but in examining the collars of the other women's dancing partners. Noticing a dingy one, she says, "Ring around the collar!" The man's wife winces and later is shown scrubbing her husband's shirt wildly (Wisk).

Obviously the overconcern with the life-styles of others, the need to live up to one's neighbors, the need to be attractive to the opposite sex, or to have the cleanest, most sparkling home on the block are ludicrous standards to emphasize and publicize; they insidiously convey the message that these are the values that count. They also decrease the amount of respect any intelligent human being could maintain for the people who are portrayed as thinking that way—invariably women!

Both sexes need to be attractive, clean, and intelligent. Both can feel the exhilaration of riding a motorcycle, waterskiing, climbing mountains, winning a tournament, or any of the human experiences usually attributed to "being a man." Unfortunately, the script writers continue to depict TV players in outmoded roles, differentiated by gender and mouthing old-fashioned lines that tend to segregate women into domestic, submissive, or sex-object roles, and men into athletic, active, successful, and achieving ones. Even toy commercials portray girls playing with dolls and boys building with erector sets.

Use the guidelines for books that was included in this chapter or the simple chart for viewing television programs that was noted earlier. Then encourage your daughter to read a great deal more than most youngsters do today and either turn off the TV or analyze its shows with her. Once she understands and *internalizes* her equality with males as a comparable human being, she should break from the passivity of *viewing* and move into the self-actualization process of *doing*.

Conclusion:
A New Beginning
for All Daughters

Once daughters have had their horizons expanded and recognize the world of opportunity that surrounds them, most of those who are intellectually able and emotionally secure will choose to explore the larger environment and test their skills and abilities in the various professions, the arts, industry, and business. These young ladies will be self-actualizing, for, in addition to the security of being self-supportive in an ever more difficult and demanding economy, they will be able to achieve, to grow, and to soar through those peak experiences one enjoys when potential and perfection blend in the successful realization of selected goals.

If your daughter decides to marry, once she has reached this elevated state, she never will have to fear desertion, divorce, or widowhood. If she becomes a mother, her own increased education will serve as an excellent model for *her* children, and your daughter's expanded knowledge and experience will assist her in raising *her* offspring as independent and self-actualizing girls (and boys). Your contribution to your daughter(s) and her daughter(s) will branch out and affect the lives of many future generations of girls—an unmatched gift to society.

On the other hand, as parents, you undoubtedly may have some concerns about "programming" your daughter's experiences in order to ensure her ability and desire to become professionally involved. You may question the legitimacy of deciding another person's fate without permitting her to exercise choice.

If you do nothing, if you do not raise your daughter according to the positive suggestions in this book, she is being programmed away from freedom to choose—toward domesticity and a limited, "boxed-in" role from which only a few escape. Is this directionless freedom of choice with its restrictive outcome better? Once your daughter has been taught to be independent and confident of her ability and continues to obtain as much education as she is capable of achieving, she will always have choices—very good ones. The only time a girl has no or few options available to her occurs when she has been led to believe that her "place is in the home," that she is capable of only comparatively menial jobs, and, therefore, that she must be dependent on others like her husband.

Another question often raised concerning girls who would be professional and independent is this: Will it be difficult for your daughter to coexist among her peers if her views of an "ideal" future life are markedly different from theirs? To the contrary, if you follow the guidelines provided in this book, she will be so secure in her own (and your) convictions that she will persuade some of her friends to consider extending their education and to seek professional involvement for themselves. Most youngsters whose backgrounds are different from their peers' believe that *theirs* is the superior one; the things with which they are familiar "make sense" to them. Consider the kindergartner whose mother was employed. When her teacher questioned her classmates about what their fathers did "for a living" and neglected to ask about their mothers —assuming that they were homemakers, the youngster spoke up without hesitation: "Teacher," she said "you forgot my mommy! She's the one that does *two* jobs in our family! She's an executive secretary in a big office and a cleaning lady in our house!"

Will your daughter find life too difficult if she does become a professional woman and also marries and raises a family of her own? Will it be taxing for her? Will it affect her youngsters adversely? Research presented in Chapter 1 documents that many working women are more healthy and content than homemakers and that their children profit from their involvement; but perhaps the views of professional women themselves will reassure you. One woman dentist related the following from her own experiences:

> When I'm tired, I drink two cups of coffee and go on. When I'm working, I forget myself. I have a terrible allergy at certain times of the year. When I work, I forget that my back is itching. I only remember when I close the office, put the children to sleep, set everything in order, and relax. *Then* my back itches!

A female general practitioner recounted a similar experience:

> I don't have time to worry about myself when I'm working. I enjoy

being busy! When things are slow and there's nothing much to do, I begin feeling all kinds of aches and pains!

A practicing woman attorney corroborated the previous accounts in her own way:

I suppose I remained within law because of the success I had in obtaining a position when women were not easily being placed. I met my husband in law school and enjoyed sharing common problems (career-wise) with him. To this day we discuss our cases together and advise each other, although we do practice separately. It's difficult to explain the enormous satisfaction derived from knowing how much I help whole families, specifically children. I know that this office "saves" many. My own children? They're adorable and delightfully adjusted! No, they don't feel deprived because I go to the office every day! They enjoy sitting around and hearing my husband and me discussing the newer cases. They know more about problems—and how to avoid them—than most teen-agers. We've never been told that they were anything other than "wonderful!"

Another woman dentist seemed to have the secret to success in both worlds when she suggested:

Any profession is "perfect" for a woman, providing that she can practice within a section of her home. She is then always near her children, can join them for lunch, arrange her professional hours to coincide with their school hours, and can plan to take vacations when they do not have school. The trick is to become a "specialist," so that your hours are "part time" and self-determined.

A third woman who has been practicing dentistry for more than thirty years shared the sentiments of her colleagues:

One of my college professors told me that dentistry would be a "lonely life for a woman." Quite the opposite. Now that our sons are grown and away at college, I would *really* be lonely were I not able to care for my patients and share their lives to some extent. Imagine if my husband were away at the office all day and I had to *find* something with which to interest myself!

Ethel Alpenfels, one of our more astute anthropologists, commented that males also play multiple roles, but that there is just less talk and public frustration about them. Outstanding professional women who wrestled with the same traditional values that seem to hypnotize our daughters today, overcame them and, after struggling successfully against society's taboos, urged parents to encourage their daughters toward becoming involved actively in medicine, law, dentistry, architecture, engineering, and other male-dominated fields. A woman physician who "never regretted" her decision, recalled:

> I told my father that one very special boy said he wanted a wife who would take care of *him,* not patients. Father said, ". . . we've both invested too much time and money in your future to give it up now. Finish [college], and then if you decide to stay home and take care of "him," no one will stop you . . . but, if you decide that the *world* needs taking care of, you'll be old enough and wise enough to then make the choice. . . ."

Another question that you, as a parent, might consider: "Is it difficult for women professionals to be accepted in their specific fields?" A woman physician, when asked the same question, responded:

> I enthusiastically encourage young (or older) women with the inclination, to go into medicine just as readily as teaching or social work. Although the preparation is long, it is no more difficult than college, and it is fun! The woman doctor is no longer resented or competed with (except in the surgical specialities). In fact, she is sought after in many fields such as pediatrics, obstetrics, and general medicine. If she combines family-rearing with medicine, she will find the specialties of anesthesiology, dermatology, opthalmology, radiology, pathology, and laboratory medicine or industrial medicine particularly suitable.
>
> In the coming years of increasing socialization of medicine, there will be many new opportunities, both administrative and practical, for women desiring to do either full-time or limited work in medicine.

It is true that, in the past, professional women were less accepted, and even rejected, by "fellow" professionals, but that is no longer the case. Resentment, prejudice, and even lack of experience in dealing with female practitioners has all but disappeared. For example, one physician vividly remembered her first few years in practice:

> I moved to a beautiful suburban area and established a practice. In four years, except for emergencies, I never received one referral. In the hospitals the male doctors passed me by with barely a nod. Finally, I decided to take "the bulls by their horns." One morning I stepped up to one of the town physicians who just happened to bypass me in the hospital corridors and asked, "If I were a male physician, would you have at least introduced yourself in the four years I've been here?" He sputtered a few words, apologized, and continued down the hall. Within two days various town physicians were calling on the phone, saying "Hello!" and requesting that we begin to "cover" for each other on weekends and during vacations. It took no time at all before they

were actually inviting my husband and me to staff parties and events. I've been here twenty years now, and I finally understand what the problem was. The male doctors just didn't know how to speak to a female doctor! They were as frightened of me as some of the patients were. It wasn't the competition—it was just the fact that it was a new role perception to which *they* hadn't adjusted!

Being accepted by one's colleagues was only part of the problem in years gone by; being trusted by patients was a more formidable concern. A petite woman dentist who met and married her husband while they were both studying dentistry explains how she gradually won the confidence of a large number of patients:

My husband and I were each graduated during the Depression, and, in order to survive, we opened an office which proudly displayed the sign: Dentist. He maintained his position at the hospital, so that we'd have a regular source of income, and I remained at the office, waiting . . . waiting . . . for patients.

Our first patient arrived in agony. He was the owner of the neighborhood butcher store and was a huge, massive man. "Are *you* the dentist?" he moaned. "I didn't know ladies *could* be dentists! You'll *never* be able to pull my tooth!"

It was due to his overwhelming pain that he consented to let me "at least *look*" into his mouth. I calmly reassured him that I could help his condition, and, before he could argue, I began working on his tooth. I worked and simultaneously prayed, "Dear Lord, *please* don't let me hurt him!"

When I was finished, he sat quietly in the chair for a few minutes and just stared at me. Finally he said, "Lady, I never had nobody treat me so gentle! Everybody in this neighborhood's gonna know about you!"

He kept his word. Every customer was told and retold the story about "the lady-dentist upstairs who don't hurt!" It got so that when my husband could finally remain in the office to practice with me, he began to be slightly disgruntled with the patients who came knocking at the door to say: "The butcher downstairs told me about the lady-dentist. Is she in?"

Professional women repeatedly described how one or both of their parents had encouraged them toward realizing their career aspirations. Each story was told with love and affection—and gratitude for their parents' faith in their daughter's ability to succeed. This account was told by a woman whose belief in her own capability was fostered by a wise father. She became a director of psychiatric nursing in New York City, despite having been reared in a rural

section of Ohio where the general level of student motivation toward professionalism was low and where few girls considered working after marriage:

> As far back as I can remember (prior to ten or eleven) I never con-
> sidered anything else . . . there was something glamorous about the
> white uniform! In those days a nurse could become an R.N. without a
> baccalaureate degree, but due to father's constant admonishments (he
> was a high school dropout who became a success working for the
> government), I couldn't consider anything apart from an academic
> degree! My mother was a teacher, and she'd say, "Let her decide for
> herself. . . ." My father always answered, "She can be anything she
> wants—*after* college!"

Another inspiring father urged his daughter away from nursing—into
medicine. This lady had been prompted toward teaching, but her "dreams" lay
elsewhere:

> When I finally became a doctor, I felt that all my dreams had
> materialized. My aunt, a principal of an elementary school, had urged
> me into teaching, insisting that a woman would face extreme difficul-
> ties in actually acquiring a medical degree. My father, on the other
> hand, consistently encouraged me. When I was nine years old, I told
> him I wanted to be a nurse, and he said, "Why a nurse? You'd be a great
> doctor!" The moment I heard his words, I knew how right they were
> for me.

One encouraging mother of an aspiring dental candidate told her, upon being
made aware of her daughter's trepidations at leaving home to enter dental
college: "No daughter of mine is afraid of anything! If anyone in this world can
do it, *you* can!" At the graduation ceremonies three years later, after her
daughter's degree had been conferred, her mother took her aside and added:

> I was frightened to death for you! I knew how difficult they could make
> it for a girl, and I didn't want you to have to experience the trauma of
> failing . . . , but I felt that not going at all *would* be failing, and I
> thought that, between the two of us, there ought to be enough "guts"
> to see you through!

Sometimes, humility is easier to express after appropriate and positive aggressiveness brings success. A district court judge, during an interview, was asked,
"Is your husband a lawyer, too?" "I'm the 'too' ", she replied gently. "My
husband is a lawyer, and I'm a lawyer, too." The daughter of that well-known
judge became an attorney and aggressively and successfully campaigned and
was elected to the State legislature—another case of a professional mother's
inspiration and example benefiting her daughter.

The many professional women interviewed often recounted that they were aware of the early matrimonial decisions of their friends and that they sometimes wondered whether they were trading one kind of life for another. Their eventual successes in marriage and the professions verify that girls need not face an "either/or" conflict; they may have the best of both wonderful worlds today.

In our century, women have been intelligent enough and administratively capable of heading railroads, colleges, broadcasting systems, newspapers, clothing and swimming pool industries, professional associations, department stores, publishing houses, banks, and manufacturing firms. They have been ambassadors, federal and state judges, Cabinet members, commissioners, and congressional leaders. They are pioneers in the fields of medicine, dentistry, law, engineering, accounting, and pharmacy. Whereas some women are content to serve only as homemakers, most intelligent human beings need constantly expanding horizons and challenges—or tedium and boredom can develop with negative emotional, psychological, and marital consequences. Moreover, the woman who is professionally qualified to change her environment may never need to do so. The intellectual woman who is restricted by her lack of qualifications eventually will feel trapped.

Your continuing education, encouragement, and example will aid your daughter to succeed and to develop the ten attributes most often listed by the professional women in the New York University research study. Those outstanding professionals described themselves as:

1. Cooperative   6. Intellectual
2. Energetic   7. Poised
3. Idealistic   8. Outgoing
4. Persistent   9. Individualistic
5. Ambitious   10. Loving

It may be that these are the attributes that characterize all professional women who challenge the narrow definition of a woman's "role," or it may be that these positive qualities serve to "stress the woman who stands out from her sisters"[1]—the outstanding, professionally successful woman.

You must decide the path your daughter will take, for it grows too late too early. "Fate" may be defined as being prepared for opportunity when it knocks.

> Four things come not back:
> The spoken word;
> The sped arrow;
> Time past;
> *The neglected opportunity.*[2]

What shall it be for your daughter? Her future is in your hands.

Notes

CHAPTER 1

[1]Signe Hammer. *Daughters and Mothers: Mothers and Daughters* (second printing). New York: Quadrangle/The New York Times Book Co. (1976); 9–10.

[2]Rita Lynne Stafford. "An Analysis of Consciously Recalled Motivating Factors and Subsequent Professional Involvement for American Women in New York State." Doctoral dissertation, New York University (1966): 173, 329.

[3]Donald E. Super and Paul B. Bachrach. *Scientific Careers and Vocational Development Theory.* "New York" Bureau of Publications, Teachers College, Columbia University (1957): 113, 118–20. Vocational Development Theory, which constitutes an approach to vocational choice, treats choice, not as an event occurring at a point in time and explainable by determinants which can be observed adequately at that same point in time, but, rather, as a process which takes place over a period and which is best explained by a combination of determinants which, themselves intact, are modified, and thus develop with time. A few of the major propositions of this theory include the concept that vocational development is an ongoing, continuous, generally irreversible process which may be described as a series of life stages, that vocational development is an orderly, patterned, and *predictable* process and that basic development of the self-concept occurs in *childhood;* that adolescence provides a period of exploratory experiences in which the concept of self is elaborated and clarified, and that interests, values, and capacities are integrated and attain vocational meaning through the development and reality testing of the self-concept.

[4]Jessie Bernard. *Academic Women*. University Park, Pennsylvania: The Pennsylvania State Press (1964): 8; George L. Groper and Robert Fitzpatrick. *Who Goes to Graduate School?* Pittsburgh, Pennsylvania: American Institute for Research (September 1959); Carol Lopate. *Women in Medicine*. Baltimore, Maryland: Johns Hopkins Press (1968): 27–28.

[5]Agatha Townsend. *College Freshmen Speak Out*. New York: Harper & Brothers (1956): 41.

[6]Hammer, op. cit.: 70.

[7]Helene Deutsch. *The Psychology of Women: A Psychologist's Interpretations*. New York: Grune & Stratton (1944): 290.

[8]John Tiedman et al. *Position Choices and Careers: Elements of a Theory*. Cambridge: Harvard Graduate School of Education (1958): 42.

[9]Margaret M. Hennig. "Family Dynamics for Developing Positive Achievement Motivation in Women: The Successful Woman Executive." *Women and Success: The Anatomy of Achievement*. Ruth B. Kindson, Sc. D., ed. New York: Morrow (1973).

[10]David Reisman. "Introduction." Bernard, op. cit.:xix

[11]Ethel J. Alpenfels. "The World of Ideas—Do Women Count?" *The Educational Record*. XLIV (January 1963): 40.

[12]Rose K. Goldsen et al. *What College Students Think*. Princeton, New Jersey: D. Van Nostrand Company, Inc. (1960): 26, 58.

[13]Caroline Bird. *Enterprising Women*. New York: W. W. Norton & Company, Inc. (1976); Frances C. Hutner. "Mother's Education and Working: Effect on the School Child." *Journal of Psychology* 82 (1972): 27–37.

[14]James A. Davis. *Great Aspirations*. Chicago: Aldine Publishing Co. (1964): 40; also see Esther Manning Westervelt. *Barriers to Women's Participation In Postsecondary Education: A Review of Research And Commentary As Of 1973–74*. Washington, D.C.: U.S. Department of Health, Education, and Welfare (1975): 50–51.

[15]*U.S. Working Women: A Chartbook*. Washington, D.C.: U.S. Department of Labor, Bureau of Labor Statistics (1975): Chart 1.

[16]*Eliminating Sex Discrimination In Schools: A Source Book*. Raleigh, North Carolina: Research and Information Center, State Department of Public Instruction (1975): 34–36; Matina S. Horner. "Fail: Bright Women." *Psychology Today*, 3 (November, 1969): 29–31 and "Toward an Understanding of Achievement-Related Conflicts in Women." *Journal of Social Issues*, 28 (1972): 157–75; Adeline Levine and Janice Crumrine. *Women and Fear Of Success: A Problem In Replication*. (presentation at American Sociological Association meeting, August 1973); Lopate, op. cit.: 95–99; Paul A. Heist. "The Motivation and Education of College Women." *Journal of the National Association of Women Deans and Counselors*, 25 (January, 1962): 51–59; Ruth E. Hartley. "Current Patterns in Sex Roles: Children's Perceptions." *Journal of the National Association of Women Deans and Counselors* (October, 1961): 3–13; Alpenfels, op. cit.; Kate Hevner Mueller. *Educating Women for a Changing World*. Minneapolis: University of Minnesota Press (1954); Joseph D. Cooper *A Woman's Guide to Part-Time Jobs*. Garden City, New York: Doubleday & Company, Inc. (1963): 19, 21; Lawrence K. Dennis. *Education and a Woman's Life*. Washington, D.C.: American Council on Education (1963): 3; M. Bunting, P.A. Graham, and E. R. Wasserman. "Academic Freedom and Incentive for Women." *Education Record*. 51 (1970): 386–91; David Reisman. "Some Dilemmas of Women's Education." *Educational Record*. 46 (1965): 424–34; J. Lever and P. Schwartz. *Women at Yale*. New York: Bobbs-Merrill (1971); Sybil Stokes. "Women Graduate Students in Political Science." *Women on Campus*. Ann Arbor, Michigan: University of Michigan Press (1970): 272; Betty Friedan. *The Feminine Mystique*. New York: Dell Publishing Company (1963): especially Chapter 7.

[17]Stafford, op. cit.: 2, 389–90; Emilie J. Hutchinson. *Women and the Ph.D.*

Greensboro, North Carolina: North Carolina College for Women (1929): Chapters 3 and 4; Betty Gene Hickey. "Factors Affecting the Plans of Gifted Girls to Go or Not to Go to College." Unpublished Ph.D. dissertation. New York: Teachers College, Columbia University (1959); Charles M. Grigg. "Who Wants to Go to Graduate School, and Why?" Research report in *Social Science*. 11, No. 1, Tallahassee: Center for Social Research, The Florida State University (February 1959); Lopate, op. cit.: 34; Emmy E. Werner. "Sex Differences Between Children's IQs and Measures of Parental Ability and Environmental Ratings." *Developmental Psychology*. 1,3 (1969) 280–85; Hutner, op. cit.: 27–37; Vaughn Crandall, Rachel Dewey, Walter Katkovsky and Anne Preston. "Parents' Attitudes and Behaviors and Grade School Children's Academic Achievements." *Journal of Genetic Psychology*. 104 (1964): 53–66.

[18]Cecilia Backlander and Ella Powell-Frith. *Women and Work*. (Kvinnor och Arbete.) Stockholm: TRU (1971); Ingrid Frederiksson. "Why Sex Roles?" (Varfor Konsroller?) In *Samlevnad i Overflod*. Lund, Sweden: RFSU (1966): 69–82; Friedan, op. cit.: Chapter 12.

[19]*The Federal Women's Program: A Point of View*. Washington, D.C.: U.S. Civil Service Commission, U.S. Government Printing Office, Stock No. 0600–27 (August 1972).

[20]Letty Cottin Pogrebin. *Getting Yours: How to Make the System Work for the Working Woman*. New York: David McKay Company, Inc. (1975): 55.

[21]Wayne Dyer. *Your Erroneous Zones*. New York: Funk & Wagnalls (1976): 214–15, 221.

[22]James W. Trent and Leland L. Medsker. *Beyond High School: A Psychological Study of 10,000 High School Graduates*. San Francisco, California: Jossey-Bass, Inc., Publishers, and the Center for Research and Development in High Education, University of California, Berkeley (1968): 139.

[23]Genevieve Pichault. "Repercussions on the family of the wife and mother who works." (Les repercussions familiales du travail professionel de la femme mariée et mere de famille.) *Population et Famille*. 22, 1 (1970): 20.

[24]T. Neal Garland. "The Better Half? The Male In The Dual Profession Family." In Constantina Safilios-Rothschild, ed., *Toward A Sociology Of Women*, Lexington, Massachusetts: Xerox College Publishing (1972): 199–215.

[25]Constantina Safilios-Rothschild. "The Influence of the Wife's Degree of Work Commitment upon Some Aspects of Family Organization and Dynamics." *Journal of Marriage and the Family*. 32, 4 (1970): 681–91.

[26]Hutner, op. cit.

[27]Per Holmberg. "The Economic and Social Consequences of Today's Sex Roles in Society." (Om de ekonomiska och sociala Konekenserna au nu Konsroller.) In *Kynne eller. Kon*. Stockholm: Raben o Sjogren (1966): 15–30.

[28]*A Statistical Portrait of Women In the United States*. Washington, D.C.: U.S. Department Of Commerce, Bureau of the Census, Special Studies, Series P-23, No. 58 (April 1976): 7–9.

[29]Cooper, op. cit.

[30]*A Statistical Portrait of Women In the United States*, op. cit.: 15–17.

[31]Abraham Maslow. *Motivation and Personality*. New York: Harper & Row, Second Edition (1970).

[32]Friedan, op. cit.: 109.

[33]Ibid.: 336.

[34]J. D. Kulken and Russell Eiseman. "The Negro in the Field of Medicine?" *The Educational Forum*. XXX, 4 (May 1966): 475–81.

[35]Phyllis Chesler. "Women as Psychiatric and Psychotherapeutic Patients." *Journal of Marriage and the Family*. 33, 4 (1971): 746–59.

[36]K. Lewin. *Resolving Social Conflicts*. New York: Harper & Row (1945).

CHAPTER 2

[1]That fathers prefer male children (and why) is expounded in the song, "Sons," from the broadway musical, *The Rothschilds,* by Jerry Block, Sheldon Harnick, and Sherman Yellen. The Western European hero, Mayer Rothschild, explains that he needs help to turn his dreams into reality. He emotes that sons extend a man's vision, reach, impact, and drive and that they are "natural allies" and grow up to be partners. Rothschild also expresses concern about the disposal of his accumulated worldly goods when he questions, "Why should strangers inherit what's not rightfully theirs?" He, as many another father both before and after him, equates his sons with "gold."

Yet, throughout history daughters successfully have "stepped into the shoes" of their fathers and husbands. Rebecca Pennock Lukens (1794–1854) inherited her father's iron mill, staved off bankruptcy, unraveled the paperwork, paid off bills, arranged credit, collected amounts receivable, saw that orders were delivered promptly, watched costs, set rates, established prices that could yield a profit, overcame male competitors' opposition, and expanded the mill into a major independent enterprise in the competitive steel industry. Similarly, Henrietta Chamberlain King (1832–1925) inherited a ranch that was besieged by debts totaling $500,000, employed new scientific developments and, gradually, built it into the King Ranch in Texas, a multinational corporation. She left an estate of $5.4 million and more than a million acres. Oil was discovered on her land after her death, adding $12 million to $18 million a year in income to the corporation formed to operate the ranch. *Many* such examples challenge the outdated concepts exemplified in "Sons," but they are provided little publicity and fail, somehow, to alter the conscious desires of many fathers for sons.

[2]The difference between a father's reaction to the prospect of a son, as opposed to a daughter, is represented also in theater depicting American dreams. In "Soliloquy," from *Carousel,* by Richard Rodgers and Oscar Hammerstein II, Billy (the male lead) contemplates the prospective birth of a son by projecting what his child eventually will do and be. He proudly plans to teach him to wrestle and to dive and projects that his son might be a heavyweight champ someday, or even President of the United States. When conjecturing that the unborn child might be a girl, Billy cries, "You can have fun with a son, but you got to be a *father* to a girl!" When he envisions a daughter, he describes her in terms of pink and white ribbons in her hair and dozens of boys pursuing her. In contrast to the many descriptions of the kinds of work his son might engage in, Billy cries in panic, that he's going to make certain that she won't grow up with a lot of "bums."

The feeling of *responsibility* (rather than "fun") comes through without any interpretation necessary when Billy sings of the need to shelter, feed, and dress a daughter "in the best that money can buy!"

Similarly, in *Shenandoah,* the lyrics of "It's a Boy," by Peter Udell, express the enthusiastic joy of the grandfather-to-be (again, the hero), as he contemplates the birth of his about-to-be-born grandchild. It does not at all occur to him that the child might be other than a boy, and his inner feelings (and those of many men) are revealed throughout the song as he proclaims jubilantly that it makes him feel immortal, that a part of him is here to stay! When told that his grandchild is a *girl,* the poor man sings, "Pour me a drink, my head is spinnin'. . . ."

[3]Howard A. Moss. "Sex, Age, and State as Determinants of Mother-Infant Interaction." Merrill-Palmer *Quarterly,* 13, 1 (1967): 19–36. Also excerpted in Judith M. Bardwick, ed. *Readings on the Psychology of Women.* New York: Harper and Row, (1972): 22–29.

[4]Lois Wladis Hoffman. "Early Childhood Experiences and Women's Achievement Motives." *Journal of Social Isues*, 28, 2 (1972): 129–55.

[5]Burton L. White. *The First Three Years of Life*. Englewood Cliffs, New Jersey: Prentice-Hall, Inc. (1975): 71.

[6]Ibid.: 73.

[7]Ibid.: 107.

[8]Esther Manning Westervelt. *Barriers To Women's Participation In Postsecondary Education: A Review of Research and Commentary as of 1973–74*. Washington, D.C.: U.S. Department of Health, Education, and Welfare (1975): 58.

[9]Loc. cit.

[10]Ibid.: 131.

CHAPTER 3

[1]Burton L. White. *The First Three Years of Life*. Englewood Cliffs, New Jersey: Prentice-Hall, Inc. (1975): 201.

[2]Ibid.: 204.

[3]Ibid.: 203.

[4]Ibid.: 206.

[5]Wayne W. Dyer. *Your Erroneous Zones*. New York: Funk & Wagnalls (1976).

[6]Ibid.: 222.

[7]Abraham Maslow. *Motivation and Personality* (second edition). New York: Harper & Row (1970): Chapter 2.

[8]Rita Lynne Stafford. "Analysis of Consciously Recalled Motivating Factors and Subsequent Professional Involvement for American Women in New York State." Doctoral dissertation, New York University (1966): 198.

[9]Joan Beck. *How to Raise A Brighter Child*. New York: Simon & Schuster (1967); Ranana Benjamin. *Origami For Everyone*. New York: Biograf Books, 5 Garber Hill, Blauvelt, New York 10913 (1973) provides paper-folding activities to be done with parents; Doreen J. Croft and Robert D. Hess. *An Activities Handbook for Teachers of Young Children*. New York: Houghton-Mifflin Company (1972); Imogene Forte and Joy Mackenzie. *Nooks, Crannies, and Corners*. Nashville, Tennessee: Incentive Publications (1972); Carl E. Frankson and Kenneth R. Benson. *Crafts Activities*. West Nyack, New York: Parker Publishing Company, Inc. (1970); Matilda J. Peck and Morton J. Schultz. *Teaching Ideas That Make Learning Fun*. West Nyack, New York: Parker Publishing Company, Inc. (1969); Jenean Romberg. *Let's Discover Tissue*. New York: The Center for Applied Research in Education (1973). This is one of an excellent series that explain how to introduce children to crayon, watercolor, paper, puppets, mobiles, tempera, printing, paper-mache, and weaving; Susan Rounds. *Teaching the Young Child*. New York: Agathon Press (1975); David H. Russel and Etta E. Karp. *Reading Aids through The Grades*. New York: Teachers College Press, Columbia University (1969).

[10]Benjamin S. Bloom. "Learning for Mastery." Evaluation Comment (Center for the Study of Evaluation, University of California at Los Angeles) 1, 2 (1968).

[11]Vivian Edmiston Todd and Helen Herffernan. *The Years Before School*. New York: The Macmillan Company (1964): Part 1.

[12]White, op. cit.: 211.

[13]Ibid.: 212.

[14]Rita Dunn and Kenneth Dunn. *Educator's Self-Teaching Guide to Individualizing Instructional Programs*. West Nyack, New York: Parker Publishing Company (1975): 86–89.

CHAPTER 4

[1]Robert F. Mager and J. McCann. *Learner-Controlled Instruction*. Palo Alto, California: Varian (1963). Research conducted by these two authors demonstrated the superiority of students who were able to control the instructional sequence of certain training tasks. It was also reported that learners' motivation increased with the amount of control they exercised over their own studies.

[2]Rita Lynne Stafford. "An Analysis of Consciously Recalled Motivating Factors and Subsequent Professional Involvement for American Women in New York State." Doctoral dissertation, New York University (1966).

[3]"Outstanding Women" refers to a direct quotation from *Who's Who of American Women* (fourth edition). Chicago: The A. M. Marquis Company (1966): 6. The passage states: "Two broad aims have characterized . . . [this] edition. . . . These aims are: . . . To present *women outstanding as women* without regard to their accomplishments or positions in relation to men; in other words, to stress the woman who stands out from her sisters.

[4]Ibid.: 369.

[5]Ibid.: 317.

[6]Ibid.: 217.

[7]David R. Krathwohl, Benjamin S. Bloom, and Bertram B. Masia. *Taxonomy Of Educational Objectives: Handbook II: Affective Domain*. New York: David McKay Company, Inc. (1964).

[8]Stafford, op. cit.: 389–90.

[9]Eleanor E. Maccoby. "Sex Differences in Intellectual Functioning," in Eleanor E. Maccoby, ed. *The Development of Sex Differences*. Stanford, California: Stanford University Press (1966): 51.

[10]Ibid.: 142.

[11]Loc. cit.

[12]Ibid.: 192–93.

[13]Ibid.: 173.

[14]Rita Dunn and Kenneth Dunn. *Educator's Self-Teaching Guide to Individualizing Instructional Programs*. West Nyack, New York: Parker Publishing Company (1975): 95–110.

CHAPTER 5

[1]The research *facts* verify that girls achieve better than boys in every academic area during the elementary school years. Researchers have interpreted these findings in a variety of ways, including the following: The higher achievement is due to (1) genetic differences, (2) the type of skills being tested, (3) physiological maturity, (4) differences between the treatment of girls and boys, (5) differences in societal expectations, (6) role conflicts, and/or (7) teacher preferences. Whatever the reasons (and those cited above have not been substantiated), girls achieve better than boys during the first seven to ten years of school.

[2]*Eliminating Sex Discrimination in Schools: A Source Book*. Raleigh, North Carolina: Research and Information Center, State Department of Public Instruction (May, 1975): 33.

[3]Ibid.: 34.

[4]James W. Trent and Leland L. Medsker. *Beyond High School: A Psychological Study of 10,000 High School Graduates.* San Francisco, California: Jossey-Bass, Inc., and the Center for Research and Development in Higher Education, University of California, Berkeley (1968): 139.

[5]Ibid.: 131–32.

[6]Ibid.: 176–77.

[7]James Block, ed. *Schools, Society and Mastery Learning.* New York: Holt, Rinehart and Winston (1974); Robert M. Gagne, ed. *Learning and Individual Differences: A Symposium of the Learning Research and Development Center,* University of Pittsburgh. Columbus, Ohio: Charles E. Merrill Books (1967). (Chapter 2, "How Can Instruction Be Adapted to Individual Differences?" by Lee Cronbach and John B. Carroll is particularly interesting.); Robert F. Peck. *Promoting Self-Disciplined Learning: A Researchable Revolution.* Washington, D.C.: U.S. Office of Education (1970); John I. Goodlad. "Diagnosis and Prescription in Educational Practice." *New Approaches to Individualizing Instruction.* Princeton, New Jersey: Educational Testing Service (1965): 27–37; Doris M. Lee. *Diagnostic Teaching.* Washington, D.C.; National Education Association (1966); Madeline C. Hunter. "When the Teacher Diagnoses Learning." *Educational Leadership* (1965): 545–49. In addition, at least two major commissions specifically emphasized the need for individualizing instruction. Their explicit recommendations are available in *The National Commission on Reform of Secondary Education,* edited by B. Frank Brown. *The Reform of Secondary Education: A Report to the Public and the Profession.* New York: McGraw-Hill Book Company (1973) and *The Rise Report: Report of the California Commission for Reform of Intermediate and Secondary Education.* Sacramento, California: California State Department of Education (1975).

[8]*Eliminating Sex Discrimination* . . . : 32.

[9]Ibid.: 35–36.

[10]Joan Beck. *How to Raise a Brighter Child.* New York: Trident Press (1967): 256.

[11]Robert J. Havinghurst. "Conditions Productive of Superior Children." *Teachers College Record.* 62 (April, 1961).

[12]Beck, op. cit.: 257.

[13]Havinghurst, op. cit.

[14]Beck, op. cit.

[15]Havinghurst, op. cit.

[16]Beck, op. cit.

[17]Ibid.: 258.

[18]Ibid.

[19]Rita Dunn and Kenneth Dunn. "Finding the Best Fit: Learning Styles, Teaching Styles." *NASSP Bulletin.* Virgina: National Association for Secondary School Principals, 59, 390 (April, 1975): 30–36.

[20]Rita Dunn and Kenneth Dunn. "Learning Style as a Criterion for Placement in Alternative Programs." *Kappan.* Bloomington, Indiana: Phi Delta Kappa (December, 1974), 275–78.

CHAPTER 6

[1]*Eliminating Sex Discrimination In Schools: A Source Book.* Raleigh, North Carolina: Research and Information Center, State Department of Public Instruction (May, 1975): 35.

[2]Ibid.: 29.
[3]Ibid.
[4]"Developmental Characteristics of Children and Youth." Institute of Child Study, College of Education, University of Maryland, College Park, Maryland. Washington, D.C. The Association for Supervision and Curriculum Development (1975); David Elkind. *A Sympathetic Understanding of the Child: Birth to Sixteen.* Boston: Allyn & Bacon (1974); R. Havinghurst. *Developmental Tasks and Education.* New York: David McKay Company, Inc. (1972); P. Mussen, et al. *Child Development and Personality.* New York: Harper & Row (1974); H. Perkins. *Human Development and Learning.* Belmont, California: Wadsworth Publishing Company (1974).

[5]Rita Lynne Stafford. "An Analysis of Consciously Recalled Motivating Factors and Subsequent Professional Involvement for American Women in New York State." Doctoral dissertation, New York University (1966): 329.

[6]Rita Dunn and Kenneth Dunn. *Practical Approaches to Individualizing Instruction: Contracts and Other Effective Teaching Strategies.* West Nyack, New York: Parker Publishing Company (1972): Chapter 7.

[7]Ibid.: Chapter 6.
[8]Ibid.

CHAPTER 7

[1]Betty Friedan. *The Feminine Mystique.* New York: Dell Publishing Company (1963): 27.

[2]Abraham Maslow. *Toward a Psychology of Being.* Princeton, New Jersey: D. Van Nostrand Company, Inc. (1962): 25.

[3]Abraham Maslow. *Motivation and Personality.* New York: Harper & Row (1970).

[4]Abraham Maslow. *Toward a Psychology of Being.* Princeton, New Jersey: D. Van Nostrand Company Inc. (1962): 23–24.

[5]Dr. Catherine Macfarlane, then professor emeritus and vice president of the board of Women's Medical College, is quoted as saying, "College vocational counselors are the single most potent force steering women away from medicine. They exaggerate the difficulties, inspire false fears of professional handicaps, advise incorrectly that men are given preference, and indicate that the odds are not worth fighting." In "Women in Health." *Medicine At Work.* 5 (November, 1965). The authors tend to believe that high school counselors exert a more negative influence on girls' aspirations than do college personnel, essentially because of the extensive documentation that professional career choices for most girls are made *prior* to college.

[6]Margaret Mead and Frances Balgley Kaplan, eds. *American Women: A Report on the President's Commission on the Status of Women* and other publications of the Commission. New York: Charles Scribner's Sons (1965): 31. Similar charges were made in *Eliminating Sex Discrimination in Schools: A Source Book.* Research and Information Center, State Department of Public Instruction, Raleigh, North Carolina (1975): 61. It was stated that many high school guidance counselors (1) do not encourage girls to develop and value their intellectual abilities, (2) do not help girls to realize that a career may be important for their future economic survival and personal fulfillment, (3) fail to encourage students to explore all career opportunities, (4) fail to inform students that many jobs are now open to both sexes which were formerly open to only one sex, and (5) fail to encourage students to prepare for "non-traditional" jobs.

[7]Carol Lopate. *Women in Medicine.* Baltimore, Maryland: The Johns Hopkins Press (1968): 45.

[8]Ruth Weinstock. *The Greening of the High School.* New York: Educational Facilities Corporation (1973): 71.

[9]Davis G. Johnson and Edwin B. Hutchins. "Doctor or Dropout? A Study of Medical School Attrition." *Journal of Medical Education.* 41, 12 (1966): 1240.

[10]Rita Lynne Stafford. "An Analysis of Consciously Recalled Motivating Factors and Subsequent Professional Involvement for American Women in New York State." Doctoral dissertation, New York University (1966): 329.

[11]Natalie Rugoff. "The Decision to Study Medicine." In R. Merton, J. Reader, and P. Kendall, eds. *The Student Physician.* Cambridge: Harvard University Press (1957): 109–30.

[12]Lopate, op. cit: 48.

[13]Ibid.

[14]Mead and Kaplan, eds. op. cit.: 224.

[15]Margaret Anderson. *Children of the South.* New York: Farrar, Straus, and Giroux (1966).

[16]*U.S. Working Women: A Chartbook.* Washington, D.C.: U.S. Department of Labor, Bureau of Labor Statistics, Bulletin 1880 (1975): Chart 56.

[17]Caroline Bird. *Enterprising Women.* New York: W. W. Norton & Company, Inc. (1976).

[18]*Medicine as a Career for Women.* New York: American Medical Women's Association (1965). Also see Elinor Bluemel. *Florence Sabine: Colorado Woman of the Century.* Boulder, Colorado: University of Colorado Press (1959).

[19]Lopate, op. cit.: 54–55.

[20]Stafford, op cit.: 161.

[21]*The Reform of Secondary Education: A Report of the National Commission on the Reform of Secondary Education.* New York: McGraw-Hill Book Company (1973): 157.

[22]Loc. cit.

[23]Loc. cit.

[24]"Recommendations." National Federation of State High School Athletic Associations Official Handbook (1972–73): 28.

[25]Patrick C. Lee and Robert Sussman Stewart. *Sex Differences: Cultural & Developmental Dimensions.* New York: Urizen Books (1976): 14–22.

CHAPTER 8

[1]*Dick And Jane as Victims.* Princeton, New Jersey: Women on Words and Images (1975): 10.

[2]Ibid.: 66.

[3]Judith L. Weinstein. Letter to The Editor. *New York Times* (May 23, 1976).

[4]R. M. Liebert, J. M. Neale, and E. S. Davidson. *The Early Window: Effects of Television on Children and Youth.* New York: Pergamon Press (1973): 5.

[5]*Dick And Jane As Victims:* 74–75.

[6]Masha Kabakow Rudman. *Children's Literature: An Issues Approach.* Lexington, Massachusetts: D. C. Heath and Company (1976).

[7]Betty Miles. *Channeling Children.* Princeton, New Jersey: Women on Words and Images (1975).

[8]Ibid.: 77–78.

[9]Ibid.: 80.

[10]Ibid.: 81.

[11]G. Gerbner. "Violence in Television Drama: Trends and Dyabolic Functions." In G. A. Comstock and E. A. Rubenstein, eds. *Television And Social Behavior. Reports and Papers 1: Media Content and Control.* Washington, D.C.: U.S. Printing Office (1972): 28–187.

[12]Evelyn Kaye. *The Family Guide to Children's Television.* New York: Pantheon Books (1974).

[13]*Television for the Family.* Los Angeles, California: National Association For Better Broadcasting (Winter 1974).

[14]*Television for The Family.* Los Angeles, California: National Association for Better Broadcasting (Winter 1976): 3–11.

[15]J. Nicholson, J. Hennessee, and D. Brile. *Analysis of the Function and Roles of Males and Females in Television Advertising on WABC–TV April 24, 1971–May 7, 1971.* Manuscript prepared for NOW, New York City Chapter (1972).

[16]Miles, op. cit.: 44.

IN CONCLUSION

[1]*Who's Who of American Women,* fourth edition (1966–67). Chicago: The A. N. Marquis Company (1966): 6.

[2]Ali Halif. "The Second Caliph." *Bartlett's Familiar Quotations.* Boston: Little, Brown & Company (1955): 42. Note: Author's italics added.

Selected Bibliography and Sources of Additional Information

Ahlum, Carol, and Jacqueline M. Fralley. *Feminist Resources for Schools and Colleges. A Guide to Curricular Materials.* Old Westbury, New York: Feminist Press, 1973.

A Working Woman's Guide To Her Job Rights. Washington, D.C.: U.S. Department of Labor, Women's Bureau, U.S. Government Printing Office, Stock No. 029-016-00031-3, Catalog No. L 36. 110.55-½, 1975.

Career Counseling for Women in the Federal Government: A Handbook. Washington, D.C.: U.S. Civil Service Commission, U.S. Government Printing Office Stock No. 006-000-00894-1/Catalog No. CS 1.54:27, Personnel Management Series No. 27, 1976.

Channeling Children: Sex Stereotyping on Prime Time TV. Princeton, New Jersey: Women on Words and Images, 1975.

Cohen, Martha. *Stop Sex Role Stereotypes in Elementary Education. A Handbook for Parents and Teachers.* Hartford, Connecticut: Connecticut Public Interest Research Group, 1974.

Dick & Jane as Victims: Sex Stereotyping in Children's Readers. Princeton, New Jersey. Women on Words & Images, 1975.

Dinnerstein, Dorothy. *Sexual Arrangements and Human Malaise.* New York: Harper & Row (1976).

Dunn, Rita, and Kenneth Dunn. *Educator's Self-Teaching Guide to Individualizing Instructional Programs.* West Nyack, New York: Parker Publishing Company, 1975.

Dyer, Wayne W. *Your Erroneous Zones.* New York: Funk & Wagnalls, 1976.

Faber, Adele, and Elaine Mazlish. *Liberated Parents/Liberated Children.* New York: Grosset & Dunlap, 1974.

Frazier, Nancy, and Myra Sadker. *Sexism in School and Society.* New York: Harper & Row, 1973. Pb.

Friedan, Betty. *The Feminine Mystique.* New York: Dell Publishers, 1963.

Ginott, Haim G. *Between Parent & Child.* New York: The Macmillan Company, 1968.

Gordon, Thomas. *P.E.T.: Parent Effectiveness Training.* New York: New American Library, 1970.

Greenleaf, Phyllis Taube. *Liberating Young Children from Sex Roles.* Somerville, Massachusetts: New England Free Press, 1972.

Help Wanted: Sexism in Career Education Materials. Princeton, New Jersey: Women on Words & Images, 1975.

Kaye, Evelyn. *The Family Guide to Children's Television: What to Watch, What to Miss, What to Change and How to Do It.* New York: Pantheon, 1975.

Little Miss Muffet Fights Back: A Bibliography of Recommended Non-Sexist Books About Girls for Young Readers. Revised edition. Whitestone, New York: Feminist Book Mart, 1974.

Martin, John Henry, *Report of the National Panel on High Schools and Adolescent Education.* Washington, D.C.: U.S. Office of Education, 1974.

Maslow, Abraham H., *Toward a Psychology of Being.* New York: Van Nostrand Reinhold Company, 1968.

Mattfield, Jacquelin A., and Carol G. Van Aken, eds. *Women and the Scientific Professions.* Massachusetts: The Massachusetts Institute of Technology Press, 1965.

O'Neil, Barbara Powell. *Careers for Women after Marriage and Children.* New York: The Macmillan Company, 1965.

Pogrebin, Letty Cottin. *Getting Yours: How to Make the System Work for the Working Woman.* New York: David McKay Company, Inc., 1975.

Rudman, Masha Kabakow. *Children's Literature: An Issues Approach.* Lexington, Massachusetts: D. C. Heath and Company, 1976.

The Reform of Secondary Education: A Report of The National Commission on The Reform of Secondary Education. B. Frank Brown, ch. New York: McGraw-Hill Book Company, 1973.

The Rise Report: Report of the California Commission for Reform of Intermediate and Secondary Education. Sacramento, California: California State Department of Education, 1975.

Truman, Margaret. *Women of Courage.* New York: William Morrow and Co., 1976.

White, Burton L., *The First Three Years of Life.* Englewood Cliffs, New Jersey: Prentice-Hall, Inc., 1975.

Index

Avocations, achievement of pleasure in, 172

Babies
    comforting of, 31–32
    handling of, 30
    holding and grasping by, 31
    looking by, 31
    preparations before birth of, 27–29
    reaching by, 31
    smiling at, 31
    speaking to, 30
    stimulating interest in learning for, 36–49
        from three-and-one-half to
            five-and-one-half months, 36–37
        from five-and-one-half to eight months,
            37–40
        from eight to fourteen months, 40–44
        from fourteen to twenty-four months,
            44–49
    toys for, 32–36
Baby and Child Care (Spock), 76
Backaches, 15
*Barriers to Women's Participation in
    Postsecondary Education*
    (Westervelt), 11
Bicycles, 51
Bird, Caroline, 221–23
Books
    for babies, 48
    guidelines for selection of, 192
        nonsexist textbooks, 192–94
    recommended, 196–223
        for ages three through eight, 197–205
        for ages six through twelve, 205–17
        for ages twelve and up, 217–21
    sexist stereotyping in, 190–91
Building blocks, 52
Building play equipment, 47
Business and Professional Women's
    Foundation, 221

Career
    adolescent choices of, 154–55
    appreciation of rewards of, 171
    See also Professional involvement
Career clubs, 181–82
Career counseling
    lack of, 173–79
    supplements and replacements for
        traditional, 179–84
        analysis of local library offerings,
            180–81
        consideration of jobs and placement
            practices, 182
        establishment of career clubs, 181–82
        expansion of counseling information,
            182

Career counseling *(continued)*
    interaction with professional role
        models, 179–80
Chanel, Coco, 171
Channeling Children (Miles), 225
Chesler, Phyllis, 23
Children's television programs
    assessment of, 233–40
    on public television, 240
    standards for, 232–33
Children's Television Workshop, 240
Chinese foot-binding, 1
Classroom activities, nonsexist, 194
Classroom practices, sexism in, 194
Cleanliness, 144
Clichés
    danger of, 17–19
    overused and underrefuted, 6
    sex bias inventory concerning frequently
        used, 6–17
Clothing
    for adolescents, 142–43
    for babies, 27–29
        colors of, 27–28
        comfort and practicality of, 28–29
Clubs, career, 181–82
Commercials, television, 253–55
Community Family Guidance Center, 175
Comparing, skill of, 65
Compatibility, social, 126
Competition, preschoolers and, 60–63
Comprehensive Guide to Family Viewing
    (NABB), 231
Contraceptives, 148–49
Contribution to lives of others, 172
Convictions, firmness of, 83–84
Counseling, *see* Career counseling
Counting, 65
Crawling babies, safe area for, 38
Crib gym, 37
Creative arts, introduction of preschoolers to,
    63
Creativity, 65, 169
Curie, Marie, 168

Decision-making, 10
Declaration of Independence, 222
Department of Labor, U.S., 8, 11, 13
Design of learning environment, 87, 97
Desire for privacy, 166
Detachment, 166
Developmental stages, toys for, 34, 35
Dictionaries, nonsexist, 224
Divestment of girls, 5–6
Divorce, 14, 15
Doctor, visits to, 46
Doll carriages, 46–47
Dolls, 47–48